DYLAN MARLAIS THOMAS was born in Swansea in 1914. After leaving school he worked briefly as a junior reporter on the *South Wales Evening Post* before embarking on a literary career in London. Here he rapidly established himself as one of the finest poets of his generation. *Eighteen Poems* appeared in 1934, *Twenty-five Poems* in 1936, and *Deaths and Entrances* in 1946; his *Collected Poems* was published in 1952. Throughout his life Thomas wrote short stories, his most famous collection being *Portrait of the Artist as a Young Dog*. He also wrote film-scripts, broadcast stories and talks, lectured in America, and wrote the radio play *Under Milk Wood*. In 1953, shortly after his thirty-ninth birthday, he collapsed and died in New York. His body is buried in Laugharne, Wales, his home for many years.

PROFESSOR WALFORD DAVIES is Director of the Department of Extra-Mural Studies at the University College of Wales, Aberystwyth. His previous work on Dylan Thomas includes the following editions – *Dylan Thomas: Early Prose Writings* (1971); *Dylan Thomas: New Critical Essays* (1972); *Dylan Thomas: Selected Poems* (1974).

RALPH MAUD is Professor of English at Simon Fraser University, Burnaby, British Columbia. Among his previous works on Dylan Thomas is *Entrances to Dylan Thomas' Poetry* and he has also edited and fully revised *Dylan Thomas: The Notebook Poems 1930–1934*, which was first published as *Poet in the Making: The Notebooks of Dylan Thomas* (1968).

Overleaf: a facsimile of the first of two pages of the verse "Prologue" as written out by Dylan Thomas for Dent's in 1952.

# PROLOGUE

This day winding down now
At God speeded summer's end
In the torrent salmon sun,
In my seashaken house
On a breakneck of rocks
Tangled with chirrup and fruit,
Froth, flute, brushwood and branch
At a wood's dancing hoof,
By scummed, starfish sands
With their fishwife cross
Gulls, pipers, cockles, and sails,
Out there, birdlike, men
Tackled with clouds, who kneel
To the sunset nets,
Geese nearly in heaven, boys
Stabbing, and herons, and shells
That speak seven seas,
Eternal waters away
From the cities of nine
Days' night whose towers will catch
In the religious wind
Like stalks of tall, dry straw,
At poor peace I sing
To you, strangers, (though song
Is a burning and crested act,
The fire of birds in,
The world's turning wood,
For my sawn, splay sounds),
Out of these seathumbed leaves
That will fly and fall
Like leaves of trees and as soon
Crumble and undie
Into the dogdayed night.
Seaward the salmon, sucked sun slips,
And the dumb swans drub blue
My dabbed bay's dusk, as I hack
This rumpus of shapes
For you to know
How I, a spinning man,
Glory also this star, bird
Roared, sea born, man torn, blood blest.
Hark: I trumpet the place,
From fish to jumping hill! Look:
I build my bellowing ark
To the best of my love
As the flood begins,
Out of the fountainhead
Of fear, rage red, manalive,/
Molten and mountainous to stream
Over the wound asleep
Sheep white hollow farms

# DYLAN THOMAS

## Collected Poems
## 1934–1953

Edited by
Professor Walford Davies
*The University College of Wales, Aberystwyth*
and
Professor Ralph Maud
*Simon Fraser University, British Columbia*

J. M. Dent & Sons Ltd: London
EVERYMAN'S LIBRARY

First published by J.M. Dent & Sons Ltd, 1988
First published in Everyman by J.M. Dent & Sons Ltd, 1989

This book is set in Photina
Made in Great Britain by
The Guernsey Press Co. Ltd, Guernsey, C.I.
for
J.M. Dent & Sons Ltd,
Orion Publishing Group, Orion House,
5 Upper St. Martin's Lane, London WC2H 9EA

British Library Cataloguing in Publication Data

Thomas, Dylan, *1914-1953*
Collected poems 1934-1953. – (Everyman classic)
I. Title   II. Davies, Walford   III. Maud, Ralph
1928
821'.912

ISBN 0 460 87054 8

# Contents

# Contents

# Preface

In his introductory note to *Collected Poems 1934–1952*, Dylan Thomas said that he had included all the poems that he wished, up to that time, to preserve. The present volume has been entitled *Collected Poems 1934–1953* because it reflects almost totally Thomas's own choice, but adds two poems that Thomas was working on up to the year of his death in 1953.

Other kinds of changes that the editors have incorporated in order to make this volume as definitive as present scholarship allows are explained fully in the Notes at the end.

The publication of this edition happily coincides with the centenary of J. M. Dent and Sons, who published Thomas's second volume of poems in 1936, further volumes in 1939 and 1946, and the original *Collected Poems* in 1952, as well as many other volumes associated with the poet.

The editors wish gratefully to acknowledge the specific help given them in the preparation of the edition by the following persons and institutions: Alan Clodd, James Laughlin, Peter Shellard, Jeff Towns and Gwen Watkins; the Department of Manuscripts of the British Library, the Library of the University of Chicago, the Harry Ransom Humanities Research Center of the University of Texas, the Houghton Library of Harvard University, the Lilly Library of Indiana University, the Special Collection Library of the State University of New York at Buffalo, the Library of Ohio State University, the Pierpont Morgan Library, Simon Fraser University, British Columbia, the Library of Southern Illinois University, the University College of Wales, Aberystwyth, the Department of Manuscripts and Records of the National Library of Wales, the Royal Commission on the Historical Monuments of England (for permission to reproduce the illustration of the Cerne Abbas giant on page 257), and Aled Jenkins (for his photograph on page 252).

The editors are also grateful for grants awarded by the British Academy, the British Council, and the Social Sciences and Humanities Research Council of Canada, in support of research work on both sides of the Atlantic.

# The Poems

# Prologue

This day winding down now
At God speeded summer's end
In the torrent salmon sun,
In my seashaken house
On a breakneck of rocks
Tangled with chirrup and fruit,
Froth, flute, fin and quill
At a wood's dancing hoof,
By scummed, starfish sands
With their fishwife cross
Gulls, pipers, cockles, and sails,
Out there, crow black, men
Tackled with clouds, who kneel
To the sunset nets,
Geese nearly in heaven, boys
Stabbing, and herons, and shells
That speak seven seas,
Eternal waters away
From the cities of nine
Days' night whose towers will catch
In the religious wind
Like stalks of tall, dry straw,
At poor peace I sing
To you, strangers, (though song
Is a burning and crested act,
The fire of birds in
The world's turning wood,
For my sawn, splay sounds),
Out of these seathumbed leaves
That will fly and fall
Like leaves of trees and as soon
Crumble and undie
Into the dogdayed night.
Seaward the salmon, sucked sun slips,
And the dumb swans drub blue
My dabbed bay's dusk, as I hack
This rumpus of shapes

For you to know
How I, a spinning man,
Glory also this star, bird
Roared, sea born, man torn, blood blest.
Hark: I trumpet the place,
From fish to jumping hill! Look:
I build my bellowing ark
To the best of my love
As the flood begins,
Out of the fountainhead
Of fear, rage red, manalive,
Molten and mountainous to stream
Over the wound asleep
Sheep white hollow farms

To Wales in my arms.
Hoo, there, in castle keep,
You king singsong owls, who moonbeam
The flickering runs and dive
The dingle furred deer dead!
Huloo, on plumbed bryns,
O my ruffled ring dove
In the hooting, nearly dark
With Welsh and reverent rook,
Coo rooing the woods' praise,
Who moons her blue notes from her nest
Down to the curlew herd!
Ho, hullaballoing clan
Agape, with woe
In your beaks, on the gabbing capes!
Heigh, on horseback hill, jack
Whisking hare! who
Hears, there, this fox light, my flood ship's
Clangour as I hew and smite
(A clash of anvils for my
Hubbub and fiddle, this tune
On a tongued puffball)

But animals thick as thieves
On God's rough tumbling grounds
(Hail to His beasthood!).
Beasts who sleep good and thin,
Hist, in hogsback woods! The haystacked
Hollow farms in a throng
Of waters cluck and cling,
And barnroofs cockcrow war!
O kingdom of neighbours, finned
Felled and quilled, flash to my patch
Work ark and the moonshine
Drinking Noah of the bay,
With pelt, and scale, and fleece:
Only the drowned deep bells
Of sheep and churches noise
Poor peace as the sun sets
And dark shoals every holy field.
We shall ride out alone, and then,
Under the stars of Wales,
Cry, Multitudes of arks! Across
The water lidded lands,
Manned with their loves they'll move,
Like wooden islands, hill to hill.
Huloo, my prowed dove with a flute!
Ahoy, old, sea-legged fox,
Tom tit and Dai mouse!
My ark sings in the sun
At God speeded summer's end
And the flood flowers now.

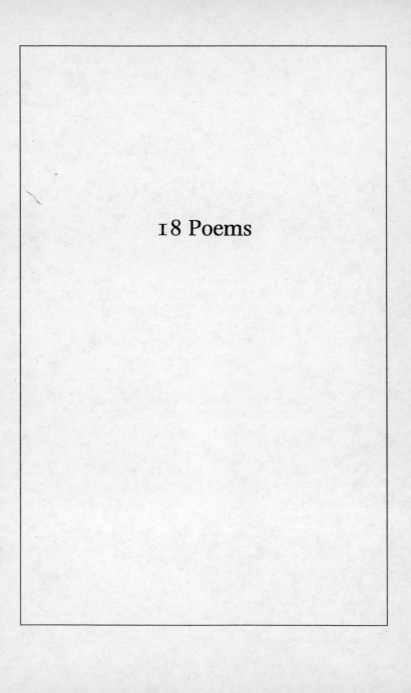

# 18 Poems

# I see the boys of summer

I

I see the boys of summer in their ruin
Lay the gold tithings barren,
Setting no store by harvest, freeze the soils;
There in their heat the winter floods
Of frozen loves they fetch their girls,
And drown the cargoed apples in their tides.

These boys of light are curdlers in their folly,
Sour the boiling honey;
The jacks of frost they finger in the hives;
There in the sun the frigid threads
Of doubt and dark they feed their nerves;
The signal moon is zero in their voids.

I see the summer children in their mothers
Split up the brawned womb's weathers,
Divide the night and day with fairy thumbs;
There in the deep with quartered shades
Of sun and moon they paint their dams
As sunlight paints the shelling of their heads.

I see that from these boys shall men of nothing
Stature by seedy shifting,
Or lame the air with leaping from its heats;
There from their hearts the dogdayed pulse
Of love and light bursts in their throats.
O see the pulse of summer in the ice.

## II

But seasons must be challenged or they totter
Into a chiming quarter
Where, punctual as death, we ring the stars;
There, in his night, the black-tongued bells
The sleepy man of winter pulls,
Nor blows back moon-and-midnight as she blows.

We are the dark deniers, let us summon
Death from a summer woman,
A muscling life from lovers in their cramp,
From the fair dead who flush the sea
The bright-eyed worm on Davy's lamp,
And from the planted womb the man of straw.

We summer boys in this four-winded spinning,
Green of the seaweeds' iron,
Hold up the noisy sea and drop her birds,
Pick the world's ball of wave and froth
To choke the deserts with her tides,
And comb the county gardens for a wreath.

In spring we cross our foreheads with the holly,
Heigh ho the blood and berry,
And nail the merry squires to the trees;
Here love's damp muscle dries and dies,
Here break a kiss in no love's quarry.
O see the poles of promise in the boys.

## III

I see you boys of summer in your ruin.
Man in his maggot's barren.
And boys are full and foreign in the pouch.
I am the man your father was.
We are the sons of flint and pitch.
O see the poles are kissing as they cross.

8

## When once the twilight locks

When once the twilight locks no longer
Locked in the long worm of my finger
Nor dammed the sea that sped about my fist,
The mouth of time sucked, like a sponge,
The milky acid on each hinge,
And swallowed dry the waters of the breast.

When the galactic sea was sucked
And all the dry seabed unlocked,
I sent my creature scouting on the globe,
That globe itself of hair and bone
That, sewn to me by nerve and brain,
Had stringed my flask of matter to his rib.

My fuses timed to charge his heart,
He blew like powder to the light
And held a little sabbath with the sun,
But when the stars, assuming shape,
Drew in his eyes the straws of sleep,
He drowned his father's magics in a dream.

All issue armoured, of the grave,
The redhaired cancer still alive,
The cataracted eyes that filmed their cloth;
Some dead undid their bushy jaws,
And bags of blood let out their flies;
He had by heart the Christ-cross-row of death.

Sleep navigates the tides of time;
The dry Sargasso of the tomb
Gives up its dead to such a working sea;
And sleep rolls mute above the beds
Where fishes' food is fed the shades
Who periscope through flowers to the sky.

The hanged who lever from the limes
Ghostly propellers for their limbs,

The cypress lads who wither with the cock,
These, and the others in sleep's acres,
Of dreaming men make moony suckers,
And snipe the fools of vision in the back.

When once the twilight screws were turned,
And mother milk was stiff as sand,
I sent my own ambassador to light;
By trick or chance he fell asleep
And conjured up a carcase shape
To rob me of my fluids in his heart.

Awake, my sleeper, to the sun,
A worker in the morning town,
And leave the poppied pickthank where he lies;
The fences of the light are down,
All but the briskest riders thrown,
And worlds hang on the trees.

## A process in the weather of the heart

A process in the weather of the heart
Turns damp to dry; the golden shot
Storms in the freezing tomb.
A weather in the quarter of the veins
Turns night to day; blood in their suns
Lights up the living worm.

A process in the eye forwarns
The bones of blindness; and the womb
Drives in a death as life leaks out.

A darkness in the weather of the eye
Is half its light; the fathomed sea

Breaks on unangled land.
The seed that makes a forest of the loin
Forks half its fruit; and half drops down,
Slow in a sleeping wind.

A weather in the flesh and bone
Is damp and dry; the quick and dead
Move like two ghosts before the eye.

A process in the weather of the world
Turns ghost to ghost; each mothered child
Sits in their double shade.
A process blows the moon into the sun,
Pulls down the shabby curtains of the skin;
And the heart gives up its dead.

## Before I knocked

Before I knocked and flesh let enter,
With liquid hands tapped on the womb,
I who was shapeless as the water
That shaped the Jordan near my home
Was brother to Mnetha's daughter
And sister to the fathering worm.

I who was deaf to spring and summer,
Who knew not sun nor moon by name,
Felt thud beneath my flesh's armour,
As yet was in a molten form,
The leaden stars, the rainy hammer
Swung by my father from his dome.

I knew the message of the winter,
The darted hail, the childish snow,

And the wind was my sister suitor;
Wind in me leaped, the hellborn dew;
My veins flowed with the Eastern weather;
Ungotten I knew night and day.

As yet ungotten, I did suffer;
The rack of dreams my lily bones
Did twist into a living cipher,
And flesh was snipped to cross the lines
Of gallow crosses on the liver
And brambles in the wringing brains.

My throat knew thirst before the structure
Of skin and vein around the well
Where words and water make a mixture
Unfailing till the blood runs foul;
My heart knew love, my belly hunger;
I smelt the maggot in my stool.

And time cast forth my mortal creature
To drift or drown upon the seas
Acquainted with the salt adventure
Of tides that never touch the shores.
I who was rich was made the richer
By sipping at the vine of days.

I, born of flesh and ghost, was neither
A ghost nor man, but mortal ghost.
And I was struck down by death's feather.
I was mortal to the last
Long breath that carried to my father
The message of his dying christ.

You who bow down at cross and altar,
Remember me and pity Him
Who took my flesh and bone for armour
And doublecrossed my mother's womb.

## The force that through the green fuse

The force that through the green fuse drives the flower
Drives my green age; that blasts the roots of trees
Is my destroyer.
And I am dumb to tell the crooked rose
My youth is bent by the same wintry fever.

The force that drives the water through the rocks
Drives my red blood; that dries the mouthing streams
Turns mine to wax.
And I am dumb to mouth unto my veins
How at the mountain spring the same mouth sucks.

The hand that whirls the water in the pool
Stirs the quicksand; that ropes the blowing wind
Hauls my shroud sail.
And I am dumb to tell the hanging man
How of my clay is made the hangman's lime.

The lips of time leech to the fountain head;
Love drips and gathers, but the fallen blood
Shall calm her sores.
And I am dumb to tell a weather's wind
How time has ticked a heaven round the stars.

And I am dumb to tell the lover's tomb
How at my sheet goes the same crooked worm.

## My hero bares his nerves

My hero bares his nerves along my wrist
That rules from wrist to shoulder,
Unpacks the head that, like a sleepy ghost,
Leans on my mortal ruler,
The proud spine spurning turn and twist.

13

And these poor nerves so wired to the skull
Ache on the lovelorn paper
I hug to love with my unruly scrawl
That utters all love hunger
And tells the page the empty ill.

My hero bares my side and sees his heart
Tread, like a naked Venus,
The beach of flesh, and wind her bloodred plait;
Stripping my loin of promise,
He promises a secret heat.

He holds the wire from this box of nerves
Praising the mortal error
Of birth and death, the two sad knaves of thieves,
And the hunger's emperor;
He pulls the chain, the cistern moves.


## Where once the waters of your face

Where once the waters of your face
Spun to my screws, your dry ghost blows,
The dead turns up its eye;
Where once the mermen through your ice
Pushed up their hair, the dry wind steers
Through salt and root and roe.

Where once your green knots sank their splice
Into the tided cord, there goes
The green unraveller,
His scissors oiled, his knife hung loose
To cut the channels at their source
And lay the wet fruits low.

Invisible, your clocking tides
Break on the lovebeds of the weeds;

14

The weed of love's left dry;
There round about your stones the shades
Of children go who, from their voids,
Cry to the dolphined sea.

Dry as a tomb, your coloured lids
Shall not be latched while magic glides
Sage on the earth and sky;
There shall be corals in your beds,
There shall be serpents in your tides,
Till all our sea-faiths die.


## If I were tickled by the rub of love

If I were tickled by the rub of love,
A rooking girl who stole me for her side,
Broke through her straws, breaking my bandaged string,
If the red tickle as the cattle calve
Still set to scratch a laughter from my lung,
I would not fear the apple nor the flood
Nor the bad blood of spring.

Shall it be male or female? say the cells,
And drop the plum like fire from the flesh.
If I were tickled by the hatching hair,
The winging bone that sprouted in the heels,
The itch of man upon the baby's thigh,
I would not fear the gallows nor the axe
Nor the crossed sticks of war.

Shall it be male or female? say the fingers
That chalk the walls with green girls and their men.
I would not fear the muscling-in of love
If I were tickled by the urchin hungers
Rehearsing heat upon a raw-edged nerve.
I would not fear the devil in the loin
Nor the outspoken grave.

15

If I were tickled by the lovers' rub
That wipes away not crow's-foot nor the lock
Of sick old manhood on the fallen jaws,
Time and the crabs and the sweethearting crib
Would leave me cold as butter for the flies,
The sea of scums could drown me as it broke
Dead on the sweethearts' toes.

This world is half the devil's and my own,
Daft with the drug that's smoking in a girl
And curling round the bud that forks her eye.
An old man's shank one-marrowed with my bone,
And all the herrings smelling in the sea,
I sit and watch the worm beneath my nail
Wearing the quick away.

And that's the rub, the only rub that tickles.
The knobbly ape that swings along his sex
From damp love-darkness and the nurse's twist
Can never raise the midnight of a chuckle,
Nor when he finds a beauty in the breast
Of lover, mother, lovers, or his six
Feet in the rubbing dust.

And what's the rub? Death's feather on the nerve?
Your mouth, my love, the thistle in the kiss?
My Jack of Christ born thorny on the tree?
The words of death are dryer than his stiff,
My wordy wounds are printed with your hair.
I would be tickled by the rub that is:
Man be my metaphor.

# Our eunuch dreams

## I

Our eunuch dreams, all seedless in the light,
Of light and love, the tempers of the heart,
Whack their boys' limbs,
And, winding-footed in their shawl and sheet,
Groom the dark brides, the widows of the night
Fold in their arms.

The shades of girls, all flavoured from their shrouds,
When sunlight goes are sundered from the worm,
The bones of men, the broken in their beds,
By midnight pulleys that unhouse the tomb.

## II

In this our age the gunman and his moll,
Two one-dimensioned ghosts, love on a reel,
Strange to our solid eye,
And speak their midnight nothings as they swell;
When cameras shut they hurry to their hole
Down in the yard of day.

They dance between their arclamps and our skull,
Impose their shots, throwing the nights away;
We watch the show of shadows kiss or kill,
Flavoured of celluloid give love the lie.

## III

Which is the world? Of our two sleepings, which
Shall fall awake when cures and their itch
Raise up this red-eyed earth?
Pack off the shapes of daylight and their starch,
The sunny gentlemen, the Welshing rich,
Or drive the night-geared forth.

17

The photograph is married to the eye,
Grafts on its bride one-sided skins of truth;
The dream has sucked the sleeper of his faith
That shrouded men might marrow as they fly.

IV

This is the world: the lying likeness of
Our strips of stuff that tatter as we move
Loving and being loth;
The dream that kicks the buried from their sack
And lets their trash be honoured as the quick.
This is the world. Have faith.

For we shall be a shouter like the cock,
Blowing the old dead back; our shots shall smack
The image from the plates;
And we shall be fit fellows for a life,
And who remain shall flower as they love,
Praise to our faring hearts.

## Especially when the October wind

Especially when the October wind
With frosty fingers punishes my hair,
Caught by the crabbing sun I walk on fire
And cast a shadow crab upon the land,
By the sea's side, hearing the noise of birds,
Hearing the raven cough in winter sticks,
My busy heart who shudders as she talks
Sheds the syllabic blood and drains her words.

Shut, too, in a tower of words, I mark
On the horizon walking like the trees
The wordy shapes of women, and the rows
Of the star-gestured children in the park.
Some let me make you of the vowelled beeches,
Some of the oaken voices, from the roots

Of many a thorny shire tell you notes,
Some let me make you of the water's speeches.

Behind a pot of ferns the wagging clock
Tells me the hour's word, the neural meaning
Flies on the shafted disc, declaims the morning
And tells the windy weather in the cock.
Some let me make you of the meadow's signs;
The signal grass that tells me all I know
Breaks with the wormy winter through the eye.
Some let me tell you of the raven's sins.

Especially when the October wind
(Some let me make you of autumnal spells,
The spider-tongued, and the loud hill of Wales)
With fist of turnips punishes the land,
Some let me make you of the heartless words.
The heart is drained that, spelling in the scurry
Of chemic blood, warned of the coming fury.
By the sea's side hear the dark-vowelled birds.

## When, like a running grave

When, like a running grave, time tracks you down,
Your calm and cuddled is a scythe of hairs,
Love in her gear is slowly through the house,
Up naked stairs, a turtle in a hearse,
Hauled to the dome,

Comes, like a scissors stalking, tailor age,
Deliver me who, timid in my tribe,
Of love am barer than Cadaver's trap
Robbed of the foxy tongue, his footed tape
Of the bone inch,

Deliver me, my masters, head and heart,
Heart of Cadaver's candle waxes thin,

19

When blood, spade-handed, and the logic time
Drive children up like bruises to the thumb,
From maid and head,

For, sunday faced, with dusters in my glove,
Chaste and the chaser, man with the cockshut eye,
I, that time's jacket or the coat of ice
May fail to fasten with a virgin o
In the straight grave,

Stride through Cadaver's country in my force,
My pickbrain masters morsing on the stone
Despair of blood, faith in the maiden's slime,
Halt among eunuchs, and the nitric stain
On fork and face.

Time is a foolish fancy, time and fool.
No, no, you lover skull, descending hammer
Descends, my masters, on the entered honour.
You hero skull, Cadaver in the hangar
Tells the stick 'fail'.

Joy is no knocking nation, sir and madam,
The cancer's fusion, or the summer feather
Lit on the cuddled tree, the cross of fever,
Nor city tar and subway bored to foster
Man through macadam.

I damp the waxlights in your tower dome.
Joy is the knock of dust, Cadaver's shoot
Of bud of Adam through his boxy shift,
Love's twilit nation and the skull of state,
Sir, is your doom.

Everything ends, the tower ending and,
(Have with the house of wind) the leaning scene,
Ball of the foot depending from the sun,
(Give, summer, over) the cemented skin,
The actions' end.

All, men my madmen, the unwholesome wind
With whistler's cough contages, time on track
Shapes in a cinder death; love for his trick,
Happy Cadaver's hunger as you take
The kissproof world.

# From love's first fever

From love's first fever to her plague, from the soft second
And to the hollow minute of the womb,
From the unfolding to the scissored caul,
The time for breast and the green apron age
When no mouth stirred about the hanging famine,
All world was one, one windy nothing,
My world was christened in a stream of milk.
And earth and sky were as one airy hill,
The sun and moon shed one white light.

From the first print of the unshodden foot, the lifting
Hand, the breaking of the hair,
And to the miracle of the first rounded word,
From the first secret of the heart, the warning ghost,
And to the first dumb wonder at the flesh,
The sun was red, the moon was grey,
The earth and sky were as two mountains meeting.

The body prospered, teeth in the marrowed gums,
The growing bones, the rumour of manseed
Within the hallowed gland, blood blessed the heart,
And the four winds, that had long blown as one,
Shone in my ears the light of sound,
Called in my eyes the sound of light.
And yellow was the multiplying sand,
Each golden grain spat life into its fellow,
Green was the singing house.

The plum my mother picked matured slowly,

The boy she dropped from darkness at her side
Into the sided lap of light grew strong,
Was muscled, matted, wise to the crying thigh
And to the voice that, like a voice of hunger,
Itched in the noise of wind and sun.

And from the first declension of the flesh
I learnt man's tongue, to twist the shapes of thoughts
Into the stony idiom of the brain,
To shade and knit anew the patch of words
Left by the dead who, in their moonless acre,
Need no word's warmth.
The root of tongues ends in a spentout cancer,
That but a name, where maggots have their X.

I learnt the verbs of will, and had my secret;
The code of night tapped on my tongue;
What had been one was many sounding minded.

One womb, one mind, spewed out the matter,
One breast gave suck the fever's issue;
From the divorcing sky I learnt the double,
The two-framed globe that spun into a score;
A million minds gave suck to such a bud
As forks my eye;
Youth did condense; the tears of spring
Dissolved in summer and the hundred seasons;
One sun, one manna, warmed and fed.

## In the beginning

In the beginning was the three-pointed star,
One smile of light across the empty face;
One bough of bone across the rooting air,
The substance forked that marrowed the first sun;
And, burning ciphers on the round of space,
Heaven and hell mixed as they spun.

22

In the beginning was the pale signature,
Three-syllabled and starry as the smile;
And after came the imprints on the water,
Stamp of the minted face upon the moon;
The blood that touched the crosstree and the grail
Touched the first cloud and left a sign.

In the beginning was the mounting fire
That set alight the weathers from a spark,
A three-eyed, red-eyed spark, blunt as a flower;
Life rose and spouted from the rolling seas,
Burst in the roots, pumped from the earth and rock
The secret oils that drive the grass.

In the beginning was the word, the word
That from the solid bases of the light
Abstracted all the letters of the void;
And from the cloudy bases of the breath
The word flowed up, translating to the heart
First characters of birth and death.

In the beginning was the secret brain.
The brain was celled and soldered in the thought
Before the pitch was forking to a sun;
Before the veins were shaking in their sieve,
Blood shot and scattered to the winds of light
The ribbed original of love.


## Light breaks where no sun shines

Light breaks where no sun shines;
Where no sea runs, the waters of the heart
Push in their tides;
And, broken ghosts with glow-worms in their heads,
The things of light
File through the flesh where no flesh decks the bones.

A candle in the thighs
Warms youth and seed and burns the seeds of age;
Where no seed stirs,
The fruit of man unwrinkles in the stars,
Bright as a fig;
Where no wax is, the candle shows its hairs.

Dawn breaks behind the eyes;
From poles of skull and toe the windy blood
Slides like a sea;
Nor fenced, nor staked, the gushers of the sky
Spout to the rod
Divining in a smile the oil of tears.

Night in the sockets rounds,
Like some pitch moon, the limit of the globes;
Day lights the bone;
Where no cold is, the skinning gales unpin
The winter's robes;
The film of spring is hanging from the lids.

Light breaks on secret lots,
On tips of thought where thoughts smell in the rain;
When logics die,
The secret of the soil grows through the eye,
And blood jumps in the sun;
Above the waste allotments the dawn halts.

# I fellowed sleep

I fellowed sleep who kissed me in the brain,
Let fall the tear of time; the sleeper's eye,
Shifting to light, turned on me like a moon.
So, 'planing-heeled, I flew along my man
And dropped on dreaming and the upward sky.

I fled the earth and, naked, climbed the weather,
Reaching a second ground far from the stars;
And there we wept, I and a ghostly other,
My mothers-eyed, upon the tops of trees;
I fled that ground as lightly as a feather.

'My fathers' globe knocks on its nave and sings.'
'This that we tread was, too, your fathers' land.'
'But this we tread bears the angelic gangs,
Sweet are their fathered faces in their wings.'
'These are but dreaming men. Breathe, and they fade.'

Faded my elbow ghost, the mothers-eyed,
As, blowing on the angels, I was lost
On that cloud coast to each grave-gabbing shade;
I blew the dreaming fellows to their bed
Where still they sleep unknowing of their ghost.

Then all the matter of the living air
Raised up a voice, and, climbing on the words,
I spelt my vision with a hand and hair,
How light the sleeping on this soily star,
How deep the waking in the worlded clouds.

There grows the hours' ladder to the sun,
Each rung a love or losing to the last,
The inches monkeyed by the blood of man.
An old, mad man still climbing in his ghost,
My fathers' ghost is climbing in the rain.

## I dreamed my genesis

I dreamed my genesis in sweat of sleep, breaking
Through the rotating shell, strong
As motor muscle on the drill, driving
Through vision and the girdered nerve.

From limbs that had the measure of the worm, shuffled
Off from the creasing flesh, filed
Through all the irons in the grass, metal
Of suns in the man-melting night.

Heir to the scalding veins that hold love's drop, costly
A creature in my bones I
Rounded my globe of heritage, journey
In bottom gear through night-geared man.

I dreamed my genesis and died again, shrapnel
Rammed in the marching heart, hole
In the stitched wound and clotted wind, muzzled
Death on the mouth that ate the gas.

Sharp in my second death I marked the hills, harvest
Of hemlock and the blades, rust
My blood upon the tempered dead, forcing
My second struggling from the grass.

And power was contagious in my birth, second
Rise of the skeleton and
Rerobing of the naked ghost. Manhood
Spat up from the resuffered pain.

I dreamed my genesis in sweat of death, fallen
Twice in the feeding sea, grown
Stale of Adam's brine until, vision
Of new man strength, I seek the sun.

# My world is pyramid

## I

Half of the fellow father as he doubles
His sea-sucked Adam in the hollow hulk,
Half of the fellow mother as she dabbles
Tomorrow's diver in her horny milk,
Bisected shadows on the thunder's bone
Bolt for the salt unborn.

The fellow half was frozen as it bubbled
Corrosive spring out of the iceberg's crop,
The fellow seed and shadow as it babbled
The swing of milk was tufted in the pap,
For half of love was planted in the lost,
And the unplanted ghost.

The broken halves are fellowed in a cripple,
The crutch that marrow taps upon their sleep,
Limp in the street of sea, among the rabble
Of tide-tongued heads and bladders in the deep,
And stake the sleepers in the savage grave
That the vampire laugh.

The patchwork halves were cloven as they scudded
The wild pigs' wood, and slime upon the trees,
Sucking the dark, kissed on the cyanide,
And loosed the braiding adders from their hairs;
Rotating halves are horning as they drill
The arterial angel.

What colour is glory? death's feather? tremble
The halves that pierce the pin's point in the air,
And prick the thumb-stained heaven through the thimble.
The ghost is dumb that stammered in the straw,
The ghost that hatched his havoc as he flew
Blinds their cloud-tracking eye.

## II

My world is pyramid. The padded mummer
Weeps on the desert ochre and the salt
Incising summer.
My Egypt's armour buckling in its sheet,
I scrape through resin to a starry bone
And a blood parhelion.

My world is cypress, and an English valley.
I piece my flesh that rattled on the yards
Red in an Austrian volley.
I hear, through dead men's drums, the riddled lads,
Strewing their bowels from a hill of bones,
Cry Eloi to the guns.

My grave is watered by the crossing Jordan.
The Arctic scut, and basin of the South,
Drip on my dead house garden.
Who seek me landward, marking in my mouth
The straws of Asia, lose me as I turn
Through the Atlantic corn.

The fellow halves that, cloven as they swivel
On casting tides, are tangled in the shells,
Bearding the unborn devil,
Bleed from my burning fork and smell my heels.
The tongues of heaven gossip as I glide
Binding my angel's hood.

Who blows death's feather? What glory is colour?
I blow the stammel feather in the vein.
The loin is glory in a working pallor.
My clay unsuckled and my salt unborn,
The secret child, I shift about the sea
Dry in the half-tracked thigh.

# All all and all

## I

All all and all the dry worlds lever,
Stage of the ice, the solid ocean,
All from the oil, the pound of lava.
City of spring, the governed flower,
Turns in the earth that turns the ashen
Towns around on a wheel of fire.

How now my flesh, my naked fellow,
Dug of the sea, the glanded morrow,
Worm in the scalp, the staked and fallow.
All all and all, the corpse's lover,
Skinny as sin, the foaming marrow,
All of the flesh, the dry worlds lever.

## II

Fear not the working world, my mortal,
Fear not the flat, synthetic blood,
Nor the heart in the ribbing metal.
Fear not the tread, the seeded milling,
The trigger and scythe, the bridal blade,
Nor the flint in the lover's mauling.

Man of my flesh, the jawbone riven,
Know now the flesh's lock and vice,
And the cage for the scythe-eyed raven.
Know, O my bone, the jointed lever,
Fear not the screws that turn the voice,
And the face to the driven lover.

## III

All all and all the dry worlds couple,
Ghost with her ghost, contagious man
With the womb of his shapeless people.

29

All that shapes from the caul and suckle,
Stroke of mechanical flesh on mine,
Square in these worlds the mortal circle.

Flower, flower the people's fusion,
O light in zenith, the coupled bud,
And the flame in the flesh's vision.
Out of the sea, the drive of oil,
Socket and grave, the brassy blood,
Flower, flower, all all and all.

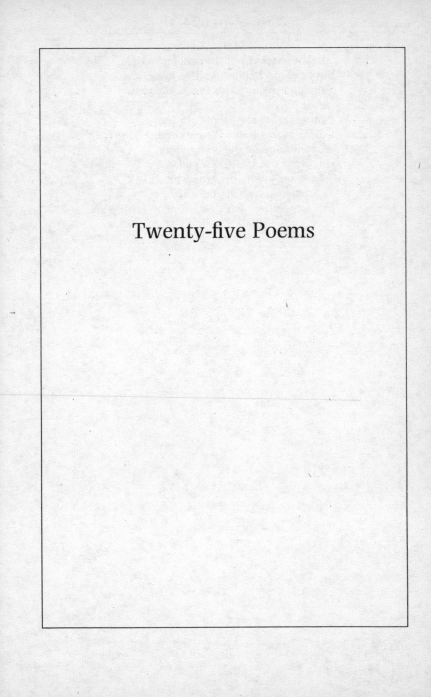

# Twenty-five Poems

# I, in my intricate image

I

I, in my intricate image, stride on two levels,
Forged in man's minerals, the brassy orator
Laying my ghost in metal,
The scales of this twin world tread on the double,
My half ghost in armour hold hard in death's corridor,
To my man-iron sidle.

Beginning with doom in the bulb, the spring unravels,
Bright as her spinning-wheels, the colic season
Worked on a world of petals;
She threads off the sap and needles, blood and bubble
Casts to the pine roots, raising man like a mountain
Out of the naked entrail.

Beginning with doom in the ghost, and the springing marvels,
Image of images, my metal phantom
Forcing forth through the harebell,
My man of leaves and the bronze root, mortal, unmortal,
I, in my fusion of rose and male motion,
Create this twin miracle.

This is the fortune of manhood: the natural peril,
A steeplejack tower, bonerailed and masterless,
No death more natural;
Thus the shadowless man or ox, and the pictured devil,
In seizure of silence commit the dead nuisance:
The natural parallel.

My images stalk the trees and the slant sap's tunnel,
No tread more perilous, the green steps and spire
Mount on man's footfall,
I with the wooden insect in the tree of nettles,
In the glass bed of grapes with snail and flower,
Hearing the weather fall.

33

Intricate manhood of ending, the invalid rivals,
Voyaging clockwise off the symboled harbour,
Finding the water final,
On the consumptives' terrace taking their two farewells,
Sail on the level, the departing adventure,
To the sea-blown arrival.


II


They climb the country pinnacle,
Twelve winds encounter by the white host at pasture,
Corner the mounted meadows in the hill corral;
They see the squirrel stumble,
The haring snail go giddily round the flower,
A quarrel of weathers and trees in the windy spiral.

As they dive, the dust settles,
The Cadaverous gravels, falls thick and steadily,
The highroad of water where the seabear and mackerel
Turn the long sea arterial
Turning a petrol face blind to the enemy
Turning the riderless dead by the channel wall.

(Death instrumental,
Splitting the long eye open, and the spiral turnkey,
Your corkscrew grave centred in navel and nipple,
The neck of the nostril,
Under the mask and the ether, they making bloody
The tray of knives, the antiseptic funeral;

Bring out the black patrol,
Your monstrous officers and the decaying army,
The sexton sentinel, garrisoned under thistles,
A cock-on-a-dunghill
Crowing to Lazarus the morning is vanity,
Dust be your saviour under the conjured soil.)

As they drown, the chime travels,
Sweetly the diver's bell in the steeple of spindrift
Rings out the Dead Sea scale;
And, clapped in water till the triton dangles,
Strung by the flaxen whale-weed, from the hangman's raft,
Hear they the salt glass breakers and the tongues of burial.

(Turn the sea-spindle lateral,
The grooved land rotating, that the stylus of lightning
Dazzle this face of voices on the moon-turned table,
Let the wax disc babble
Shames and the damp dishonours, the relic scraping.
These are your years' recorders. The circular world stands still.)

### III

They suffer the undead water where the turtle nibbles,
Come unto sea-stuck towers, at the fibre scaling,
The flight of the carnal skull
And the cell-stepped thimble;
Suffer, my topsy-turvies, that a double angel
Sprout from the stony lockers like a tree on Aran.

Be by your one ghost pierced, his pointed ferrule,
Brass and the bodiless image, on a stick of folly
Star-set at Jacob's angle,
Smoke hill and hophead's valley,
And the five-fathomed Hamlet on his father's coral,
Thrusting the tom-thumb vision up the iron mile.

Suffer the slash of vision by the fin-green stubble,
Be by the ships' sea broken at the manstring anchored
The stoved bones' voyage downward
In the shipwreck of muscle;
Give over, lovers, locking, and the seawax struggle,
Love like a mist or fire through the bed of eels.

35

And in the pincers of the boiling circle,
The sea and instrument, nicked in the locks of time,
My great blood's iron single
In the pouring town,
I, in a wind on fire, from green Adam's cradle,
No man more magical, clawed out the crocodile.

Man was the scales, the death birds on enamel,
Tail, Nile, and snout, a saddler of the rushes,
Time in the hourless houses
Shaking the sea-hatched skull,
And, as for oils and ointments on the flying grail,
All-hallowed man wept for his white apparel.

Man was Cadaver's masker, the harnessing mantle,
Windily master of man was the rotten fathom,
My ghost in his metal neptune
Forged in man's mineral.
This was the god of beginning in the intricate seawhirl,
And my images roared and rose on heaven's hill.

## This bread I break

This bread I break was once the oat,
This wine upon a foreign tree
Plunged in its fruit;
Man in the day or wind at night
Laid the crops low, broke the grape's joy.

Once in this wine the summer blood
Knocked in the flesh that decked the vine,
Once in this bread
The oat was merry in the wind;
Man broke the sun, pulled the wind down.

This flesh you break, this blood you let
Make desolation in the vein,
Were oat and grape
Born of the sensual root and sap;
My wine you drink, my bread you snap.


## Incarnate devil

Incarnate devil in a talking snake,
The central plains of Asia in his garden,
In shaping-time the circle stung awake,
In shapes of sin forked out the bearded apple,
And God walked there who was a fiddling warden
And played down pardon from the heavens' hill.

When we were strangers to the guided seas,
A handmade moon half holy in a cloud,
The wisemen tell me that the garden gods
Twined good and evil on an eastern tree;
And when the moon rose windily it was
Black as the beast and paler than the cross.

We in our Eden knew the secret guardian
In sacred waters that no frost could harden,
And in the mighty mornings of the earth;
Hell in a horn of sulphur and the cloven myth,
All heaven in a midnight of the sun,
A serpent fiddled in the shaping-time.

# Today, this insect

Today, this insect, and the world I breathe,
Now that my symbols have outelbowed space,
Time at the city spectacles, and half
The dear, daft time I take to nudge the sentence,
In trust and tale have I divided sense,
Slapped down the guillotine, the blood-red double
Of head and tail made witnesses to this
Murder of Eden and green genesis.

The insect certain is the plague of fables.

This story's monster has a serpent caul,
Blind in the coil scrams round the blazing outline,
Measures his own length on the garden wall
And breaks his shell in the last shocked beginning;
A crocodile before the chrysalis,
Before the fall from love the flying heartbone,
Winged like a sabbath ass this children's piece
Uncredited blows Jericho on Eden.

The insect fable is the certain promise.

Death: death of Hamlet and the nightmare madmen,
An air-drawn windmill on a wooden horse,
John's beast, Job's patience, and the fibs of vision,
Greek in the Irish sea the ageless voice:
'Adam I love, my madmen's love is endless,
No tell-tale lover has an end more certain,
All legends' sweethearts on a tree of stories,
My cross of tales behind the fabulous curtain.'

## The seed-at-zero

The seed-at-zero shall not storm
That town of ghosts, the trodden womb
With her rampart to his tapping,
No god-in-hero tumble down
Like a tower on the town
Dumbly and divinely stumbling
Over the manwaging line.

The seed-at-zero shall not storm
That town of ghosts, the manwaged womb
With her rampart to his tapping,
No god-in-hero tumble down
Like a tower on the town
Dumbly and divinely leaping
Over the warbearing line.

Through the rampart of the sky
Shall the star-flanked seed be riddled,
Manna for the rumbling ground,
Quickening for the riddled sea;
Settled on a virgin stronghold
He shall grapple with the guard
And the keeper of the key.

Through the rampart of the sky
Shall the star-flanked seed be riddled,
Manna for the guarded ground,
Quickening for the virgin sea;
Settling on a riddled stronghold
He shall grapple with the guard
And the loser of the key.

May a humble village labour
And a continent deny?
A hemisphere may scold him
And a green inch be his bearer;
Let the hero seed find harbour,

Seaports by a drunken shore
Have their thirsty sailors hide him.

May a humble planet labour
And a continent deny?
A village green may scold him
And a high sphere be his bearer;
Let the hero seed find harbour,
Seaports by a thirsty shore
Have their drunken sailors hide him.

Man-in-seed, in seed-at-zero,
From the foreign fields of space,
Shall not thunder on the town
With a star-flanked garrison,
Nor the cannons of his kingdom
Shall the hero-in-tomorrow
Range on the sky-scraping place.

Man-in-seed, in seed-at-zero,
From the star-flanked fields of space,
Thunders on the foreign town
With a sand-bagged garrison,
Nor the cannons of his kingdom
Shall the hero-in-tomorrow
Range from the grave-groping place.


## Shall gods be said

Shall gods be said to thump the clouds
When clouds are cursed by thunder,
Be said to weep when weather howls?
Shall rainbows be their tunics' colour?

When it is rain where are the gods?
Shall it be said they sprinkle water

From garden cans, or free the floods?

Shall it be said that, venuswise,
An old god's dugs are pressed and pricked,
The wet night scolds me like a nurse?

It shall be said that gods are stone.
Shall a dropped stone drum on the ground,
Flung gravel chime? Let the stones speak
With tonges that talk all tongues.


## Here in this spring

Here in this spring, stars float along the void;
Here in this ornamental winter
Down pelts the naked weather;
This summer buries a spring bird.

Symbols are selected from the years'
Slow rounding of four seasons' coasts,
In autumn teach three seasons' fires
And four birds' notes.

I should tell summer from the trees, the worms
Tell, if at all, the winter's storms
Or the funeral of the sun;
I should learn spring by the cuckooing,
And the slug should teach me destruction.

A worm tells summer better than the clock,
The slug's a living calendar of days;
What shall it tell me if a timeless insect
Says the world wears away?

41

# Do you not father me

Do you not father me, nor the erected arm
For my tall tower's sake cast in her stone?
Do you not mother me, nor, as I am,
The lovers' house, lie suffering my stain?
Do you not sister me, nor the erected crime
For my tall turrets carry as your sin?
Do you not brother me, nor, as you climb,
Adore my windows for their summer scene?

Am I not father, too, and the ascending boy,
The boy of woman and the wanton starer
Marking the flesh and summer in the bay?
Am I not sister, too, who is my saviour?
Am I not all of you by the directed sea
Where bird and shell are babbling in my tower?
Am I not you who front the tidy shore,
Nor roof of sand, nor yet the towering tiler?

You are all these, said she who gave me the long suck,
All these, he said who sacked the children's town,
Up rose the Abraham-man, mad for my sake,
They said, who hacked and humoured, they were mine.
I am, the tower told, felled by a timeless stroke,
Who razed my wooden folly stands aghast,
For man-begetters in the dry-as-paste,
The ringed-sea ghost, rise grimly from the wrack.

Do you not father me on the destroying sand?
You are your sisters' sire, said seaweedy,
The salt sucked dam and darlings of the land
Who play the proper gentleman and lady.
Shall I still be love's house on the widdershin earth,
Woe to the windy masons at my shelter?
Love's house, they answer, and the tower death
Lie all unknowing of the grave sin-eater.

# Out of the sighs

Out of the sighs a little comes,
But not of grief, for I have knocked down that
Before the agony; the spirit grows,
Forgets, and cries;
A little comes, is tasted and found good;
All could not disappoint;
There must, be praised, some certainty,
If not of loving well, then not,
And that is true after perpetual defeat.

After such fighting as the weakest know,
There's more than dying;
Lose the great pains or stuff the wound,
He'll ache too long
Through no regret of leaving woman waiting
For her soldier stained with spilt words
That spill such acrid blood.

Were that enough, enough to ease the pain,
Feeling regret when this is wasted
That made me happy in the sun,
And, sleeping, made me dream
How much was happy while it lasted,
Were vaguenesses enough and the sweet lies plenty,
The hollow words could bear all suffering
And cure me of ills.

Were that enough, bone, blood, and sinew,
The twisted brain, the fair-formed loin,
Groping for matter under the dog's plate,
Man should be cured of distemper.
For all there is to give I offer:
Crumbs, barn, and halter.

## Hold hard, these ancient minutes

Hold hard, these ancient minutes in the cuckoo's month,
Under the lank, fourth folly on Glamorgan's hill,
As the green blooms ride upward, to the drive of time;
Time, in a folly's rider, like a county man
Over the vault of ridings with his hound at heel,
Drives forth my men, my children, from the hanging south.

Country, your sport is summer, and December's pools
By crane and water-tower by the seedy trees
Lie this fifth month unskated, and the birds have flown;
Hold hard, my country children in the world of tales,
The greenwood dying as the deer fall in their tracks,
This first and steepled season, to the summer's game.

And now the horns of England, in the sound of shape,
Summon your snowy horsemen, and the four-stringed hill,
Over the sea-gut loudening, sets a rock alive;
Hurdles and guns and railings, as the boulders heave,
Crack like a spring in a vice, bone breaking April,
Spill the lank folly's hunter and the hard-held hope.

Down fall four padding weathers on the scarlet lands,
Stalking my children's faces with a tail of blood,
Time, in a rider rising, from the harnessed valley;
Hold hard, my county darlings, for a hawk descends,
Golden Glamorgan straightens, to the falling birds.
Your sport is summer as the spring runs angrily.

## Was there a time

Was there a time when dancers with their fiddles
In children's circuses could stay their troubles?
There was a time they could cry over books,
But time has set its maggot on their track.

44

Under the arc of the sky they are unsafe.
What's never known is safest in this life.
Under the skysigns they who have no arms
Have cleanest hands, and, as the heartless ghost
Alone's unhurt, so the blind man sees best.

## Now

Now
Say nay,
Man dry man,
Dry lover mine
The deadrock base and blow the flowered anchor,
Should he, for centre sake, hop in the dust,
Forsake, the fool, the hardiness of anger.

Now
Say nay,
Sir no say,
Death to the yes,
The yes to death, the yesman and the answer,
Should he who split his children with a cure
Have brotherless his sister on the handsaw.

Now
Say nay,
No say sir
Yea the dead stir,
And this, nor this, is shade, the landed crow,
He lying low with ruin in his ear,
The cockerel's tide upcasting from the fire.

Now
Say nay,
So star fall,
So the ball fail,

So solve the mystic sun, the wife of light,
The sun that leaps on petals through a nought,
The come-a-cropper rider of the flower.

Now
Say nay
A fig for
The seal of fire,
Death hairy-heeled, and the tapped ghost in wood,
We make me mystic as the arm of air,
The two-a-vein, the foreskin, and the cloud.


## Why east wind chills

Why east wind chills and south wind cools
Shall not be known till windwell dries
And west's no longer drowned
In winds that bring the fruit and rind
Of many a hundred falls;
Why silk is soft and the stone wounds
The child shall question all his days,
Why night-time rain and the breast's blood
Both quench his thirst he'll have a black reply.

When cometh Jack Frost? the children ask.
Shall they clasp a comet in their fists?
Not till, from high and low, their dust
Sprinkles in children's eyes a long-last sleep
And dusk is crowded with the children's ghosts,
Shall a white answer echo from the rooftops.

All things are known: the stars' advice
Calls some content to travel with the winds,
Though what the stars ask as they round
Time upon time the towers of the skies
Is heard but little till the stars go out.

I hear content, and 'Be content'
Ring like a handbell through the corridors,
And 'Know no answer,' and I know
No answer to the children's cry
Of echo's answer and the man of frost
And ghostly comets over the raised fists.

# A grief ago

A grief ago,
She who was who I hold, the fats and flower,
Or, water-lammed, from the scythe-sided thorn,
Hell wind and sea,
A stem cementing, wrestled up the tower,
Rose maid and male,
Or, masted venus, through the paddler's bowl
Sailed up the sun;

Who is my grief,
A chrysalis unwrinkling on the iron,
Wrenched by my fingerman, the leaden bud
Shot through the leaf,
Was who was folded on the rod the aaron
Rose cast to plague,
The horn and ball of water on the frog
Housed in the side.

And she who lies,
Like exodus a chapter from the garden,
Brand of the lily's anger on her ring,
Tugged through the days
Her ropes of heritage, the wars of pardon,
On field and sand
The twelve triangles of the cherub wind
Engraving going.

47

Who then is she,
She holding me? The people's sea drives on her,
Drives out the father from the caesared camp;
The dens of shape
Shape all her whelps with the long voice of water,
That she I have,
The country-handed grave boxed into love,
Rise before dark.

The night is near,
A nitric shape that leaps her, time and acid;
I tell her this: before the suncock cast
Her bone to fire,
Let her inhale her dead, through seed and solid
Draw in their seas,
So cross her hand with their grave gipsy eyes,
And close her fist.

## How soon the servant sun

How soon the servant sun
(Sir morrow mark)
Can time unriddle, and the cupboard stone
(Fog has a bone
He'll trumpet into meat)
Unshelve that all my gristles have a gown
And the naked egg stand straight,

Sir morrow at his sponge,
(The wound records)
The nurse of giants by the cut sea basin,
(Fog by his spring
Soaks up the sewing tides)
Tells you and you, my masters, as his strange
Man morrow blows through food.

All nerves to serve the sun,
The rite of light,
A claw I question from the mouse's bone,
The long-tailed stone
Trap I with coil and sheet,
Let the soil squeal I am the biting man
And the velvet dead inch out.

How soon my level, lord,
(Sir morrow stamps
Two heels of water on the floor of seed)
Shall raise a lamp
Or spirit up a cloud,
Erect a walking centre in the shroud,
Invisible on the stump

A leg as long as trees,
This inward sir,
Mister and master, darkness for his eyes,
The womb-eyed, cries,
And all sweet hell, deaf as an hour's ear,
Blasts back the trumpet voice.

## Ears in the turrets hear

Ears in the turrets hear
Hands grumble on the door,
Eyes in the gables see
The fingers at the locks.
Shall I unbolt or stay
Alone till the day I die
Unseen by stranger-eyes
In this white house?
Hands, hold you poison or grapes?

Beyond this island bound
By a thin sea of flesh
And a bone coast,

49

The land lies out of sound
And the hills out of mind.
No bird or flying fish
Disturbs this island's rest.

Ears in this island hear
The wind pass like a fire,
Eyes in this island see
Ships anchor off the bay.
Shall I run to the ships
With the wind in my hair,
Or stay till the day I die
And welcome no sailor?
Ships, hold you poison or grapes?

Hands grumble on the door,
Ships anchor off the bay,
Rain beats the sand and slates.
Shall I let in the stranger,
Shall I welcome the sailor,
Or stay till the day I die?

Hands of the stranger and holds of the ships,
Hold you poison or grapes?


## Foster the light

Foster the light nor veil the manshaped moon,
Nor weather winds that blow not down the bone,
But strip the twelve-winded marrow from his circle;
Master the night nor serve the snowman's brain
That shapes each bushy item of the air
Into a polestar pointed on an icicle.

Murmur of spring nor crush the cockerel's eggs,
Nor hammer back a season in the figs,
But graft these four-fruited ridings on your country;

Farmer in time of frost the burning leagues,
By red-eyed orchards sow the seeds of snow,
In your young years the vegetable century.

And father all nor fail the fly-lord's acre,
Nor sprout on owl-seed like a goblin-sucker,
But rail with your wizard's ribs the heart-shaped planet;
Of mortal voices to the ninnies' choir,
High lord esquire, speak up the singing cloud,
And pluck a mandrake music from the marrowroot.

Roll unmanly over this turning tuft,
O ring of seas, nor sorrow as I shift
From all my mortal lovers with a starboard smile;
Nor when my love lies in the cross-boned drift
Naked among the bow-and-arrow birds
Shall you turn cockwise on a tufted axle.

Who gave these seas their colour in a shape
Shaped my clayfellow, and the heaven's ark
In time at flood filled with his coloured doubles;
O who is glory in the shapeless maps,
Now make the world of me as I have made
A merry manshape of your walking circle.


## The hand that signed the paper

The hand that signed the paper felled a city;
Five sovereign fingers taxed the breath,
Doubled the globe of dead and halved a country;
These five kings did a king to death.

The mighty hand leads to a sloping shoulder,
The finger joints are cramped with chalk;
A goose's quill has put an end to murder
That put an end to talk.

The hand that signed the treaty bred a fever,
And famine grew, and locusts came;
Great is the hand that holds dominion over
Man by a scribbled name.

The five kings count the dead but do not soften
The crusted wound nor stroke the brow;
A hand rules pity as a hand rules heaven;
Hands have no tears to flow.


## Should lanterns shine

Should lanterns shine, the holy face,
Caught in an octagon of unaccustomed light,
Would wither up, and any boy of love
Look twice before he fell from grace.
The features in their private dark
Are formed of flesh, but let the false day come
And from her lips the faded pigments fall,
The mummy cloths expose an ancient breast.

I have been told to reason by the heart,
But heart, like head, leads helplessly;
I have been told to reason by the pulse,
And, when it quickens, alter the actions' pace
Till field and roof lie level and the same
So fast I move defying time, the quiet gentleman
Whose beard wags in Egyptian wind.

I have heard many years of telling,
And many years should see some change.

The ball I threw while playing in the park
Has not yet reached the ground.

# I have longed to move away

I have longed to move away
From the hissing of the spent lie
And the old terrors' continual cry
Growing more terrible as the day
Goes over the hill into the deep sea;
I have longed to move away
From the repetition of salutes,
For there are ghosts in the air
And ghostly echoes on paper,
And the thunder of calls and notes.

I have longed to move away but am afraid;
Some life, yet unspent, might explode
Out of the old lie burning on the ground,
And, crackling into the air, leave me half-blind.
Neither by night's ancient fear,
The parting of hat from hair,
Pursed lips at the receiver,
Shall I fall to death's feather.
By these I would not care to die,
Half convention and half lie.

# Find meat on bones

'Find meat on bones that soon have none,
And drink in the two milked crags,
The merriest marrow and the dregs
Before the ladies' breasts are hags
And the limbs are torn.
Disturb no winding-sheets, my son,
But when the ladies are cold as stone
Then hang a ram rose over the rags.

Rebel against the binding moon
And the parliament of sky,
The kingcrafts of the wicked sea,
Autocracy of night and day,
Dictatorship of sun.
Rebel against the flesh and bone,
The word of the blood, the wily skin,
And the maggot no man can slay.'

'The thirst is quenched, the hunger gone,
And my heart is cracked across;
My face is haggard in the glass,
My lips are withered with a kiss,
My breasts are thin.
A merry girl took me for man,
I laid her down and told her sin,
And put beside her a ram rose.

The maggot that no man can kill
And the man no rope can hang
Rebel against my father's dream
That out of a bower of red swine
Howls the foul fiend to heel.
I cannot murder, like a fool,
Season and sunshine, grace and girl,
Nor can I smother the sweet waking.

Black night still ministers the moon,
And the sky lays down her laws,
The sea speaks in a kingly voice,
Light and dark are no enemies
But one companion.
"War on the spider and the wren!
War on the destiny of man!
Doom on the sun!"
Before death takes you, O take back this.'

## Grief thief of time

Grief thief of time crawls off,
The moon-drawn grave, with the seafaring years,
The knave of pain steals off
The sea-halved faith that blew time to his knees,
The old forget the cries,
Lean time on tide and times the wind stood rough,
Call back the castaways
Riding the sea light on a sunken path,
The old forget the grief,
Hack of the cough, the hanging albatross,
Cast back the bone of youth
And salt-eyed stumble bedward where she lies
Who tossed the high tide in a time of stories
And timelessly lies loving with the thief.

Now Jack my fathers let the time-faced crook,
Death flashing from his sleeve,
With swag of bubbles in a seedy sack
Sneak down the stallion grave,
Bull's-eye the outlaw through a eunuch crack
And free the twin-boxed grief,
No silver whistles chase him down the weeks'
Dayed peaks to day to death,
These stolen bubbles have the bites of snakes
And the undead eye-teeth,
No third eye probe into a rainbow's sex
That bridged the human halves,
All shall remain and on the graveward gulf
Shape with my fathers' thieves.

# And death shall have no dominion

And death shall have no dominion.
Dead men naked they shall be one
With the man in the wind and the west moon;
When their bones are picked clean and the clean bones gone,
They shall have stars at elbow and foot;
Though they go mad they shall be sane,
Though they sink through the sea they shall rise again;
Though lovers be lost love shall not;
And death shall have no dominion.

And death shall have no dominion.
Under the windings of the sea
They lying long shall not die windily;
Twisting on racks when sinews give way,
Strapped to a wheel, yet they shall not break;
Faith in their hands shall snap in two,
And the unicorn evils run them through;
Split all ends up they shan't crack;
And death shall have no dominion.

And death shall have no dominion.
No more may gulls cry at their ears
Or waves break loud on the seashores;
Where blew a flower may a flower no more
Lift its head to the blows of the rain;
Though they be mad and dead as nails,
Heads of the characters hammer through daisies;
Break in the sun till the sun breaks down,
And death shall have no dominion.

# Then was my neophyte

Then was my neophyte,
Child in white blood bent on its knees
Under the bell of rocks,
Ducked in the twelve, disciple seas
The winder of the water-clocks
Calls a green day and night.
My sea hermaphrodite,
Snail of man in His ship of fires
That burn the bitten decks,
Knew all His horrible desires
The climber of the water sex
Calls the green rock of light.

Who in these labyrinths,
This tidethread and the lane of scales,
Twine in a moon-blown shell,
Escapes to the flat cities' sails
Furled on the fishes' house and hell,
Nor falls to His green myths?
Stretch the salt photographs,
The landscape grief, love in His oils
Mirror from man to whale
That the green child see like a grail
Through veil and fin and fire and coil
Time on the canvas paths.

He films my vanity.
Shot in the wind, by tilted arcs,
Over the water come
Children from homes and children's parks
Who speak on a finger and thumb,
And the masked, headless boy.
His reels and mystery
The winder of the clockwise scene
Wound like a ball of lakes
Then threw on that tide-hoisted screen
Love's image till my heartbone breaks
By a dramatic sea.

Who kills my history?
The year-hedged row is lame with flint,
Blunt scythe and water blade.
'Who could snap off the shapeless print
From your tomorrow-treading shade
With oracle for eye?'
Time kills me terribly.
'Time shall not murder you,' He said,
'Nor the green nought be hurt;
Who could hack out your unsucked heart,
O green and unborn and undead?'
I saw time murder me.


## Altarwise by owl-light

### I

Altarwise by owl-light in the halfway-house
The gentleman lay graveward with his furies;
Abaddon in the hang-nail cracked from Adam,
And, from his fork, a dog among the fairies,
The atlas-eater with a jaw for news,
Bit out the mandrake with tomorrow's scream.
Then, penny-eyed, that gentleman of wounds,
Old cock from nowheres and the heaven's egg,
With bones unbuttoned to the halfway winds,
Hatched from the windy salvage on one leg,
Scraped at my cradle in a walking word
That night of time under the Christward shelter,
I am the long world's gentleman, he said,
And share my bed with Capricorn and Cancer.

## II

Death is all metaphors, shape in one history;
The child that sucketh long is shooting up,
The planet-ducted pelican of circles
Weans on an artery the gender's strip;
Child of the short spark in a shapeless country
Soon sets alight a long stick from the cradle;
The horizontal cross-bones of Abaddon,
You by the cavern over the black stairs,
Rung bone and blade, the verticals of Adam,
And, manned by midnight, Jacob to the stars;
Hairs of your head, then said the hollow agent,
Are but the roots of nettles and of feathers
Over these groundworks thrusting through a pavement
And hemlock-headed in the wood of weathers.

## III

First there was the lamb on knocking knees
And three dead seasons on a climbing grave
That Adam's wether in the flock of horns,
Butt of the tree-tailed worm that mounted Eve,
Horned down with skullfoot and the skull of toes
On thunderous pavements in the garden time;
Rip of the vaults, I took my marrow-ladle
Out of the wrinkled undertaker's van,
And, Rip Van Winkle from a timeless cradle,
Dipped me breast-deep in the descended bone;
The black ram, shuffling of the year, old winter,
Alone alive among his mutton fold,
We rung our weathering changes on the ladder,
Said the antipodes, and twice spring chimed.

## IV

What is the metre of the dictionary?
The size of genesis? the short spark's gender?
Shade without shape? the shape of Pharaoh's echo?
(My shape of age nagging the wounded whisper).
Which sixth of wind blew out the burning gentry?
(Questions are hunchbacks to the poker marrow).
What of a bamboo man among your acres?
Corset the boneyards for a crooked lad?
Button your bodice on a hump of splinters,
My camel's eye will needle through the shroud.
Love's a reflection of the mushroom features,
Stills snapped by night in the bread-sided field,
Once close-up smiling in the wall of pictures,
Ark-lamped thrown back upon the cutting flood.

## V

And from the windy West came two-gunned Gabriel,
From Jesu's sleeve trumped up the king of spots,
The sheath-decked jacks, queen with a shuffled heart;
Said the fake gentleman in suit of spades,
Black-tongued and tipsy from salvation's bottle,
Rose my Byzantine Adam in the night;
For loss of blood I fell on Ishmael's plain,
Under the milky mushrooms slew my hunger,
A climbing sea from Asia had me down
And Jonah's Moby snatched me by the hair;
Cross-stroked salt Adam to the frozen angel
Pin-legged on pole-hills with a black medusa
By waste seas where the white bear quoted Virgil
And sirens singing from our lady's sea-straw.

## VI

Cartoon of slashes on the tide-traced crater,
He in a book of water tallow-eyed
By lava's light split through the oyster vowels
And burned sea silence on a wick of words:
Pluck, cock, my sea eye, said medusa's scripture,
Lop, love, my fork tongue, said the pin-hilled nettle;
And love plucked out the stinging siren's eye,
Old cock from nowheres lopped the minstrel tongue
Till tallow I blew from the wax's tower
The fats of midnight when the salt was singing;
Adam, time's joker, on a witch of cardboard
Spelt out the seven seas, an evil index,
The bagpipe-breasted ladies in the deadweed
Blew out the blood gauze through the wound of manwax.

## VII

Now stamp the Lord's Prayer on a grain of rice,
A Bible-leaved of all the written woods
Strip to this tree: a rocking alphabet,
Genesis in the root, the scarecrow word,
And one light's language in the book of trees;
Doom on deniers at the wind-turned statement.
Time's tune my ladies with the teats of music,
The scaled sea-sawers, fix in a naked sponge
Who sucks the bell-voiced Adam out of magic,
Time, milk, and magic, from the world beginning.
Time is the tune my ladies lend their heartbreak,
From bald pavilions and the house of bread
Time tracks the sound of shape on man and cloud,
On rose and icicle the ringing handprint.

## VIII

This was the crucifixion on the mountain,
Time's nerve in vinegar, the gallow grave
As tarred with blood as the bright thorns I wept;
The world's my wound, God's Mary in her grief,
Bent like three trees and bird-papped through her shift,
With pins for teardrops is the long wound's woman.
This was the sky, Jack Christ, each minstrel angle
Drove in the heaven-driven of the nails
Till the three-coloured rainbow from my nipples
From pole to pole leapt round the snail-waked world.
I by the tree of thieves, all glory's sawbones
Unsex the skeleton this mountain minute,
And by this blowclock witness of the sun
Suffer the heaven's children through my heartbeat.

## IX

From the oracular archives and the parchment,
Prophets and fibre kings in oil and letter,
The lamped calligrapher, the queen in splints,
Buckle to lint and cloth their natron footsteps,
Draw on the glove of prints, dead Cairo's henna
Pour like a halo on the caps and serpents.
This was the resurrection in the desert,
Death from a bandage, rants the mask of scholars
Gold on such features, and the linen spirit
Weds my long gentleman to dusts and furies;
With priest and pharaoh bed my gentle wound,
World in the sand, on the triangle landscape,
With stones of odyssey for ash and garland
And rivers of the dead around my neck.

## X

Let the tale's sailor from a Christian voyage
Atlaswise hold halfway off the dummy bay
Time's ship-racked gospel on the globe I balance:
So shall winged harbours through the rockbirds' eyes
Spot the blown word, and on the seas I image
December's thorn screwed in a brow of holly.
Let the first Peter from a rainbow's quayrail
Ask the tall fish swept from the bible east,
What rhubarb man peeled in her foam-blue channel
Has sown a flying garden round that sea-ghost?
Green as beginning, let the garden diving
Soar, with its two bark towers, to that Day
When the worm builds with the gold straws of venom
My nest of mercies in the rude, red tree.

# The Map of Love

# Because the pleasure-bird whistles

Because the pleasure-bird whistles after the hot wires,
Shall the blind horse sing sweeter?
Convenient bird and beast lie lodged to suffer
The supper and knives of a mood.
In the sniffed and poured snow on the tip of the tongue of the year
That clouts the spittle like bubbles with broken rooms,
An enamoured man alone by the twigs of his eyes, two fires,
Camped in the drug-white shower of nerves and food,
Savours the lick of the times through a deadly wood of hair
In a wind that plucked a goose,
Nor ever, as the wild tongue breaks its tombs,
Rounds to look at the red, wagged root.
Because there stands, one story out of the bum city,
That frozen wife whose juices drift like a fixed sea
Secretly in statuary,
Shall I, struck on the hot and rocking street,
Not spin to stare at an old year
Toppling and burning in the muddle of towers and galleries
Like the mauled pictures of boys?
The salt person and blasted place
I furnish with the meat of a fable;
If the dead starve, their stomachs turn to tumble
An upright man in the antipodes
Or spray-based and rock-chested sea:
Over the past table I repeat this present grace.

# I make this in a warring absence

I make this in a warring absence when
Each ancient, stone-necked minute of love's season
Harbours my anchored tongue, slips the quaystone,
When, praise is blessed, her pride in mast and fountain
Sailed and set dazzling by the handshaped ocean,
In that proud sailing tree with branches driven
Through the last vault and vegetable groyne,
And this weak house to marrow-columned heaven,

Is corner-cast, breath's rag, scrawled weed, a vain
And opium head, crow stalk, puffed, cut, and blown,
Or like the tide-looped breastknot reefed again
Or rent ancestrally the roped sea-hymen,
And, pride is last, is like a child alone
By magnet winds to her blind mother drawn,
Bread and milk mansion in a toothless town.

She makes for me a nettle's innocence
And a silk pigeon's guilt in her proud absence,
In the molested rocks the shell of virgins,
The frank, closed pearl, the sea-girls' lineaments
Glint in the staved and siren-printed caverns,
Is maiden in the shameful oak, omens
Whalebed and bulldance, the gold bush of lions
Proud as a sucked stone and huge as sandgrains.

There are her contraries: the beast who follows
With priest's grave foot and hand of five assassins
Her molten flight up cinder-nesting columns,
Calls the starved fire herd, is cast in ice,
Lost in a limp-treed and uneating silence,
Who scales a hailing hill in her cold flintsteps
Falls on a ring of summers and locked noons.

I make a weapon of an ass's skeleton
And walk the warring sands by the dead town,
Cudgel great air, wreck east, and topple sundown,

Storm her sped heart, hang with beheaded veins
Its wringing shell, and let her eyelids fasten.
Destruction, picked by birds, brays through the jawbone,
And, for that murder's sake, dark with contagion
Like an approaching wave I sprawl to ruin.

Ruin, the room of errors, one rood dropped
Down the stacked sea and water-pillared shade,
Weighed in rock shroud, is my proud pyramid;
Where, wound in emerald linen and sharp wind,
The hero's head lies scraped of every legend,
Comes love's anatomist with sun-gloved hand
Who picks the live heart on a diamond.

'His mother's womb had a tongue that lapped up mud,'
Cried the topless, inchtaped lips from hank and hood
In that bright anchorground where I lay linened,
'A lizard darting with black venom's thread
Doubled, to fork him back, through the lockjaw bed
And the breath-white, curtained mouth of seed.'
'See,' drummed the taut masks, 'how the dead ascend:
In the groin's endless coil a man is tangled.'

These once-blind eyes have breathed a wind of visions,
The cauldron's root through this once-rindless hand
Fumed like a tree, and tossed a burning bird;
With loud, torn tooth and tail and cobweb drum
The crumpled packs fled past this ghost in bloom,
And, mild as pardon from a cloud of pride,
The terrible world my brother bares his skin.

Now in the cloud's big breast lie quiet countries,
Delivered seas my love from her proud place
Walks with no wound, nor lightning in her face,
A calm wind blows that raised the trees like hair
Once where the soft snow's blood was turned to ice.
And though my love pulls the pale, nippled air,
Prides of tomorrow suckling in her eyes,
Yet this I make in a forgiving presence.

# When all my five and country senses

When all my five and country senses see,
The fingers will forget green thumbs and mark
How, through the halfmoon's vegetable eye,
Husk of young stars and handfull zodiac,
Love in the frost is pared and wintered by,
The whispering ears will watch love drummed away
Down breeze and shell to a discordant beach,
And, lashed to syllables, the lynx tongue cry
That her fond wounds are mended bitterly.
My nostrils see her breath burn like a bush.

My one and noble heart has witnesses
In all love's countries, that will grope awake;
And when blind sleep drops on the spying senses,
The heart is sensual, though five eyes break.

# We lying by seasand

We lying by seasand, watching yellow
And the grave sea, mock who deride
Who follow the red rivers, hollow
Alcove of words out of cicada shade,
For in this yellow grave of sand and sea
A calling for colour calls with the wind
That's grave and gay as grave and sea
Sleeping on either hand.
The lunar silences, the silent tide
Lapping the still canals, the dry tide-master
Ribbed between desert and water storm,
Should cure our ills of the water
With a one-coloured calm;
The heavenly music over the sand
Sounds with the grains as they hurry
Hiding the golden mountains and mansions

Of the grave, gay, seaside land.
Bound by a sovereign strip, we lie,
Watch yellow, wish for wind to blow away
The strata of the shore and drown red rock;
But wishes breed not, neither
Can we fend off rock arrival,
Lie watching yellow until the golden weather
Breaks, O my heart's blood, like a heart and hill.


## It is the sinners' dust-tongued bell

It is the sinners' dust-tongued bell claps me to churches
When, with his torch and hourglass, like a sulphur priest,
His beast heel cleft in a sandal,
Time marks a black aisle kindle from the brand of ashes,
Grief with dishevelled hands tear out the altar ghost
And a firewind kill the candle.

Over the choir minute I hear the hour chant:
Time's coral saint and the salt grief drown a foul sepulchre
And a whirlpool drives the prayerwheel;
Moonfall and sailing emperor, pale as their tideprint,
Hear by death's accident the clocked and dashed-down spire
Strike the sea hour through bellmetal.

There is loud and dark directly under the dumb flame,
Storm, snow, and fountain in the weather of fireworks,
Cathedral calm in the pulled house;
Grief with drenched book and candle christens the cherub time
From the emerald, still bell; and from the pacing weathercock
The voice of bird on coral prays.

Forever it is a white child in the dark-skinned summer
Out of the font of bone and plants at that stone tocsin
Scales the blue wall of spirits;
From blank and leaking winter sails the child in colour,

Shakes, in crabbed burial shawl, by sorcerer's insect woken,
Ding dong from the mute turrets.

I mean by time the cast and curfew rascal of our marriage,
At nightbreak born in the fat side, from an animal bed
In a holy room in a wave;
And all love's sinners in sweet cloth kneel to a hyleg image,
Nutmeg, civet, and sea-parsley serve the plagued groom and bride
Who have brought forth the urchin grief.

## O make me a mask

O make me a mask and a wall to shut from your spies
Of the sharp, enamelled eyes and the spectacled claws
Rape and rebellion in the nurseries of my face,
Gag of a dumbstruck tree to block from bare enemies
The bayonet tongue in this undefended prayerpiece,
The present mouth, and the sweetly blown trumpet of lies,
Shaped in old armour and oak the countenance of a dunce
To shield the glistening brain and blunt the examiners,
And a tear-stained widower grief drooped from the lashes
To veil belladonna and let the dry eyes perceive
Others betray the lamenting lies of their losses
By the curve of the nude mouth or the laugh up the sleeve.

## The spire cranes

The spire cranes. Its statue is an aviary.
From the stone nest it does not let the feathery
Carved birds blunt their striking throats on the salt gravel,
Pierce the spilt sky with diving wing in weed and heel
An inch in froth. Chimes cheat the prison spire, pelter
In time like outlaw rains on that priest, water,

Time for the swimmers' hands, music for silver lock
And mouth. Both note and plume plunge from the spire's hook.
Those craning birds are choice for you, songs that jump back
To the built voice, or fly with winter to the bells,
But do not travel down dumb wind like prodigals.

## After the funeral

### (In memory of Ann Jones)

After the funeral, mule praises, brays,
Windshake of sailshaped ears, muffle-toed tap
Tap happily of one peg in the thick
Grave's foot, blinds down the lids, the teeth in black,
The spittled eyes, the salt ponds in the sleeves,
Morning smack of the spade that wakes up sleep,
Shakes a desolate boy who slits his throat
In the dark of the coffin and sheds dry leaves,
That breaks one bone to light with a judgment clout,
After the feast of tear-stuffed time and thistles
In a room with a stuffed fox and a stale fern,
I stand, for this memorial's sake, alone
In the snivelling hours with dead, humped Ann
Whose hooded, fountain heart once fell in puddles
Round the parched worlds of Wales and drowned each sun
(Though this for her is a monstrous image blindly
Magnified out of praise; her death was a still drop;
She would not have me sinking in the holy
Flood of her heart's fame; she would lie dumb and deep
And need no druid of her broken body).
But I, Ann's bard on a raised hearth, call all
The seas to service that her wood-tongued virtue
Babble like a bellbuoy over the hymning heads,
Bow down the walls of the ferned and foxy woods
That her love sing and swing through a brown chapel,
Bless her bent spirit with four, crossing birds.
Her flesh was meek as milk, but this skyward statue

With the wild breast and blessed and giant skull
Is carved from her in a room with a wet window
In a fiercely mourning house in a crooked year.
I know her scrubbed and sour humble hands
Lie with religion in their cramp, her threadbare
Whisper in a damp word, her wits drilled hollow,
Her fist of a face died clenched on a round pain;
And sculptured Ann is seventy years of stone.
These cloud-sopped, marble hands, this monumental
Argument of the hewn voice, gesture and psalm
Storm me forever over her grave until
The stuffed lung of the fox twitch and cry Love
And the strutting fern lay seeds on the black sill.


## Once it was the colour of saying

Once it was the colour of saying
Soaked my table the uglier side of a hill
With a capsized field where a school sat still
And a black and white patch of girls grew playing;
The gentle seaslides of saying I must undo
That all the charmingly drowned arise to cockcrow and kill.
When I whistled with mitching boys through a reservoir park
Where at night we stoned the cold and cuckoo
Lovers in the dirt of their leafy beds,
The shade of their trees was a word of many shades
And a lamp of lightning for the poor in the dark;
Now my saying shall be my undoing,
And every stone I wind off like a reel.

## Not from this anger

Not from this anger, anticlimax after
Refusal struck her loin and the lame flower
Bent like a beast to lap the singular floods
In a land strapped by hunger
Shall she receive a bellyful of weeds
And bear those tendril hands I touch across
The agonized, two seas.

Behind my head a square of sky sags over
The circular smile tossed from lover to lover
And the golden ball spins out of the skies;
Not from this anger after
Refusal struck like a bell under water
Shall her smile breed that mouth, behind the mirror,
That burns along my eyes.

## How shall my animal

How shall my animal
Whose wizard shape I trace in the cavernous skull,
Vessel of abscesses and exultation's shell,
Endure burial under the spelling wall,
The invoked, shrouding veil at the cap of the face,
Who should be furious,
Drunk as a vineyard snail, flailed like an octopus,
Roaring, crawling, quarrel
With the outside weathers,
The natural circle of the discovered skies
Draw down to its weird eyes?

How shall it magnetize,
Towards the studded male in a bent, midnight blaze
That melts the lionhead's heel and horseshoe of the heart,

A brute land in the cool top of the country days
To trot with a loud mate the haybeds of a mile,
Love and labour and kill
In quick, sweet, cruel light till the locked ground sprout out,
The black, burst sea rejoice,
The bowels turn turtle,
Claw of the crabbed veins squeeze from each red particle
The parched and raging voice?

Fishermen of mermen
Creep and harp on the tide, sinking their charmed, bent pin
With bridebait of gold bread, I with a living skein,
Tongue and ear in the thread, angle the temple-bound
Curl-locked and animal cavepools of spells and bone,
Trace out a tentacle,
Nailed with an open eye, in the bowl of wounds and weed
To clasp my fury on ground
And clap its great blood down;
Never shall beast be born to atlas the few seas
Or poise the day on a horn.

Sigh long, clay cold, lie shorn,
Cast high, stunned on gilled stone; sly scissors ground in frost
Clack through the thicket of strength, love hewn in pillars drops
With carved bird, saint, and sun, the wrackspiked maiden mouth
Lops, as a bush plumed with flames, the rant of the fierce eye,
Clips short the gesture of breath.
Die in red feathers when the flying heaven's cut,
And roll with the knocked earth:
Lie dry, rest robbed, my beast.
You have kicked from a dark den, leaped up the whinnying light,
And dug your grave in my breast.

## The tombstone told

The tombstone told when she died.
Her two surnames stopped me still.
A virgin married at rest.
She married in this pouring place,
That I struck one day by luck,
Before I heard in my mother's side
Or saw in the looking-glass shell
The rain through her cold heart speak
And the sun killed in her face.
More the thick stone cannot tell.

Before she lay on a stranger's bed
With a hand plunged through her hair,
Or that rainy tongue beat back
Through the devilish years and innocent deaths
To the room of a secret child,
Among men later I heard it said
She cried her white-dressed limbs were bare
And her red lips were kissed black,
She wept in her pain and made mouths,
Talked and tore though her eyes smiled.

I who saw in a hurried film
Death and this mad heroine
Meet once on a mortal wall
Heard her speak through the chipped beak
Of the stone bird guarding her:
I died before bedtime came
But my womb was bellowing
And I felt with my bare fall
A blazing red harsh head tear up
And the dear floods of his hair.

# On no work of words

On no work of words now for three lean months in the bloody
Belly of the rich year and the big purse of my body
I bitterly take to task my poverty and craft:

To take to give is all, return what is hungrily given
Puffing the pounds of manna up through the dew to heaven,
The lovely gift of the gab bangs back on a blind shaft.

To lift to leave from the treasures of man is pleasing death
That will rake at last all currencies of the marked breath
And count the taken, forsaken mysteries in a bad dark.

To surrender now is to pay the expensive ogre twice.
Ancient woods of my blood, dash down to the nut of the seas
If I take to burn or return this world which is each man's work.

# A saint about to fall

A saint about to fall,
The stained flats of heaven hit and razed
To the kissed kite hems of his shawl,
On the last street wave praised
The unwinding, song by rock,
Of the woven wall
Of his father's house in the sands,
The vanishing of the musical ship-work and the chucked bells,
The wound-down cough of the blood-counting clock
Behind a face of hands,
On the angelic etna of the last whirring featherlands,
Wind-heeled foot in the hole of a fireball,
Hymned his shrivelling flock,
On the last rick's tip by spilled wine-wells

Sang heaven hungry and the quick
Cut Christbread spitting vinegar and all
The mazes of his praise and envious tongue were worked in
                                        flames and shells.


Glory cracked like a flea.
The sun-leaved holy candlewoods
Drivelled down to one singeing tree
With a stub of black buds,
The sweet, fish-gilled boats bringing blood
Lurched through a scuttled sea
With a hold of leeches and straws,
Heaven fell with his fall and one crocked bell beat the left air.
O wake in me in my house in the mud
Of the crotch of the squawking shores,
Flicked from the carbolic city puzzle in a bed of sores
The scudding base of the familiar sky,
The lofty roots of the clouds.
From an odd room in a split house stare,
Milk in your mouth, at the sour floods
That bury the sweet street slowly, see
The skull of the earth is barbed with a war of burning brains
                                        and hair.


Strike in the time-bomb town,
Raise the live rafters of the eardrum,
Throw your fear a parcel of stone
Through the dark asylum,
Lapped among herods wail
As their blade marches in
That the eyes are already murdered,
The stocked heart is forced, and agony has another mouth to feed.
O wake to see, after a noble fall,
The old mud hatch again, the horrid
Woe drip from the dishrag hands and the pressed sponge of the
                                        forehead,
The breath draw back like a bolt through white oil
And a stranger enter like iron.

Cry joy that this witchlike midwife second
Bullies into rough seas you so gentle
And makes with a flick of the thumb and sun
A thundering bullring of your silent and girl-circled island.

## If my head hurt a hair's foot

'If my head hurt a hair's foot
Pack back the downed bone. If the unpricked ball of my breath
Bump on a spout let the bubbles jump out.
Sooner drop with the worm of the ropes round my throat
Than bully ill love in the clouted scene.

All game phrases fit your ring of a cockfight:
I'll comb the snared woods with a glove on a lamp,
Peck, sprint, dance on fountains and duck time
Before I rush in a crouch the ghost with a hammer, air,
Strike light, and bloody a loud room.

If my bunched, monkey coming is cruel
Rage me back to the making house. My hand unravel
When you sew the deep door. The bed is a cross place.
Bend, if my journey ache, direction like an arc or make
A limp and riderless shape to leap nine thinning months.'

'No. Not for Christ's dazzling bed
Or a nacreous sleep among soft particles and charms
My dear would I change my tears or your iron head.
Thrust, my daughter or son, to escape, there is none, none, none,
Nor when all ponderous heaven's host of waters breaks.

Now to awake husked of gestures and my joy like a cave
To the anguish and carrion, to the infant forever unfree,
O my lost love bounced from a good home;
The grain that hurries this way from the rim of the grave
Has a voice and a house, and there and here you must couch
                                        and cry.

Rest beyond choice in the dust-appointed grain,
At the breast stored with seas. No return
Through the waves of the fat streets nor the skeleton's thin ways.
The grave and my calm body are shut to your coming as stone,
And the endless beginning of prodigies suffers open.'


## Twenty-four years

Twenty-four years remind the tears of my eyes.
(Bury the dead for fear that they walk to the grave in labour.)
In the groin of the natural doorway I crouched like a tailor
Sewing a shroud for a journey
By the light of the meat-eating sun.
Dressed to die, the sensual strut begun,
With my red veins full of money,
In the final direction of the elementary town
I advance for as long as forever is.

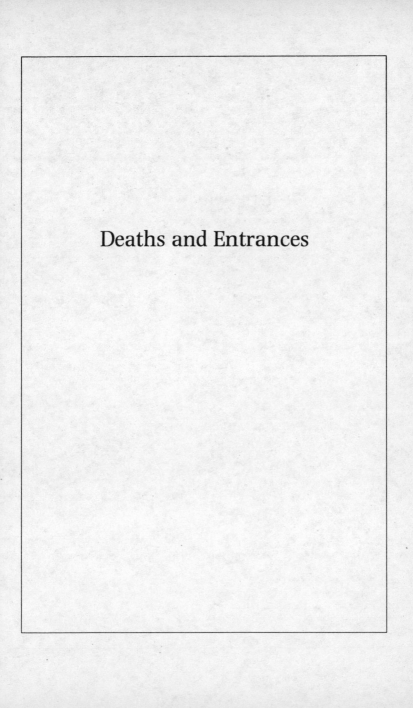

# Deaths and Entrances

## The conversation of prayers

The conversation of prayers about to be said
By the child going to bed and the man on the stairs
Who climbs to his dying love in her high room,
The one not caring to whom in his sleep he will move
And the other full of tears that she will be dead,

Turns in the dark on the sound they know will arise
Into the answering skies from the green ground,
From the man on the stairs and the child by his bed.
The sound about to be said in the two prayers
For the sleep in a safe land and the love who dies

Will be the same grief flying. Whom shall they calm?
Shall the child sleep unharmed or the man be crying?
The conversation of prayers about to be said
Turns on the quick and the dead, and the man on the stairs
Tonight shall find no dying but alive and warm

In the fire of his care his love in the high room.
And the child not caring to whom he climbs his prayer
Shall drown in a grief as deep as his true grave,
And mark the dark eyed wave, through the eyes of sleep,
Dragging him up the stairs to one who lies dead.

## A Refusal to Mourn the Death, by Fire, of a Child in London

Never until the mankind making
Bird beast and flower
Fathering and all humbling darkness
Tells with silence the last light breaking
And the still hour
Is come of the sea tumbling in harness

85

And I must enter again the round
Zion of the water bead
And the synagogue of the ear of corn
Shall I let pray the shadow of a sound
Or sow my salt seed
In the least valley of sackcloth to mourn

The majesty and burning of the child's death.
I shall not murder
The mankind of her going with a grave truth
Nor blaspheme down the stations of the breath
With any further
Elegy of innocence and youth.

Deep with the first dead lies London's daughter,
Robed in the long friends,
The grains beyond age, the dark veins of her mother,
Secret by the unmourning water
Of the riding Thames.
After the first death, there is no other.

## Poem in October

It was my thirtieth year to heaven
Woke to my hearing from harbour and neighbour wood
    And the mussel pooled and the heron
            Priested shore
            The morning beckon
With water praying and call of seagull and rook
And the knock of sailing boats on the net webbed wall
        Myself to set foot
            That second
In the still sleeping town and set forth.

My birthday began with the water-
Birds and the birds of the winged trees flying my name
    Above the farms and the white horses
            And I rose
        In rainy autumn
And walked abroad in a shower of all my days.
High tide and the heron dived when I took the road
        Over the border
           And the gates
Of the town closed as the town awoke.

    A springful of larks in a rolling
Cloud and the roadside bushes brimming with whistling
    Blackbirds and the sun of October
            Summery
        On the hill's shoulder,
Here were fond climates and sweet singers suddenly
Come in the morning where I wandered and listened
        To the rain wringing
           Wind blow cold
In the wood faraway under me.

    Pale rain over the dwindling harbour
And over the sea wet church the size of a snail
    With its horns through mist and the castle
           Brown as owls
        But all the gardens
Of spring and summer were blooming in the tall tales
Beyond the border and under the lark full cloud.
        There could I marvel
           My birthday
Away but the weather turned around.

    It turned away from the blithe country
And down the other air and the blue altered sky
    Streamed again a wonder of summer
            With apples
        Pears and red currants
And I saw in the turning so clearly a child's

Forgotten mornings when he walked with his mother
  Through the parables
    Of sun light
And the legends of the green chapels

And the twice told fields of infancy
That his tears burned my cheeks and his heart moved in mine.
  These were the woods the river and sea
    Where a boy
   In the listening
Summertime of the dead whispered the truth of his joy
To the trees and the stones and the fish in the tide.
   And the mystery
    Sang alive
Still in the water and singingbirds.

And there could I marvel my birthday
Away but the weather turned around. And the true
  Joy of the long dead child sang burning
    In the sun.
   It was my thirtieth
Year to heaven stood there then in the summer noon
Though the town below lay leaved with October blood.
   O may my heart's truth
    Still be sung
On this high hill in a year's turning.

## This side of the truth

(for Llewelyn)

This side of the truth,
You may not see, my son,
King of your blue eyes
In the blinding country of youth,
That all is undone,
Under the unminding skies,
Of innocence and guilt
Before you move to make

One gesture of the heart or head,
Is gathered and spilt
Into the winding dark
Like the dust of the dead.

Good and bad, two ways
Of moving about your death
By the grinding sea,
King of your heart in the blind days,
Blow away like breath,
Go crying through you and me
And the souls of all men
Into the innocent
Dark, and the guilty dark, and good
Death, and bad death, and then
In the last element
Fly like the stars' blood,

Like the sun's tears,
Like the moon's seed, rubbish
And fire, the flying rant
Of the sky, king of your six years.
And the wicked wish,
Down the beginning of plants
And animals and birds,
Water and light, the earth and sky,
Is cast before you move,
And all your deeds and words,
Each truth, each lie,
Die in unjudging love.

## To Others than You

Friend by enemy I call you out.

You with a bad coin in your socket,
You my friend there with a winning air
Who palmed the lie on me when you looked

Brassily at my shyest secret,
Enticed with twinkling bits of the eye
Till the sweet tooth of my love bit dry,
Rasped at last, and I stumbled and sucked,
Whom now I conjure to stand as thief
In the memory worked by mirrors,
With unforgettably smiling act,
Quickness of hand in the velvet glove
And my whole heart under your hammer,
Were once such a creature, so gay and frank
A desireless familiar
I never thought to utter or think
While you displaced a truth in the air,

That though I loved them for their faults
As much as for their good,
My friends were enemies on stilts
With their heads in a cunning cloud.


## Love in the Asylum

A stranger has come
To share my room in the house not right in the head,
A girl mad as birds

Bolting the night of the door with her arm her plume.
Strait in the mazed bed
She deludes the heaven-proof house with entering clouds

Yet she deludes with walking the nightmarish room,
At large as the dead,
Or rides the imagined oceans of the male wards.

She has come possessed
Who admits the delusive light through the bouncing wall,
Possessed by the skies

She sleeps in the narrow trough yet she walks the dust
        Yet raves at her will
On the madhouse boards worn thin by my walking tears.

And taken by light in her arms at long and dear last
        I may without fail
Suffer the first vision that set fire to the stars.


## Unluckily for a death

Unluckily for a death
Waiting with phoenix under
The pyre yet to be lighted of my sins and days,
And for the woman in shades
Saint carved and sensual among the scudding
Dead and gone, dedicate forever to my self
Though the brawl of the kiss has not occurred,
On the clay cold mouth, on the fire
Branded forehead, that could bind
Her constant, nor the winds of love broken wide
To the wind the choir and cloister
Of the wintry nunnery of the order of lust
Beneath my life, that sighs for the seducer's coming
In the sun strokes of summer,

Loving on this sea banged guilt
My holy lucky body
Under the cloud against love is caught and held and kissed
In the mill of the midst
Of the descending day, the dark our folly,
Cut to the still star in the order of the quick
But blessed by such heroic hosts in your every
Inch and glance that the wound
Is certain god, and the ceremony of souls
Is celebrated there, and communion between suns.

Never shall my self chant
About the saint in shades while the endless breviary
Turns of your prayed flesh, nor shall I shoo the bird below me:
The death biding two lie lonely.

I see the tigron in tears
In the androgynous dark,
His striped and noon maned tribe striding to holocaust,
The she mules bear their minotaurs,
The duck-billed platypus broody in a milk of birds.
I see the wanting nun saint carved in a garb
Of shades, symbol of desire beyond my hours
And guilts, great crotch and giant
Continence. I see the unfired phoenix, herald
And heaven crier, arrow now of aspiring
And the renouncing of islands.
All love but for the full assemblage in flower
Of the living flesh is monstrous or immortal,
And the grave its daughters.

Love, my fate got luckily,
Teaches with no telling
That the phoenix' bid for heaven and the desire after
Death in the carved nunnery
Both shall fail if I bow not to your blessing
Nor walk in the cool of your mortal garden
With immortality at my side like Christ the sky.
This I know from the native
Tongue of your translating eyes. The young stars told me,
Hurling into beginning like Christ the child.
Lucklessly she must lie patient
And the vaulting bird be still. O my true love, hold me.
In your every inch and glance is the globe of genesis spun,
And the living earth your sons.

# The hunchback in the park

The hunchback in the park
A solitary mister
Propped between trees and water
From the opening of the garden lock
That lets the trees and water enter
Until the Sunday sombre bell at dark

Eating bread from a newspaper
Drinking water from the chained cup
That the children filled with gravel
In the fountain basin where I sailed my ship
Slept at night in a dog kennel
But nobody chained him up.

Like the park birds he came early
Like the water he sat down
And Mister they called Hey mister
The truant boys from the town
Running when he had heard them clearly
On out of sound

Past lake and rockery
Laughing when he shook his paper
Hunchbacked in mockery
Through the loud zoo of the willow groves
Dodging the park keeper
With his stick that picked up leaves.

And the old dog sleeper
Alone between nurses and swans
While the boys among willows
Made the tigers jump out of their eyes
To roar on the rockery stones
And the groves were blue with sailors

Made all day until bell time
A woman figure without fault
Straight as a young elm

Straight and tall from his crooked bones
That she might stand in the night
After the locks and chains

All night in the unmade park
After the railings and shrubberies
The birds the grass the trees the lake
And the wild boys innocent as strawberries
Had followed the hunchback
To his kennel in the dark.

## Into her lying down head

### I

Into her lying down head
His enemies entered bed,
Under the encumbered eyelid,
Through the rippled drum of the hair-buried ear;
And Noah's rekindled now unkind dove
Flew man-bearing there.
Last night in a raping wave
Whales unreined from the green grave
In fountains of origin gave up their love,
Along her innocence glided
Juan aflame and savagely young King Lear,
Queen Catherine howling bare
And Samson drowned in his hair,
The colossal intimacies of silent
Once seen strangers or shades on a stair;
There the dark blade and wanton sighing her down
To a haycock couch and the scythes of his arms
Rode and whistled a hundred times
Before the crowing morning climbed;

94

Man was the burning England she was sleep-walking, and the
                                        enamouring island
    Made her limbs blind by luminous charms,
Sleep to a newborn sleep in a swaddling loin-leaf stroked and sang
    And his runaway beloved childlike laid in the acorned sand.


II


        There where a numberless tongue
        Wound their room with a male moan,
    His faith around her flew undone
And darkness hung the walls with baskets of snakes,
A furnace-nostrilled column-membered
            Super-or-near man
        Resembling to her dulled sense
        The thief of adolescence,
Early imaginary half remembered
        Oceanic lover alone
Jealousy cannot forget for all her sakes,
        Made his bad bed in her good
        Night, and enjoyed as he would.
Crying, white gowned, from the middle moonlit stages
        Out to the tiered and hearing tide,
Close and far she announced the theft of the heart
In the taken body at many ages,
        Trespasser and broken bride
        Celebrating at her side
All blood-signed assailings and vanished marriages in which he
                                had no lovely part
        Nor could share, for his pride, to the least
Mutter and foul wingbeat of the solemnizing nightpriest
Her holy unholy hours with the always anonymous beast.


95

III

Two sand grains together in bed,
Head to heaven-circling head,
Singly lie with the whole wide shore,
The covering sea their nightfall with no names;
And out of every domed and soil-based shell
One voice in chains declaims
The female, deadly, and male
Libidinous betrayal,
Golden dissolving under the water veil.
A she bird sleeping brittle by
Her lover's wings that fold tomorrow's flight,
Within the nested treefork
Sings to the treading hawk
Carrion, paradise, chirrup my bright yolk.
A blade of grass longs with the meadow,
A stone lies lost and locked in the lark-high hill.
Open as to the air to the naked shadow
O she lies alone and still,
Innocent between two wars,
With the incestuous secret brother in the seconds to perpetuate
the stars,
A man torn up mourns in the sole night.
And the second comers, the severers, the enemies from the deep
Forgotten dark, rest their pulse and bury their dead in her
faithless sleep.

# Paper and sticks

Paper and sticks and shovel and match
Why won't the news of the old world catch
And the fire in a temper start

Once I had a rich boy for myself
I loved his body and his navy blue wealth
And I lived in his purse and his heart

When in our bed I was tossing and turning
All I could see were his brown eyes burning
By the green of a one pound note

I talk to him as I clean the grate
O my dear it's never too late
To take me away as you whispered and wrote

I had a handsome and well-off boy
I'll share my money and we'll run for joy
With a bouncing and silver spooned kid

Sharp and shrill my silly tongue scratches
Words on the air as the fire catches
*You* never did and *he* never did.

# Deaths and Entrances

On almost the incendiary eve
    Of several near deaths,
When one at the great least of your best loved
    And always known must leave
Lions and fires of his flying breath,
    Of your immortal friends
Who'd raise the organs of the counted dust
    To shoot and sing your praise,

One who called deepest down shall hold his peace
   That cannot sink or cease
   Endlessly to his wound
In many married London's estranging grief.

On almost the incendiary eve
   When at your lips and keys,
Locking, unlocking, the murdered strangers weave,
   One who is most unknown,
Your polestar neighbour, sun of another street,
   Will dive up to his tears.
He'll bathe his raining blood in the male sea
   Who strode for your own dead
And wind his globe out of your water thread
   And load the throats of shells
   With every cry since light
Flashed first across his thunderclapping eyes.

On almost the incendiary eve
   Of deaths and entrances,
When near and strange wounded on London's waves
   Have sought your single grave,
One enemy, of many, who knows well
   Your heart is luminous
In the watched dark, quivering through locks and caves,
   Will pull the thunderbolts
To shut the sun, plunge, mount your darkened keys
   And sear just riders back,
   Until that one loved least
Looms the last Samson of your zodiac.

# A Winter's Tale

It is a winter's tale
That the snow blind twilight ferries over the lakes
And floating fields from the farm in the cup of the vales,
Gliding windless through the hand folded flakes,
The pale breath of cattle at the stealthy sail,

And the stars falling cold,
And the smell of hay in the snow, and the far owl
Warning among the folds, and the frozen hold
Flocked with the sheep white smoke of the farm house cowl
In the river wended vales where the tale was told.

Once when the world turned old
On a star of faith pure as the drifting bread,
As the food and flames of the snow, a man unrolled
The scrolls of fire that burned in his heart and head,
Torn and alone in a farm house in a fold

Of fields. And burning then
In his firelit island ringed by the winged snow
And the dung hills white as wool and the hen
Roosts sleeping chill till the flame of the cock crow
Combs through the mantled yards and the morning men

Stumble out with their spades,
The cattle stirring, the mousing cat stepping shy,
The puffed birds hopping and hunting, the milk maids
Gentle in their clogs over the fallen sky,
And all the woken farm at its white trades,

He knelt, he wept, he prayed,
By the spit and the black pot in the log bright light
And the cup and the cut bread in the dancing shade,
In the muffled house, in the quick of night,
At the point of love, forsaken and afraid.

He knelt on the cold stones,
He wept from the crest of grief, he prayed to the veiled sky
May his hunger go howling on bare white bones
Past the statues of the stables and the sky roofed sties
And the duck pond glass and the blinding byres alone

Into the home of prayers
And fires where he should prowl down the cloud
Of his snow blind love and rush in the white lairs.
His naked need struck him howling and bowed
Though no sound flowed down the hand folded air

But only the wind strung
Hunger of birds in the fields of the bread of water, tossed
In high corn and the harvest melting on their tongues.
And his nameless need bound him burning and lost
When cold as snow he should run the wended vales among

The rivers mouthed in night,
And drown in the drifts of his need, and lie curled caught
In the always desiring centre of the white
Inhuman cradle and the bride bed forever sought
By the believer lost and the hurled outcast of light.

Deliver him, he cried,
By losing him all in love, and cast his need
Alone and naked in the engulfing bride,
Never to flourish in the fields of the white seed
Or flower under the time dying flesh astride.

Listen. The minstrels sing
In the departed villages. The nightingale,
Dust in the buried wood, flies on the grains of her wings
And spells on the winds of the dead his winter's tale.
The voice of the dust of water from the withered spring

Is telling. The wizened
Stream with bells and baying water bounds. The dew rings
On the gristed leaves and the long gone glistening
Parish of snow. The carved mouths in the rock are wind swept strings.
Time sings through the intricately dead snow drop. Listen.

It was a hand or sound
In the long ago land that glided the dark door wide
And there outside on the bread of the ground
A she bird rose and rayed like a burning bride.
A she bird dawned, and her breast with snow and scarlet downed.

Look. And the dancers move
On the departed, snow bushed green, wanton in moon light
As a dust of pigeons. Exulting, the grave hooved
Horses, centaur dead, turn and tread the drenched white
Paddocks in the farms of birds. The dead oak walks for love.

The carved limbs in the rock
Leap, as to trumpets. Calligraphy of the old
Leaves is dancing. Lines of age on the stones weave in a flock.
And the harp shaped voice of the water's dust plucks in a fold
Of fields. For love, the long ago she bird rises. Look.

And the wild wings were raised
Above her folded head, and the soft feathered voice
Was flying through the house as though the she bird praised
And all the elements of the slow fall rejoiced
That a man knelt alone in the cup of the vales,

In the mantle and calm,
By the spit and the black pot in the log bright light.
And the sky of birds in the plumed voice charmed
Him up and he ran like a wind after the kindling flight
Past the blind barns and byres of the windless farm.

In the poles of the year
When black birds died like priests in the cloaked hedge row
And over the cloth of counties the far hills rode near,
Under the one leaved trees ran a scarecrow of snow
And fast through the drifts of the thickets antlered like deer,

Rags and prayers down the knee-
Deep hillocks and loud on the numbed lakes,
All night lost and long wading in the wake of the she-
Bird through the times and lands and tribes of the slow flakes.
Listen and look where she sails the goose plucked sea,

The sky, the bird, the bride,
The cloud, the need, the planted stars, the joy beyond
The fields of seed and the time dying flesh astride,
The heavens, the heaven, the grave, the burning font.
In the far ago land the door of his death glided wide,

And the bird descended.
On a bread white hill over the cupped farm
And the lakes and floating fields and the river wended
Vales where he prayed to come to the last harm
And the home of prayers and fires, the tale ended.

The dancing perishes
On the white, no longer growing green, and, minstrel dead,
The singing breaks in the snow shoed villages of wishes
That once cut the figures of birds on the deep bread
And over the glazed lakes skated the shapes of fishes

Flying. The rite is shorn
Of nightingale and centaur dead horse. The springs wither
Back. Lines of age sleep on the stones till trumpeting dawn.
Exultation lies down. Time buries the spring weather
That belled and bounded with the fossil and the dew reborn.

For the bird lay bedded
In a choir of wings, as though she slept or died,
And the wings glided wide and he was hymned and wedded,
And through the thighs of the engulfing bride,
The woman breasted and the heaven headed

Bird, he was brought low,
Burning in the bride bed of love, in the whirl-
Pool at the wanting centre, in the folds
Of paradise, in the spun bud of the world.
And she rose with him flowering in her melting snow.

## On a Wedding Anniversary

The sky is torn across
This ragged anniversary of two
Who moved for three years in tune
Down the long walks of their vows.

Now their love lies a loss
And Love and his patients roar on a chain;
From every true or crater
Carrying cloud, Death strikes their house.

Too late in the wrong rain
They come together whom their love parted:
The windows pour into their heart
And the doors burn in their brain.

103

# There was a saviour

There was a saviour
Rarer than radium,
Commoner than water, crueller than truth;
Children kept from the sun
Assembled at his tongue
To hear the golden note turn in a groove,
Prisoners of wishes locked their eyes
In the jails and studies of his keyless smiles.

The voice of children says
From a lost wilderness
There was calm to be done in his safe unrest,
When hindering man hurt
Man, animal, or bird
We hid our fears in that murdering breath,
Silence, silence to do, when earth grew loud,
In lairs and asylums of the tremendous shout.

There was glory to hear
In the churches of his tears,
Under his downy arm you sighed as he struck,
O you who could not cry
On to the ground when a man died
Put a tear for joy in the unearthly flood
And laid your cheek against a cloud-formed shell:
Now in the dark there is only yourself and myself.

Two proud, blacked brothers cry,
Winter-locked side by side,
To this inhospitable hollow year,
O we who could not stir
One lean sigh when we heard
Greed on man beating near and fire neighbour
But wailed and nested in the sky-blue wall
Now break a giant tear for the little known fall,

        For the drooping of homes
        That did not nurse our bones,
    Brave deaths of only ones but never found,
        Now see, alone in us,
        Our own true strangers' dust
    Ride through the doors of our unentered house.
    Exiled in us we arouse the soft,
    Unclenched, armless, silk and rough love that breaks all rocks.


## On the Marriage of a Virgin

Waking alone in a multitude of loves when morning's light
Surprised in the opening of her nightlong eyes
His golden yesterday asleep upon the iris
And this day's sun leapt up the sky out of her thighs
Was miraculous virginity old as loaves and fishes,
Though the moment of a miracle is unending lightning
And the shipyards of Galilee's footprints hide a navy of doves.

No longer will the vibrations of the sun desire on
Her deepsea pillow where once she married alone,
Her heart all ears and eyes, lips catching the avalanche
Of the golden ghost who ringed with his streams her mercury bone,
Who under the lids of her windows hoisted his golden luggage,
For a man sleeps where fire leapt down and she learns through his arm
That other sun, the jealous coursing of the unrivalled blood.

# In my craft or sullen art

In my craft or sullen art
Exercised in the still night
When only the moon rages
And the lovers lie abed
With all their griefs in their arms,
I labour by singing light
Not for ambition or bread
Or the strut and trade of charms
On the ivory stages
But for the common wages
Of their most secret heart.

Not for the proud man apart
From the raging moon I write
On these spindrift pages
Nor for the towering dead
With their nightingales and psalms
But for the lovers, their arms
Round the griefs of the ages,
Who pay no praise or wages
Nor heed my craft or art.

# Ceremony After a Fire Raid

I

Myselves
The grievers
Grieve
Among the street burned to tireless death
A child of a few hours
With its kneading mouth
Charred on the black breast of the grave
The mother dug, and its arms full of fires.

Begin
With singing
Sing
Darkness kindled back into beginning
When the caught tongue nodded blind,
A star was broken
Into the centuries of the child
Myselves grieve now, and miracles cannot atone.

Forgive
Us forgive
Give
Us your death that myselves the believers
May hold it in a great flood
Till the blood shall spurt,
And the dust shall sing like a bird
As the grains blow, as your death grows, through our heart.

Crying
Your dying
Cry,
Child beyond cockcrow, by the fire-dwarfed
Street we chant the flying sea
In the body bereft.
Love is the last light spoken. Oh
Seed of sons in the loin of the black husk left.

II

I know not whether
Adam or Eve, the adorned holy bullock
Or the white ewe lamb
Or the chosen virgin
Laid in her snow
On the altar of London,
Was the first to die
In the cinder of the little skull,
O bride and bride groom
O Adam and Eve together
Lying in the lull
Under the sad breast of the head stone
White as the skeleton
Of the garden of Eden.

I know the legend
Of Adam and Eve is never for a second
Silent in my service
Over the dead infants
Over the one
Child who was priest and servants,
Word, singers, and tongue
In the cinder of the little skull,
Who was the serpent's
Night fall and the fruit like a sun,
Man and woman undone,
Beginning crumbled back to darkness
Bare as the nurseries
Of the garden of wilderness.

III

Into the organpipes and steeples
Of the luminous cathedrals,
Into the weathercocks' molten mouths

Rippling in twelve-winded circles,
Into the dead clock burning the hour
Over the urn of sabbaths
Over the whirling ditch of daybreak
Over the sun's hovel and the slum of fire
And the golden pavements laid in requiems,
Into the cauldrons of the statuary,
Into the bread in a wheatfield of flames,
Into the wine burning like brandy,
The masses of the sea
The masses of the sea under
The masses of the infant-bearing sea
Erupt, fountain, and enter to utter for ever
Glory glory glory
The sundering ultimate kingdom of genesis' thunder.


## Once below a time

### I

Once below a time,
When my pinned-around-the-spirit
Cut-to-measure flesh bit,
Suit for a serial sum
On the first of each hardship,
My paid-for slaved-for own too late
In love torn breeches and blistered jacket
On the snapping rims of the ashpit,
In grottoes I worked with birds,
Spiked with a mastiff collar,
Tasselled in cellar and snipping shop
Or decked on a cloud swallower,

Then swift from a bursting sea with bottlecork boats

And out-of-perspective sailors,
In common clay clothes disguised as scales,
As a he-god's paddling water skirts,
I astounded the sitting tailors,
I set back the clock faced tailors,

Then, bushily swanked in bear wig and tails,
Hopping hot leaved and feathered
From the kangaroo foot of the earth,
From the chill, silent centre
Trailing the frost bitten cloth,
Up through the lubber crust of Wales
I rocketed to astonish
The flashing needle rock of squatters,
The criers of Shabby and Shorten,
The famous stitch droppers.

II

My silly suit, hardly yet suffered for,
Around some coffin carrying
Birdman or told ghost I hung.
And the owl hood, the heel hider,
Claw fold and hole for the rotten
Head, deceived, I believed, my maker,

The cloud perched tailors' master with nerves for cotton.
On the old seas from stories, thrashing my wings,
Combing with antlers, Columbus on fire,
I was pierced by the idol tailor's eyes,
Glared through shark mask and navigating head,
Cold Nansen's beak on a boat full of gongs,

To the boy of common thread,
The bright pretender, the ridiculous sea dandy
With dry flesh and earth for adorning and bed.
It was sweet to drown in the readymade handy water

110

With my cherry capped dangler green as seaweed
Summoning a child's voice from a webfoot stone,
Never never oh never to regret the bugle I wore
On my cleaving arm as I blasted in a wave.

Now shown and mostly bare I would lie down,
Lie down, lie down and live
As quiet as a bone.


# When I woke

When I woke, the town spoke.
Birds and clocks and cross bells
Dinned aside the coiling crowd,
The reptile profligates in a flame,
Spoilers and pokers of sleep,
The next-door sea dispelled
Frogs and satans and woman-luck,
While a man outside with a billhook,
Up to his head in his blood,
Cutting the morning off,
The warm-veined double of Time
And his scarving beard from a book,
Slashed down the last snake as though
It were a wand or subtle bough,
Its tongue peeled in the wrap of a leaf.

Every morning I make,
God in bed, good and bad,
After a water-face walk,
The death-stagged scatter-breath
Mammoth and sparrowfall
Everybody's earth.
Where birds ride like leaves and boats like ducks
I heard, this morning, waking,

111

Crossly out of the town noises
A voice in the erected air,
No prophet-progeny of mine,
Cry my sea town was breaking.
No Time, spoke the clocks, no God, rang the bells,
I drew the white sheet over the islands
And the coins on my eyelids sang like shells.


## Among those Killed in the Dawn Raid was a Man Aged a Hundred

When the morning was waking over the war
He put on his clothes and stepped out and he died,
The locks yawned loose and a blast blew them wide,
He dropped where he loved on the burst pavement stone
And the funeral grains of the slaughtered floor.
Tell his street on its back he stopped a sun
And the craters of his eyes grew springshoots and fire
When all the keys shot from the locks, and rang.
Dig no more for the chains of his grey-haired heart.
The heavenly ambulance drawn by a wound
Assembling waits for the spade's ring on the cage.
O keep his bones away from that common cart,
The morning is flying on the wings of his age
And a hundred storks perch on the sun's right hand.

# Lie still, sleep becalmed

Lie still, sleep becalmed, sufferer with the wound
In the throat, burning and turning. All night afloat
On the silent sea we have heard the sound
That came from the wound wrapped in the salt sheet.

Under the mile off moon we trembled listening
To the sea sound flowing like blood from the loud wound
And when the salt sheet broke in a storm of singing
The voices of all the drowned swam on the wind.

Open a pathway through the slow sad sail,
Throw wide to the wind the gates of the wandering boat
For my voyage to begin to the end of my wound,
We heard the sea sound sing, we saw the salt sheet tell.
Lie still, sleep becalmed, hide the mouth in the throat,
Or we shall obey, and ride with you through the drowned.

# Vision and Prayer

### I

Who
Are  you
Who  is  born
In   the   next   room
So  loud  to  my  own
That  I  can  hear  the  womb
Opening  and  the  dark  run
Over  the  ghost  and  the  dropped  son
Behind  the  wall  thin  as  a  wren's  bone?
In   the   birth   bloody   room   unknown
To  the  burn  and  turn  of  time
And  the  heart  print  of  man
Bows    no    baptism
But  dark  alone
Blessing  on
The  wild
Child.

I
Must   lie
Still   as   stone
By   the   wren   bone
Wall   hearing   the   moan
Of   the   mother   hidden
And   the   shadowed   head   of   pain
Casting   tomorrow   like   a   thorn
And   the   midwives   of   miracle   sing
Until   the   turbulent   new   born
Burns   me   his   name   and   his   flame
And   the   winged   wall   is   torn
By   his   torrid   crown
And the dark thrown
From   his   loin
To   bright
Light.

When
The  wren
Bone writhes down
And  the  first  dawn
Furied  by  his  stream
Swarms  on  the  kingdom  come
Of  the  dazzler  of  heaven
And  the  splashed  mothering  maiden
Who  bore  him  with  a  bonfire  in
His  mouth  and  rocked  him  like  a  storm
I  shall  run  lost  in  sudden
Terror  and  shining  from
The  once  hooded  room
Crying  in  vain
In  the  caldron
Of  his
Kiss

I n
the   spin
Of  the   sun
In   the   spuming
Cyclone  of  his   wing
For   I   was   lost   who   am
Crying at the man drenched throne
In   the   first   fury   of   his   stream
And   the   lightnings   of   adoration
Back  to  black  silence  melt  and  mourn
For   I   was   lost   who   have   come
To   dumbfounding   haven
And   the   finding   one
And   the   high   noon
Of   his   wound
Blinds   my
C r y.

There
Crouched bare
In the shrine
Of his blazing
Breast I shall waken
To the judge blown bedlam
Of the uncaged sea bottom
The cloud climb of the exhaling tomb
And the bidden dust upsailing
With his flame in every grain.
O spiral of ascension
From the vultured urn
Of the morning
Of man when
The land
And

The
Born sea
Praised the sun
The finding one
And upright Adam
Sang    upon    origin!
O the wings of the children!
The woundward flight of the ancient
Young from the canyons of oblivion!
The sky stride of the always slain
In battle! the happening
Of saints to their vision!
The world winding home!
And the whole pain
Flows open
And    I
Die.

II

In the name of the lost who glory in
The swinish plains of carrion
Under the burial song
Of the birds of burden
Heavy with the drowned
And the green dust
And bearing
The ghost
From
The ground
Like pollen
On the black plume
And the beak of slime
I pray though I belong
Not wholly to that lamenting
Brethren for joy has moved within
The inmost marrow of my heart bone

That he who learns now the sun and moon
Of his mother's milk may return
Before the lips blaze and bloom
To the birth bloody room
Behind the wall's wren
Bone and be dumb
And the womb
That bore
For
All men
The adored
Infant light or
The dazzling prison
Yawn to his upcoming.
In the name of the wanton
Lost on the unchristened mountain
In the centre of dark I pray him

That he let the dead lie though they moan
For his briared hands to hoist them
To the shrine of his world's wound
And the blood drop's garden
Endure    the    stone
Blind host to sleep
In  the  dark
And deep
Rock
A w a k e
No heart bone
But  let  it  break
On the mountain crown
Unbidden  by  the  sun
And the beating dust be blown
Down  to  the  river  rooting  plain
Under  the  night  forever  falling.

Forever   falling   night   is   a   known
Star   and   country   to   the   legion
Of   sleepers   whose   tongue   I   toll
To   mourn   his   deluging
Light through sea and soil
And we have come
To   know   all
Places
Ways
Mazes
Passages
Quarters and graves
Of   the   endless   fall.
Now common lazarus
Of   the   charting   sleepers   prays
Never   to   awake   and   arise
For the country of death is the heart's size

And the star of the lost the shape of the eyes.
In the name of the fatherless
In the name of the unborn
And the undesirers
Of midwiving morning's
Hands or instruments
O in the name
Of no one
Now or
No
One to
Be I pray
May the crimson
Sun spin a grave grey
And the colour of clay
Stream upon his martyrdom
In the interpreted evening
And the known dark of the earth amen.

I turn the corner of prayer and burn
In a blessing of the sudden
Sun. In the name of the damned
I would turn back and run
To the hidden land
But the loud sun
Christens down
The sky.
I
Am found.
O let him
Scald me and drown
Me in his world's wound.
His lightning answers my
Cry. My voice burns in his hand.
Now I am lost in the blinding
One. The sun roars at the prayer's end.

## Ballad of the Long-legged Bait

The bows glided down, and the coast
Blackened with birds took a last look
At his thrashing hair and whale-blue eye;
The trodden town rang its cobbles for luck.

Then goodbye to the fishermanned
Boat with its anchor free and fast
As a bird hooking over the sea,
High and dry by the top of the mast,

Whispered the affectionate sand
And the bulwarks of the dazzled quay.
For my sake sail, and never look back,
Said the looking land.

Sails drank the wind, and white as milk
He sped into the drinking dark;
The sun shipwrecked west on a pearl
And the moon swam out of its hulk.

Funnels and masts went by in a whirl.
Goodbye to the man on the sea-legged deck
To the gold gut that sings on his reel
To the bait that stalked out of the sack,

For we saw him throw to the swift flood
A girl alive with his hooks through her lips;
All the fishes were rayed in blood,
Said the dwindling ships.

Goodbye to chimneys and funnels,
Old wives that spin in the smoke,
He was blind to the eyes of candles
In the praying windows of waves

But heard his bait buck in the wake
And tussle in a shoal of loves.
Now cast down your rod, for the whole
Of the sea is hilly with whales,

She longs among horses and angels,
The rainbow-fish bend in her joys,
Floated the lost cathedral
Chimes of the rocked buoys.

Where the anchor rode like a gull
Miles over the moonstruck boat
A squall of birds bellowed and fell,
A cloud blew the rain from its throat;

He saw the storm smoke out to kill
With fuming bows and ram of ice,
Fire on starlight, rake Jesu's stream;
And nothing shone on the water's face

But the oil and bubble of the moon,
Plunging and piercing in his course
The lured fish under the foam
Witnessed with a kiss.

Whales in the wake like capes and Alps
Quaked the sick sea and snouted deep,
Deep the great bushed bait with raining lips
Slipped the fins of those humpbacked tons

And fled their love in a weaving dip.
Oh, Jericho was falling in their lungs!
She nipped and dived in the nick of love,
Spun on a spout like a long-legged ball

Till every beast blared down in a swerve
Till every turtle crushed from his shell
Till every bone in the rushing grave
Rose and crowed and fell!

127

Good luck to the hand on the rod,
There is thunder under its thumbs;
Gold gut is a lightning thread,
His fiery reel sings off its flames,

The whirled boat in the burn of his blood
Is crying from nets to knives,
Oh the shearwater birds and their boatsized brood
Oh the bulls of Biscay and their calves

Are making under the green, laid veil
The long-legged beautiful bait their wives.
Break the black news and paint on a sail
Huge weddings in the waves,

Over the wakeward-flashing spray
Over the gardens of the floor
Clash out the mounting dolphin's day,
My mast is a bell-spire,

Strike and smoothe, for my decks are drums,
Sing through the water-spoken prow
The octopus walking into her limbs
The polar eagle with his tread of snow.

From salt-lipped beak to the kick of the stern
Sing how the seal has kissed her dead!
The long, laid minute's bride drifts on
Old in her cruel bed.

Over the graveyard in the water
Mountains and galleries beneath
Nightingale and hyena
Rejoicing for that drifting death

Sing and howl through sand and anemone
Valley and sahara in a shell,
Oh all the wanting flesh his enemy
Thrown to the sea in the shell of a girl

Is old as water and plain as an eel;
Always goodbye to the long-legged bread
Scattered in the paths of his heels
For the salty birds fluttered and fed

And the tall grains foamed in their bills;
Always goodbye to the fires of the face,
For the crab-backed dead on the sea-bed rose
And scuttled over her eyes,

The blind, clawed stare is cold as sleet.
The tempter under the eyelid
Who shows to the selves asleep
Mast-high moon-white women naked

Walking in wishes and lovely for shame
Is dumb and gone with his flame of brides.
Susanna's drowned in the bearded stream
And no-one stirs at Sheba's side

But the hungry kings of the tides;
Sin who had a woman's shape
Sleeps till Silence blows on a cloud
And all the lifted waters walk and leap.

Lucifer that bird's dropping
Out of the sides of the north
Has melted away and is lost
Is always lost in her vaulted breath,

Venus lies star-struck in her wound
And the sensual ruins make
Seasons over the liquid world,
White springs in the dark.

Always goodbye, cried the voices through the shell,
Goodbye always for the flesh is cast
And the fisherman winds his reel
With no more desire than a ghost.

Always good luck, praised the finned in the feather
Bird after dark and the laughing fish
As the sails drank up the hail of thunder
And the long-tailed lightning lit his catch.

The boat swims into the six-year weather,
A wind throws a shadow and it freezes fast.
See what the gold gut drags from under
Mountains and galleries to the crest!

See what clings to hair and skull
As the boat skims on with drinking wings!
The statues of great rain stand still,
And the flakes fall like hills.

Sing and strike his heavy haul
Toppling up the boatside in a snow of light!
His decks are drenched with miracles.
Oh miracle of fishes! The long dead bite!

Out of the urn the size of a man
Out of the room the weight of his trouble
Out of the house that holds a town
In the continent of a fossil

One by one in dust and shawl,
Dry as echoes and insect-faced,
His fathers cling to the hand of the girl
And the dead hand leads the past,

Leads them as children and as air
On to the blindly tossing tops;
The centuries throw back their hair
And the old men sing from newborn lips:

*Time is bearing another son.*
*Kill Time! She turns in her pain!*
*The oak is felled in the acorn*
*And the hawk in the egg kills the wren.*

He who blew the great fire in
And died on a hiss of flames
Or walked on the earth in the evening
Counting the denials of the grains

Clings to her drifting hair, and climbs;
And he who taught their lips to sing
Weeps like the risen sun among
The liquid choirs of his tribes.

The rod bends low, divining land,
And through the sundered water crawls
A garden holding to her hand
With birds and animals

With men and women and waterfalls
Trees cool and dry in the whirlpool of ships
And stunned and still on the green, laid veil
Sand with legends in its virgin laps

And prophets loud on the burned dunes;
Insects and valleys hold her thighs hard,
Time and places grip her breast bone,
She is breaking with seasons and clouds;

Round her trailed wrist fresh water weaves,
With moving fish and rounded stones
Up and down the greater waves
A separate river breathes and runs;

Strike and sing his catch of fields
For the surge is sown with barley,
The cattle graze on the covered foam,
The hills have footed the waves away,

With wild sea fillies and soaking bridles
With salty colts and gales in their limbs
All the horses of his haul of miracles
Gallop through the arched, green farms,

Trot and gallop with gulls upon them
And thunderbolts in their manes.
O Rome and Sodom Tomorrow and London
The country tide is cobbled with towns,

And steeples pierce the cloud on her shoulder
And the streets that the fisherman combed
When his long-legged flesh was a wind on fire
And his loin was a hunting flame

Coil from the thoroughfares of her hair
And terribly lead him home alive
Lead her prodigal home to his terror,
The furious ox-killing house of love.

Down, down, down, under the ground,
Under the floating villages,
Turns the moon-chained and water-wound
Metropolis of fishes,

There is nothing left of the sea but its sound,
Under the earth the loud sea walks,
In deathbeds of orchards the boat dies down
And the bait is drowned among hayricks,

Land, land, land, nothing remains
Of the pacing, famous sea but its speech,
And into its talkative seven tombs
The anchor dives through the floors of a church.

Goodbye, good luck, struck the sun and the moon,
To the fisherman lost on the land.
He stands alone at the door of his home,
With his long-legged heart in his hand.

# Holy Spring

O
Out of a bed of love
When that immortal hospital made one more move to soothe
The cureless counted body,
And ruin and his causes
Over the barbed and shooting sea assumed an army
And swept into our wounds and houses,
I climb to greet the war in which I have no heart but only
That one dark I owe my light,
Call for confessor and wiser mirror but there is none
To glow after the god stoning night
And I am struck as lonely as a holy maker by the sun.

No
Praise that the spring time is all
Gabriel and radiant shrubbery as the morning grows joyful
Out of the woebegone pyre
And the multitude's sultry tear turns cool on the weeping wall,
My arising prodigal
Sun the father his quiver full of the infants of pure fire,
But blessed be hail and upheaval
That uncalm still it is sure alone to stand and sing
Alone in the husk of man's home
And the mother and toppling house of the holy spring,
If only for a last time.

133

# Fern Hill

Now as I was young and easy under the apple boughs
About the lilting house and happy as the grass was green,
    The night above the dingle starry,
        Time let me hail and climb
    Golden in the heydays of his eyes,
And honoured among wagons I was prince of the apple towns
And once below a time I lordly had the trees and leaves
        Trail with daisies and barley
    Down the rivers of the windfall light.


And as I was green and carefree, famous among the barns
About the happy yard and singing as the farm was home,
    In the sun that is young once only,
        Time let me play and be
    Golden in the mercy of his means,
And green and golden I was huntsman and herdsman, the calves
Sang to my horn, the foxes on the hills barked clear and cold,
        And the sabbath rang slowly
    In the pebbles of the holy streams.


All the sun long it was running, it was lovely, the hay
Fields high as the house, the tunes from the chimneys, it was air
    And playing, lovely and watery
        And fire green as grass.
    And nightly under the simple stars
As I rode to sleep the owls were bearing the farm away,
All the moon long I heard, blessed among stables, the nightjars
    Flying with the ricks, and the horses
        Flashing into the dark.


And then to awake, and the farm, like a wanderer white
With the dew, come back, the cock on his shoulder: it was all
    Shining, it was Adam and maiden,
        The sky gathered again
    And the sun grew round that very day.

So it must have been after the birth of the simple light
In the first, spinning place, the spellbound horses walking warm
    Out of the whinnying green stable
        On to the fields of praise.

And honoured among foxes and pheasants by the gay house
Under the new made clouds and happy as the heart was long,
    In the sun born over and over,
        I ran my heedless ways,
    My wishes raced through the house high hay
And nothing I cared, at my sky blue trades, that time allows
In all his tuneful turning so few and such morning songs
    Before the children green and golden
        Follow him out of grace,

Nothing I cared, in the lamb white days, that time would take me
Up to the swallow thronged loft by the shadow of my hand,
    In the moon that is always rising,
        Nor that riding to sleep
    I should hear him fly with the high fields
And wake to the farm forever fled from the childless land.
Oh as I was young and easy in the mercy of his means,
        Time held me green and dying
      Though I sang in my chains like the sea.

# In Country Sleep

# In Country Sleep

## I

Never and never, my girl riding far and near
In the land of the hearthstone tales, and spelled asleep,
Fear or believe that the wolf in a sheepwhite hood
Loping and bleating roughly and blithely shall leap,
          My dear, my dear,
Out of a lair in the flocked leaves in the dew dipped year
To eat your heart in the house in the rosy wood.

Sleep, good, for ever, slow and deep, spelled rare and wise,
My girl ranging the night in the rose and shire
Of the hobnail tales: no gooseherd or swine will turn
Into a homestall king or hamlet of fire
          And prince of ice
To court the honeyed heart from your side before sunrise
In a spinney of ringed boys and ganders, spike and burn,

Nor the innocent lie in the rooting dingle wooed
And staved, and riven among plumes my rider weep.
From the broomed witch's spume you are shielded by fern
And flower of country sleep and the greenwood keep.
          Lie fast and soothed,
Safe be and smooth from the bellows of the rushy brood.
Never, my girl, until tolled to sleep by the stern

Bell believe or fear that the rustic shade or spell
Shall harrow and snow the blood while you ride wide and near,
For who unmanningly haunts the mountain ravened eaves
Or skulks in the dell moon but moonshine echoing clear
          From the starred well?
A hill touches an angel. Out of a saint's cell
The nightbird lauds through nunneries and domes of leaves

Her robin breasted tree, three Marys in the rays.
Sanctum sanctorum the animal eye of the wood
In the rain telling its beads, and the gravest ghost
The owl at its knelling. Fox and holt kneel before blood.
                Now the tales praise
The star rise at pasture and nightlong the fables graze
On the lord's table of the bowing grass. Fear most

For ever of all not the wolf in his baaing hood
Nor the tusked prince, in the ruttish farm, at the rind
And mire of love, but the Thief as meek as the dew.
The country is holy: O bide in that country kind,
                Know the green good,
Under the prayer wheeling moon in the rosy wood
Be shielded by chant and flower and gay may you

Lie in grace. Sleep spelled at rest in the lowly house
In the squirrel nimble grove, under linen and thatch
And star: held and blessed, though you scour the high four
Winds, from the dousing shade and the roarer at the latch,
                Cool in your vows.
Yet out of the beaked, web dark and the pouncing boughs
Be you sure the Thief will seek a way sly and sure

And sly as snow and meek as dew blown to the thorn,
This night and each vast night until the stern bell talks
In the tower and tolls to sleep over the stalls
Of the hearthstone tales my own, last love; and the soul walks
                The waters shorn.
This night and each night since the falling star you were born,
Ever and ever he finds a way, as the snow falls,

As the rain falls, hail on the fleece, as the vale mist rides
Through the haygold stalls, as the dew falls on the wind-
Milled dust of the apple tree and the pounded islands
Of the morning leaves, as the star falls, as the winged
                Apple seed glides,
And falls, and flowers in the yawning wound at our sides,
As the world falls, silent as the cyclone of silence.

## II

Night and the reindeer on the clouds above the haycocks
And the wings of the great roc ribboned for the fair!
The leaping saga of prayer! And high, there, on the hare-
               Heeled winds the rooks
Cawing from their black bethels soaring, the holy books
Of birds! Among the cocks like fire the red fox

Burning! Night and the vein of birds in the winged, sloe wrist
Of the wood! Pastoral beat of blood through the laced leaves!
The stream from the priest black wristed spinney and sleeves
               Of thistling frost
Of the nightingale's din and tale! The upgiven ghost
Of the dingle torn to singing and the surpliced

Hill of cypresses! The din and tale in the skimmed
Yard of the buttermilk rain on the pail! The sermon
Of blood! The bird loud vein! The saga from mermen
               To seraphim
Leaping! The gospel rooks! All tell, this night, of him
Who comes as red as the fox and sly as the heeled wind.

Illumination of music! the lulled black backed
Gull, on the wave with sand in its eyes! And the foal moves
Through the shaken greensward lake, silent, on moonshod
                    hooves,
             In the winds' wakes.
Music of elements, that a miracle makes!
Earth, air, water, fire, singing into the white act,

The haygold haired, my love asleep, and the rift blue
Eyed, in the haloed house, in her rareness and hilly
High riding, held and blessed and true, and so stilly
               Lying the sky
Might cross its planets, the bell weep, night gather her eyes,
The Thief fall on the dead like the willynilly dew,

Only for the turning of the earth in her holy
Heart! Slyly, slowly, hearing the wound in her side go
Round the sun, he comes to my love like the designed snow,
           And truly he
Flows to the strand of flowers like the dew's ruly sea,
And surely he sails like the ship shape clouds. Oh he

Comes designed to my love to steal not her tide raking
Wound, nor her riding high, nor her eyes, nor kindled hair,
But her faith that each vast night and the saga of prayer
           He comes to take
Her faith that this last night for his unsacred sake
He comes to leave her in the lawless sun awaking

Naked and forsaken to grieve he will not come.
Ever and ever by all your vows believe and fear
My dear this night he comes and night without end my dear
           Since you were born:
And you shall wake, from country sleep, this dawn and each
                             first dawn,
Your faith as deathless as the outcry of the ruled sun.

## Over Sir John's hill

Over Sir John's hill,
The hawk on fire hangs still;
In a hoisted cloud, at drop of dusk, he pulls to his claws
And gallows, up the rays of his eyes the small birds of the bay
And the shrill child's play
Wars
Of the sparrows and such who swansing, dusk, in wrangling hedges.
And blithely they squawk
To fiery tyburn over the wrestle of elms until
The flash the noosed hawk

142

Crashes, and slowly the fishing holy stalking heron
In the river Towy below bows his tilted headstone.


Flash, and the plumes crack,
And a black cap of jack-
Daws Sir John's just hill dons, and again the gulled birds hare
To the hawk on fire, the halter height, over Towy's fins,
In a whack of wind.
There
Where the elegiac fisherbird stabs and paddles
In the pebbly dab filled
Shallow and sedge, and 'dilly dilly,' calls the loft hawk,
'Come and be killed,'
I open the leaves of the water at a passage
Of psalms and shadows among the pincered sandcrabs prancing


And read, in a shell,
Death clear as a buoy's bell:
All praise of the hawk on fire in hawk-eyed dusk be sung,
When his viperish fuse hangs looped with flames under the brand
Wing, and blest shall
Young
Green chickens of the bay and bushes cluck, 'dilly dilly,
Come let us die.'
We grieve as the blithe birds, never again, leave shingle and elm,
The heron and I,
I young Aesop fabling to the near night by the dingle
Of eels, saint heron hymning in the shell-hung distant


Crystal harbour vale
Where the sea cobbles sail,
And wharves of water where the walls dance and the white cranes
                                                    stilt.
It is the heron and I, under judging Sir John's elmed
Hill, tell-tale the knelled
Guilt
Of the led-astray birds whom God, for their breast of whistles,

Have mercy on,
God in his whirlwind silence save, who marks the sparrows hail,
For their souls' song.
Now the heron grieves in the weeded verge. Through windows
Of dusk and water I see the tilting whispering

Heron, mirrored, go,
As the snapt feathers snow,
Fishing in the tear of the Towy. Only a hoot owl
Hollows, a grassblade blown in cupped hands, in the looted elms,
And no green cocks or hens
Shout
Now on Sir John's hill. The heron, ankling the scaly
Lowlands of the waves,
Makes all the music; and I who hear the tune of the slow,
Wear-willow river, grave,
Before the lunge of the night, the notes on this time-shaken
Stone for the sake of the souls of the slain birds sailing.

## Poem on his Birthday

In the mustardseed sun,
By full tilt river and switchback sea
Where the cormorants scud,
In his house on stilts high among beaks
And palavers of birds
This sandgrain day in the bent bay's grave
He celebrates and spurns
His driftwood thirty-fifth wind turned age;
Herons spire and spear.

Under and round him go
Flounders, gulls, on their cold, dying trails,
Doing what they are told,

Curlews aloud in the congered waves
    Work at their ways to death,
And the rhymer in the long tongued room,
    Who tolls his birthday bell,
Toils towards the ambush of his wounds;
    Herons, steeple stemmed, bless.

    In the thistledown fall,
He sings towards anguish; finches fly
    In the claw tracks of hawks
On a seizing sky; small fishes glide
    Through wynds and shells of drowned
Ship towns to pastures of otters. He
    In his slant, racking house
And the hewn coils of his trade perceives
    Herons walk in their shroud,

    The livelong river's robe
Of minnows wreathing around their prayer;
    And far at sea he knows,
Who slaves to his crouched, eternal end
    Under a serpent cloud,
Dolphins dive in their turnturtle dust,
    The rippled seals streak down
To kill and their own tide daubing blood
    Slides good in the sleek mouth.

    In a cavernous, swung
Wave's silence, wept white angelus knells.
    Thirty-five bells sing struck
On skull and scar where his loves lie wrecked,
    Steered by the falling stars.
And tomorrow weeps in a blind cage
    Terror will rage apart
Before chains break to a hammer flame
    And love unbolts the dark

    And freely he goes lost
In the unknown, famous light of great

145

And fabulous, dear God.
Dark is a way and light is a place,
  Heaven that never was
Nor will be ever is always true,
  And, in that brambled void,
Plenty as blackberries in the woods
  The dead grow for His joy.


  There he might wander bare
With the spirits of the horseshoe bay
  Or the stars' seashore dead,
Marrow of eagles, the roots of whales
  And wishbones of wild geese,
With blessed, unborn God and His Ghost,
  And every soul His priest,
Gulled and chanter in young Heaven's fold
  Be at cloud quaking peace,


  But dark is a long way.
He, on the earth of the night, alone
  With all the living, prays,
Who knows the rocketing wind will blow
  The bones out of the hills,
And the scythed boulders bleed, and the last
  Rage shattered waters kick
Masts and fishes to the still quick stars,
  Faithlessly unto Him


  Who is the light of old
And air shaped Heaven where souls grow wild
  As horses in the foam:
Oh, let me midlife mourn by the shrined
  And druid herons' vows
The voyage to ruin I must run,
  Dawn ships clouted aground,

146

Yet, though I cry with tumbledown tongue,
  Count my blessings aloud:

  Four elements and five
Senses, and man a spirit in love
  Tangling through this spun slime
To his nimbus bell cool kingdom come
  And the lost, moonshine domes,
And the sea that hides his secret selves
  Deep in its black, base bones,
Lulling of spheres in the seashell flesh,
  And this last blessing most,

  That the closer I move
To death, one man through his sundered hulks,
  The louder the sun blooms
And the tusked, ramshackling sea exults;
  And every wave of the way
And gale I tackle, the whole world then
  With more triumphant faith
Than ever was since the world was said
  Spins its morning of praise,

  I hear the bouncing hills
Grow larked and greener at berry brown
  Fall and the dew larks sing
Taller this thunderclap spring, and how
  More spanned with angels ride
The mansouled fiery islands! Oh,
  Holier then their eyes,
And my shining men no more alone
  As I sail out to die.

# Do not go gentle into that good night

Do not go gentle into that good night,
Old age should burn and rave at close of day;
Rage, rage against the dying of the light.

Though wise men at their end know dark is right,
Because their words had forked no lightning they
Do not go gentle into that good night.

Good men, the last wave by, crying how bright
Their frail deeds might have danced in a green bay,
Rage, rage against the dying of the light.

Wild men who caught and sang the sun in flight,
And learn, too late, they grieved it on its way,
Do not go gentle into that good night.

Grave men, near death, who see with blinding sight
Blind eyes could blaze like meteors and be gay,
Rage, rage against the dying of the light.

And you, my father, there on the sad height,
Curse, bless, me now with your fierce tears, I pray.
Do not go gentle into that good night.
Rage, rage against the dying of the light.

# Lament

When I was a windy boy and a bit
And the black spit of the chapel fold,
(Sighed the old ram rod, dying of women),
I tiptoed shy in the gooseberry wood,
The rude owl cried like a telltale tit,
I skipped in a blush as the big girls rolled
Ninepin down on the donkeys' common,

And on seesaw sunday nights I wooed
Whoever I would with my wicked eyes,
The whole of the moon I could love and leave
All the green leaved little weddings' wives
In the coal black bush and let them grieve.

When I was a gusty man and a half
And the black beast of the beetles' pews,
(Sighed the old ram rod, dying of bitches),
Not a boy and a bit in the wick-
Dipping moon and drunk as a new dropped calf,
I whistled all night in the twisted flues,
Midwives grew in the midnight ditches,
And the sizzling beds of the town cried, Quick! –
Whenever I dove in a breast high shoal,
Wherever I ramped in the clover quilts,
Whatsoever I did in the coal-
Black night, I left my quivering prints.

When I was a man you could call a man
And the black cross of the holy house,
(Sighed the old ram rod, dying of welcome),
Brandy and ripe in my bright, bass prime,
No springtailed tom in the red hot town
With every simmering woman his mouse
But a hillocky bull in the swelter
Of summer come in his great good time
To the sultry, biding herds, I said,
Oh, time enough when the blood creeps cold,
And I lie down but to sleep in bed,
For my sulking, skulking, coal black soul!

When I was a half of the man I was
And serve me right as the preachers warn,
(Sighed the old ram rod, dying of downfall),
No flailing calf or cat in a flame
Or hickory bull in milky grass
But a black sheep with a crumpled horn,
At last the soul from its foul mousehole

Slunk pouting out when the limp time came;
And I gave my soul a blind, slashed eye,
Gristle and rind, and a roarer's life,
And I shoved it into the coal black sky
To find a woman's soul for a wife.

Now I am a man no more no more
And a black reward for a roaring life,
(Sighed the old ram rod, dying of strangers),
Tidy and cursed in my dove cooed room
I lie down thin and hear the good bells jaw –
For, oh, my soul found a sunday wife
In the coal black sky and she bore angels!
Harpies around me out of her womb!
Chastity prays for me, piety sings,
Innocence sweetens my last black breath,
Modesty hides my thighs in her wings,
And all the deadly virtues plague my death!

## In the White Giant's Thigh

Through throats where many rivers meet, the curlews cry,
Under the conceiving moon, on the high chalk hill,
And there this night I walk in the white giant's thigh
Where barren as boulders women lie longing still

To labour and love though they lay down long ago.

Through throats where many rivers meet, the women pray,
Pleading in the waded bay for the seed to flow
Though the names on their weed grown stones are rained away,

And alone in the night's eternal, curving act
They yearn with tongues of curlews for the unconceived
And immemorial sons of the cudgelling, hacked

Hill. Who once in gooseskin winter loved all ice leaved

In the courters' lanes, or twined in the ox roasting sun
In the wains tonned so high that the wisps of the hay
Clung to the pitching clouds, or gay with anyone
Young as they in the after milking moonlight lay

Under the lighted shapes of faith and their moonshade
Petticoats galed high, or shy with the rough riding boys,
Now clasp me to their grains in the gigantic glade,

Who once, green countries since, were a hedgerow of joys.

Time by, their dust was flesh the swineherd rooted sly,
Flared in the reek of the wiving sty with the rush
Light of his thighs, spreadeagle to the dunghill sky,
Or with their orchard man in the core of the sun's bush
Rough as cows' tongues and thrashed with brambles their
                                        buttermilk
Manes, under his quenchless summer barbed gold to the bone,

Or rippling soft in the spinney moon as the silk
And ducked and draked white lake that harps to a hail stone.

Who once were a bloom of wayside brides in the hawed house
And heard the lewd, wooed field flow to the coming frost,
The scurrying, furred small friars squeal, in the dowse
Of day, in the thistle aisles, till the white owl crossed

Their breast, the vaulting does roister, the horned bucks climb
Quick in the wood at love, where a torch of foxes foams,
All birds and beasts of the linked night uproar and chime

And the mole snout blunt under his pilgrimage of domes,

Or, butter fat goosegirls, bounced in a gambo bed,
Their breasts full of honey, under their gander king
Trounced by his wings in the hissing shippen, long dead
And gone that barley dark where their clogs danced in the spring,

And their firefly hairpins flew, and the ricks ran round –

(But nothing bore, no mouthing babe to the veined hives
Hugged, and barren and bare on Mother Goose's ground
They with the simple Jacks were a boulder of wives) –

Now curlew cry me down to kiss the mouths of their dust.

The dust of their kettles and clocks swings to and fro
Where the hay rides now or the bracken kitchens rust
As the arc of the billhooks that flashed the hedges low
And cut the birds' boughs that the minstrel sap ran red.
They from houses where the harvest kneels, hold me hard,
Who heard the tall bell sail down the Sundays of the dead
And the rain wring out its tongues on the faded yard,
Teach me the love that is evergreen after the fall leaved
Grave, after Beloved on the grass gulfed cross is scrubbed
Off by the sun and Daughters no longer grieved
Save by their long desirers in the fox cubbed
Streets or hungering in the crumbled wood: to these
Hale dead and deathless do the women of the hill
Love forever meridian through the courters' trees

And the daughters of darkness flame like Fawkes fires still.

In Country Heaven
*and*
Elegy

## In Country Heaven

Always when He, in country heaven,
    (Whom my heart hears),
Crosses the breast of the praising east and kneels,
    Humble in all his planets,
    And weeps on the abasing crest,

Then in the last ward and joy of beasts and birds
    And the canonized valley
    Where all sings, that was made and is dead,
    And the angels whirr like pheasants
      Through naves of leaves,

Light and His tears dewfall together
    (O hand in hand)
Out of the pierced eyes and the cataract sky,
    He cries his blood, and the suns
    Dissolve and run down the raggèd

Gutters of his face: Heaven is blind and black.

## Elegy

Too proud to die, broken and blind he died
The darkest way, and did not turn away,
A cold, kind man brave in his burning pride

On that darkest day. Oh, forever may
He live lightly, at last, on the last, crossed
Hill, and there grow young, under the grass, in love,

Among the long flocks, and never lie lost
Or still all the days of his death, though above
All he longed all dark for his mother's breast

Which was rest and dust, and in the kind ground
The darkest justice of death, blind and unblessed.
Let him find no rest but be fathered and found,

I prayed in the crouching room, by his blind bed,
In the muted house, one minute before
Noon, and night, and light. The rivers of the dead

Moved in his poor hand I held, and I saw
Through his faded eyes to the roots of the sea.
Go calm to your crucifixed hill, I told

The air that drew away from him.

# The Notes

# General Preface to the Notes

What needs to be described first of all is the exact sense in which the present edition is a *Collected Poems 1934–1953*. In 1952 Dylan Thomas authorized *Collected Poems 1934–1952*, which he said contained 'most of the poems I have written, and all, up to the present year, that I wish to preserve'. In any simple sense, it was clearly wrong to describe those 91 poems as comprising most of the poems he had written: the early notebooks (1930–1934) alone contain another 164 poems which Thomas left either unpublished, or published but uncollected. But Thomas was probably thinking of the canon as consisting only of poems of a stylistic homogeneity that, by 1952, he would certainly have been able to consider as recognizable and recognized, and therefore expected by a large body of readers. Although some 37 of those 'Collected' poems had sprung from early notebook beginnings, other notebook poems had been in a different style (more dilute, 'mainly free verse' as he wrote on one notebook) from what had soon – via published poems from 1934 onwards – come to be recognized as his formal, stylistic and textual trademarks.

More significant is Thomas's opinion that the *Collected* volume of 1952 represented 'all, up to the present year, that I wish to preserve'. The range on which Thomas himself set his sights in 1952 represented decisions he had already made in his publishing history over the previous two decades: *Collected Poems 1934–1952* was, with the exceptions mentioned below, the aggregate of all his previously and individually published volumes – *18 Poems* (1934), *Twenty-five Poems* (1936), *The Map of Love* (1939 – minus the prose), *Deaths and Entrances* (1946) and *In Country Sleep* (1952). The present edition respects Thomas's decision to make the *Collected Poems* a confirmation of his previous publishing decisions.

Indeed, our respect for Thomas's aggregate policy has led to the restoration, here, of "Paper and sticks", a poem Thomas originally included in *Deaths and Entrances* (1946) but excluded from *Collected Poems 1934–1952*. "Paper and sticks" was not included in 1952 because Thomas, as he said in a letter to his publisher, suddenly had the 'horrors' of it (*Letters* p. 839). The present editors, however, feel that Thomas's policy of keeping the original volumes whole was correct, and that his last-minute aversion to that one poem is something to bear in mind but not sufficient to condemn it to oblivion.

Thomas allowed one other variation to occur in his policy on assembling the 1952 *Collected* volume. It is a variation the reverse, as it were, of that which cut out "Paper and sticks": he allowed into *Collected Poems 1934–1952* one poem, "Once below a time", that he had *not* included in its period volume, *Deaths and Entrances*. He had apparently by 1952 become satisfied that its characteristic qualities had earned it access. Admittedly, "Paper and sticks" does not have this same relatedness to the style and themes of its period; it is essentially a minor dramatic monologue, impersonative of a character who might very well have figured, later, in *Under Milk Wood*. But, as such, it can usefully stand as the first example of new tendencies that were, increasingly in the 1940s, to enter Thomas's work as a whole: a more dilute style and a racy realism.

Not only the general policy of aggregation, but also several accidental inadequacies in the text of *Collected Poems 1934–1952* have decided us in taking as our copy-text for this present edition the five previous individual volumes, plus the extra poem, "Once below a time", plus the "Prologue" written by Thomas expressly for his *Collected* volume. We were determined that any further poems we added to those which Thomas had said constituted 'all, up to the present year, that I wish to preserve' should be severely limited. In the upshot, we have included only two others: the unfinished "Elegy" on his father's death, which was added by Vernon Watkins to later printings of the 1952 volume, though in a different form from that which we print here; and "In Country Heaven", whose incompletion is especially disappointing because it was to have been an over-arching structure for three of Thomas's finest late poems ("In Country Sleep", "Over Sir John's hill" and "In the White Giant's Thigh"). The "Elegy" and "In Country Heaven", both here taken from manuscripts in progress at Thomas's death, merit being preserved as accurately as possible in those parts that Thomas had, at least provisionally, brought to some degree of completion. It is in this sense that the present volume is an edition of *Collected Poems 1934–1953*, not 1952.

The profile given to Thomas's achievement by our decision to remain, otherwise, within the parameters of Thomas's own choice in 1952 seems to us to be the right one. Thirty-five years after his death, the basic integrity of that collection has come to carry its own persuasiveness. That is not to say that its persuasiveness is that of mere historic fact. The publication of the poet's notebooks in 1968 made visible the early context, the reservoir from which the main flow of the career took its force for the first of its two decades,

1934 to 1941 (when the notebooks were sold to Buffalo University Library). After 1941, the poems by Thomas that did not reach publication are very few in number. To augment the *Collected* volume with poems selected editorially from the notebooks or elsewhere would have damaged the integrity of two discrete bodies of poetry, each with its own rationale.

Two books – as it happens, by the same author – have greatly eased the path of anyone interested in Thomas's achievement: Paul Ferris's *Life* (1977) and his edition of the *Collected Letters* (1985). This is attested by the high frequency with which the *Collected Letters*, especially, has been referred to in the present edition.

The great number of critical studies of the poet's work – in the form of detailed reader's guides as well as of more general assessments – has also eased the path. However, in an edition of this kind, the sign-posting of all the highways, detours and by-ways that that path leads on to in the matter of explication of meanings or elucidation of allusions is undesirable. Reviewing Thomas's *Collected Poems 1934–1952* in the *New Statesman* on 15 May 1954, William Empson prefigured a central concern that has also exercised the editors of this present edition. Commenting on the different kinds of obscurity to be found in Thomas's early poems, Empson revealed that he had been puzzling over the word 'Mnetha' in the opening stanza of "Before I knocked":

> Miss Kathleen Raine has at last told me that Mnetha is a suitable character in one of Blake's Prophetic Books; but this acts only as a reassurance that the line meant the kind of thing you wanted it to, not really as an explanation of it. 'That'll do very well,' as Alice said when she was told the meaning of a word in the 'Jabberwocky', because she knew already what it ought to fit in with. I think an annotated edition of Dylan Thomas ought to be prepared as soon as possible, and that a detail like that ought to go in briefly ...

But Empson then added –

> it would be hard to decide what else ought to go in.

Alice's 'That'll do very well' is very often one's reaction to an explanation of an allusion in a Thomas poem, because it is indeed true, as Empson implies, that other factors (rhythm, image, connotation) have already pointed us adequately in the right direction. A healthy scepticism as to any help needed is particularly relevant to the more obscure early poems, in which the element of irreducibility – the poet's aim that his poem should remain what it says, and not what it can be made to say in other words – is strongest. Nevertheless, even in the early poetry, there is a consistent level of allusion, ranging from the relatively obvious to the highly private, that has merited annotation in this edition. Our policy has been to work always from the specific and the

161

concrete. Thus in our notes we have not attempted to supply paraphrases of the general meaning of poems. We have, rather, allowed the broad parameters of a poem's subject-area to be evoked tangentially by notes that are keyed into specific, local points of difficulty or interest. Proper names are glossed; most words that can be found in a dictionary are not. Another way in which we have sought to anchor each note is to allow generous access to any explication that stems from Thomas himself, especially if it survives in Thomas's own words. The poet is not often as explicit or accommodating in his explanations as another commentator might be, but we have felt that a comment by Thomas himself is more likely, whether in relation to a whole poem or to a part, to keep the reader within reach of the original impulse that drove the poem along or determined, say, the selection of an image. In terms of interpretation, this edition is meant to be specifically enabling, rather than comprehensive and prescriptive. We have tried to bear in mind in the explanatory notes what Thomas told Richard Church of Dent's in an early letter. He acknowledged as one of his main faults 'a very much overweighted imagery that leads too often to incoherence. But' – he immediately added – 'every line *is* meant to be understood; the reader *is* meant to understand every poem by thinking and feeling about it, not by sucking it in through his pores' (*Letters* p. 205).

In preparing this volume, the editors have felt not only a confidence in that last remark, but a renewed respect for the remarkable achievement of so many of these poems, in terms of seriousness of theme, richness of texture, and memorability.

# Textual Preface to the Notes

In the case of Dylan Thomas's poems, the question of textual emendation becomes complicated exactly where it should be most clear-cut. If one could work by the generally accepted rule-of-thumb that the text which received an author's latest attention is that of highest validity, the Dent *Collected Poems* of 1952 could be reprinted without qualms. But we must ask what kind of attention that volume received from Thomas. In the absence of the author's marked proofs of the *Collected Poems*, we can only make conjectures on circumstantial evidence. And, immediately, we encounter the eagle-eyed T. A. Sinclair, who wrote to Thomas about a misprint in the poem "This bread I break" when *Twenty-five Poems* first came out. Thomas's reply is dated 20 January 1937:

> Thank you so much for asking J. M. Dent whether the line 'Once in this *wind*' was not a misprint for 'Once in this *wine*.' Of course it is, though no-one at all, including myself, spotted it. I'm letting Dent's know at once. Thanks again. I *do* appreciate the fact that someone has read my poems so carefully (*Letters* pp. 243–4).

The poet exhibited a natural concern; but, on the other side of the ledger, he not only allowed the misprint to continue through two further printings of *Twenty-five Poems*, but also forgot to change it in the *Collected Poems*. Only after T. A. Sinclair wrote to the *Times Literary Supplement* (10 September 1954) did the alerted Dent's correct 'wind' to 'wine' for subsequent printings. Thomas's attention to the text of the *Collected Poems* is shown to be in this instance non-existent. Another glaring error was not caught in the production of the volume: 'desires' was printed instead of 'desirers' in the last section of "In the White Giant's Thigh". These, and other lapses listed below, have made us cautious in accepting the 1952 text of the *Collected Poems* as the best copy-text. Even the last-minute changes to the page proofs that could only be Thomas's come under some suspicion. There are so few of them – a couple of deleted passages, a few word changes – that they are barely enough to give minimum credence to Thomas's remark about his poems in the "Note" at the front of the *Collected Poems*: 'Some of them I have revised a little' – especially if the remark is meant to imply a discriminating and sustained effort on the text. E. F. Bozman, who was in charge of editorial matters at Dent's at the time, wrote:

> Undoubtedly the publishing event that meant most to him was the issue
> of his *Collected Poems*. But in putting together, and revising them, he
> lost all interest periodically, even going so far as to lose the actual
> material on several occasions (*Dent typescript*).

One of the things Bozman is referring to is Thomas's needing, at as late a date as June 1952, a new set of proofs, having misplaced the set previously sent to him (*Letters* p. 830).

What can we discern about Thomas's attitude to the page proofs of his *Collected Poems* while they were sitting through the summer of 1952 on the table in his writing shed at Laugharne? The main thing on his mind was the preface he had promised to write. In a letter of 28 June 1952 to his agent, David Higham, Thomas confessed that he had made Dent's the impossible promise of writing a preface within a week, and then illness had intervened, and now: 'I can't write an ordinary prose-preface at all' (*Letters* p. 830). He had done about 80 lines of what he envisaged as 'about 160 to 200 short lines of verse' and what ultimately became, by the time it was submitted to Bozman on 10 September 1952, the tortuously rhymed 102-line "Prologue" to the *Collected Poems*. 'Why I acrosticked myself like this,' he wrote in the accompanying letter, 'don't ask me' (*Letters* p. 838). The answer to why Thomas chose to act like a juggler for those twelve weeks might come from the psychological theory nearest to hand: the poet's need to procrastinate. He apparently felt compelled to fill the time with a demanding poetic preface until it was too late to make a responsible review of the poems themselves. He squeezed out of himself one last-minute plea: 'Proofreading the Collected Poems, I have the horrors of "Paper and Sticks" on page 116. It's *awful*' (*Letters* p. 839). What else he had similar aversion to we can deduce from the differences between copies of the page proofs (as we have said, none of the extant copies is the poet's) and the final published text. Thomas apparently cut out a stanza of "When once the twilight locks" and a line of "From love's first fever". He altered 'pat the brow' to 'stroke the brow' in "The hand that signed the paper"; 'lad' to 'boy' in sonnet IV of "Altarwise by owl-light"; 'hear in a shell' to 'read in a shell' in "Over Sir John's hill"; 'bows' to 'kneels' in "In the White Giant's Thigh"; and a few words in "Lament". The impulsiveness of these unsystematic changes makes one uneasy. Most of them are acceptable; but former readings, we consider, could be preferable in some cases. In his dash through the proofs, Thomas was in a state of mind in which he altered 'pat' to 'stroke' in a minor poem, while overlooking an appalling mistake ('Because their words has forked no lightning') in a very important poem.

The above considerations have caused us to give less weight to the final stages of the production of the *Collected Poems* and more weight to the poet's original intention for the volume: that it should be an amalgamation of his five previously published collections. Collation of those individual volumes with the *Collected Poems* has built up the conviction that they should be our copy-texts, the texts from which we depart only when we have compelling reasons for doing so. At the same time, before the present edition, the Dent *Collected Poems* of 1952 has been the nearest thing to a standard text, and we have made sure that all deviations from that volume are noted. We have had to ignore the variants in the New Directions edition of *Collected Poems* (New York 1953) and the Dent's Everyman paperback printing, both of which volumes have corrected certain details, but have also introduced a number of misprints and variants of their own. These have no force in textual decisions; therefore they are not listed. (The existence of variants in those two volumes should be mentioned here, however, in case owners of them notice discrepancies and are puzzled.)

The specific demonstration of Thomas's intention for his *Collected Poems* comes from a document arising from the meeting at Dent's on 30 November 1951 when Thomas and Bozman first got down to details about a collection. In the Harry Ransom Humanities Research Center at the University of Texas is a typed sheet, headed 'Contents', listing all the titles in his previous volumes, with the volume named in the margin, viz. '(From *18 Poems*)'; '(From TWENTY-FIVE POEMS file copy)'; '(From MAP OF LOVE file copy)'; '(From DEATHS & ENTRANCES)'. The final six titles were typed separately:

> In Country Sleep
> Over Sir John's hill
> Poem on his Birthday
> Do not go gentle into that good night
> Lament
> In the White Giant's Thigh.

These are the poems of *In Country Sleep*, but that volume was not to be published for another three months, and only in the United States; so it is not mentioned by title in this sheet typed at Dent's. It is indicated, instead, that Thomas will supply typescripts or manuscripts for these six poems.

One other singularity of this typed Contents page was the inclusion, within the titles of the *Deaths and Entrances* volume, of a note: 'Shabby and Shorten (copy still to come)' – with the proper title "Once below a time" added by

165

hand later, presumably after Dent's had received the poem. 'Enclosed, is the Poem I imagined incorrectly was entitled "Shabby and Shorten". Can you let Bozman have it?' Thomas wrote to his agent three days after the meeting (*Letters* p. 818). "Once below a time" was included in the *Collected Poems* (1952); and we likewise include it among the poems of *Deaths and Entrances*, according to the poet's wishes. The evidence is that he intended it to go in that volume in the first place.

This typed Contents page has been our guide. As has been said, we have added the "Prologue" poem, and two late poems, "In Country Heaven" and "Elegy", whose textual problems are taken up in the notes to those poems below. We can now look at our copy-texts, the five individual volumes, seriatim.

## *18 Poems* (1934)

Anyone who has followed Thomas's correspondence with Pamela Hansford Johnson during the year 1934 will realize how seriously the young poet of nineteen set about determining the direction of his career and the specific contents of his first book of poems. When the *Sunday Referee* Poet's Corner invited him in April 1934 to put together a volume, Thomas selected only those poems that would maintain the energy of the volume at all points. He had finished thirty poems in the previous seven months; he selected thirteen of them. Five poems were completed between May and October 1934, and could be included as the book was delayed. The *18 Poems* which appeared on 18 December 1934 was obviously a cared-for volume. Thomas was in London to see it through the press, and there appear to be no typographical errors in the first edition. We have utilized this first edition as our copy-text, and have followed it in every particular, except for one hyphenation.

Dent did not apparently have the first edition for the compositor to use in setting up the *Collected Poems* in 1952, but fell back on the Fortune Press reprint, which had been available in good supply since 1942 when Thomas had sold the rights. The Fortune Press resetting introduced a number of misprints which we see copied exactly in the proofs of the Dent *Collected Poems*. Most of them were caught, either by Thomas or by a copy editor; but two undesirable variants from the Fortune Press edition (see 'damned' and 'fists' below) survived into the published *Collected Poems*.

The other differences between *18 Poems* (first edition) and the *Collected Poems* (1952) were due to Dent's 1952 compositor or to last-minute changes to the page proofs. In all cases (except 'glow-worm', see below), the first edition reading has been restored in the present edition.

|  | *18 Poems* (1934) | *18 Poems* (Fortune) | *Collected* (proofs) | *Collected* (1952) | Present edition |
|---|---|---|---|---|---|
| "When once the twilight locks" |  |  |  |  |  |
| (l. 3) | dammed | damned | damned | damned | dammed |
| (st. 6) | (included) | (included) | (included) | (dropped) | (restored) |
| (st. 7, l. 5) | carcase | carcase | carcass | carcass | carcase |
|  |  |  |  |  |  |
| "Especially when the October wind" |  |  |  |  |  |
| (st. 3, l. 3) | disc | disc | disk | disk | disc |
| (st. 4, l. 4) | fist | fists | fists | fists | fist |
|  |  |  |  |  |  |
| "When, like a running grave" |  |  |  |  |  |
| (st. 6, l. 5) | stick | stick | stick | stick, | stick |
|  | 'fail'. | 'fail'. | 'fail.' | 'fail.' | 'fail'. |
| (st. 9, ll. 2, 4 after parentheses) | (no commas) | (no commas) | (no commas) | (commas added) | (no commas) |
|  |  |  |  |  |  |
| "From love's first fever" |  |  |  |  |  |
| (st. 2, l. 3) | (included) | (included) | (included) | (dropped) | (restored) |
|  |  |  |  |  |  |
| "Light breaks where no sun shines" |  |  |  |  |  |
| (l. 4) | glowworms | glowworms | glow-worms | glow-worms | glow-worms |
|  |  |  |  |  |  |
| "I fellowed sleep" |  |  |  |  |  |
| (l. 4) | 'planing- | 'planing- | 'planing- | planing- | 'planing- |

## *Twenty-five Poems* (1936)

On 17 March 1936, fifteen months after *18 Poems*, Thomas sent to Richard Church at Dent's a manuscript volume, *Twenty-three Poems* – almost as an act of defiance: 'As you'll see,' he wrote, 'most of the poems are the very recent ones you have, in the past, objected to' (*Letters* p. 219). Church had wanted a volume of 'simple poems', and there were a number of those included (mainly revisions of early notebook poems); but Thomas would not sacrifice the heavier, obscure poems, and Church relented: 'I have decided to put myself aside and let you and the public face each other. I am accordingly taking steps to have the book set up in type' (*Dent typescript*). This volume, one concludes, was not undertaken lightly, on either side.

The advance proof of the preliminary *Twenty-three Poems* reveals, in comparison with the final *Twenty-five Poems*, that several misprints were corrected and several lines changed at proof stage. Thomas was in London for substantial visits during that period, and gave the volume his attention. The celebrated misprint, 'wind' instead of 'wine', escaped him. A line seems to have dropped from a poem by accident; we restore it from manuscript; and also on the basis of manuscript we move the final quotation marks in "Find meat on bones" to their proper place at the end of the poem.

| | MS | 25 Poems (1936) | Collected (proofs) | Collected (1952) | Present edition |
|---|---|---|---|---|---|
| **"I, in my intricate image"** | | | | | |
| (pt. ii, st. 2, l. 2) | Cadaverous | cadaverous | cadaverous | cadaverous | Cadaverous |
| (pt. ii, st. 6, l. 4) | disc | disc | disk | disk | disc |
| | | | | | |
| **"This bread I break"** | | | | | |
| (st. 2, l. 1) | wine | wind | wind | wind (early printings) | wine |
| **"Out of the sighs"** | | | | | |
| (st. 3, l. 4) | (included) | (dropped) | (dropped) | (dropped) | (restored) |
| | | | | | |
| **"How soon the servant sun"** | | | | | |
| (ll. 1, 2, 3, 5, 9, 12, 24) | (no commas) | (no commas) | (no commas) | (commas added) | (no commas) |
| | | | | | |
| **"Ears in the turrets hear"** | | | | | |
| (st. 2, l. 6) | bird | bird | birds | birds | bird |
| | | | | | |
| **"Foster the light"** | | | | | |
| (st. 5, l. 1) | (no comma) | (no comma) | (no comma) | (comma added) | (no comma) |
| | | | | | |
| **"The hand that signed the paper"** | | | | | |
| (st. 4, l. 2) | pat | pat | pat | stroke | stroke |
| | | | | | |
| **"Find meat on bones"** | | | | | |
| (final quotation mark) | end of poem | end of st. 4 | end of st. 4 | end of st. 4 | end of poem |
| | | | | | |
| **"Altarwise by owl-light"** | | | | | |
| (I, l. 1) | halfway- | | half-way | half-way | halfway- |
| (I, l. 3) | hang-nail | | hangnail | hangnail | hang-nail |
| (I, l. 9) | halfway | | half-way | half-way | halfway |
| (I, l. 12) | (end comma) | | (end comma) | (end colon) | (end comma) |
| (II, l. 10) | (end semi-colon) | | (end semi-colon) | (end period) | (end semi-colon) |
| (IV, l. 8) | lad | | lad | boy | lad |
| (IV, l. 11) | Love's | | Love's | Love's | Love's a |

|  | 25 Poems (1936) | Collected (proofs) | Collected (1952) | Present edition |
|---|---|---|---|---|
| (IV, l. 14) | Ark- | Arc- | Arc- | Ark- |
| (V, l. 5) | (end comma) | (end comma) | (end period) | (end comma) |
| (V, l. 6) | (end semi-colon) | (end semi-colon) | (end period) | (end semi-colon) |
| (V, l. 10) | (end semi-colon) | (end semi-colon) | (end comma) | (end semi-colon) |
| (VI, l. 4) | (end colon) | (end colon) | (end period) | (end colon) |
| (VII, l. 5) | (end semi-colon) | (end semi-colon) | (end period) | (end semi-colon) |
| (VIII, l. 11) | (no end comma) | (no end comma) | (end comma) | (no end comma) |
| (X, l. 2) | halfway | half-way | half-way | halfway |

The emendation of sonnet IV (l. 11) to read 'Love's a reflection' is a reversion to the first printing of the poem in *Life and Letters Today*; it is confirmed by Thomas's marginal gloss of the line in a copy of *Twenty-five Poems*: 'Love is a reflection' (see note to the poem).

## *The Map of Love* (1939)

The page proofs of this volume, corrected in Thomas's hand, have been deposited by New Directions Publishers in the Houghton Library, Harvard University. The poet caught four typographical errors, and made no other changes.

In the *Map of Love* printing there are two occasions where a stanza break coincides with the bottom of a page, and this fact was not recognized by the compositor of the 1952 *Collected Poems*. We have followed Thomas's intention in restoring the stanza break in "Not from this anger", and after l. 14 of "The tombstone told".

|  | The Map of Love (1939) | Collected (proof) | Collected (1952) | Present edition |
|---|---|---|---|---|
| "I make this in a warring absence" | | | | |
| (st. 3, l. 7) | (no end comma) | (no end comma) | (end comma added) | (no end comma) |
| (st. 5, l. 6) | jaw-/bone | jaw-bone | jaw-bone | jawbone |
| (st. 5, ll. 7–8) | (added to st. 6) | (added to st. 6) | (added to st. 6) | (restored to st. 5) |
| "It is the sinners' dust-tongued bell" | | | | |
| (st. 2, l. 4) | tide-/print | tide-print | tide-print | tideprint |
| "After the funeral" | | | | |
| (4th line from end) | (no end comma) | (end comma) | (end comma) | (no end comma) |

## *Deaths and Entrances* (1946)

According to a manuscript at Buffalo, a volume to be called *Deaths and Entrances* was being planned as far back as July 1941. The war delayed everything, and the possibility of a volume was not raised again until 1944, a book-length manuscript being submitted to Dent's in October of that year. Thomas added new poems after that date; proofs of *Deaths and Entrances* were sent to him on 30 May 1945. Thomas apparently could not get to them until the end of the summer, and when he returned them on 18 September 1945, he had a new poem, "Fern Hill", to add. He also enclosed "In my craft or sullen art", and a revised "Unluckily for a death". Thomas returned final proof on 6 November 1945, and the volume was officially published in February 1946.

No proofsheets have survived, so we cannot say what kind of proof reader Thomas was in this case. We know he missed a misprint on the first page, and a couple in "Vision and Prayer". But, on the whole, *Deaths and Entrances* provides us with a good copy-text. We have made one major emendation to it, restoring lines from the periodical printing of "Ceremony After a Fire Raid" that were unaccountably dropped in *Deaths and Entrances* and were not restored later.

"Once below a time" (a poem not originally included in *Deaths and Entrances*) had stanza breaks after l.18 and three lines from the end in a manuscript now at Texas and in its *Life and Letters Today* printing. These stanza breaks were omitted in *Collected Poems* (1952) but are restored in the present edition.

| | MS | *Deaths &*<br>*Entrances* | *Collected*<br>(proofs) | *Collected*<br>(1952) | Present<br>edition |
|---|---|---|---|---|---|
| "The conversation of prayers" | | | | | |
| (st. 3, l. 5) | Tonight | To night | To-night | To-night | Tonight |
| | | | | | |
| "Unluckily for a death" | | | | | |
| (l. 7) | (comma) | (comma) | (no comma) | (no comma) | (comma) |
| (st. 3, l. 5) | duck-/Billed | duck billed | duck-billed | duck-billed | duck-billed |
| | | | | | |
| "A Winter's Tale" | | | | | |
| (st. 5, l. 3) | milk maids | milk maids | milkmaids | milkmaids | milk maids |
| | | | | | |
| "Ceremony After a Fire Raid" | | | | | |
| (pt. ii, l. 3) | (included) | (missing) | (missing) | (missing) | (restored) |
| (pt. iii, l. 10) | (included) | (missing) | (missing) | (missing) | (restored) |

| | MS | Deaths & Entrances | Collected (proofs) | Collected (1952) | Present edition |
|---|---|---|---|---|---|
| **"Vision and Prayer"** | | | | | |
| (st. 4, l. 6) | | I lost was | I lost was | I was lost | I was lost |
| (pt. ii, st. 3, l. 1) | | Then he | Then he | That he | That he |
| | | | | | |
| **"Ballad of the Long-legged Bait"** | | | | | |
| (st. 27, l. 3) | Susannah's | Sussanah's | Sussanah's | Sussanah's | Susanna's |

## *In Country Sleep* (1952)

The marked proofs of *In Country Sleep* are apparently not extant. But we know that Thomas read proofs, and read them under interesting circumstances. He wrote to his agent on 14 December 1951, just ready to forward them to New Directions in New York: 'I am posting Laughlin's proofs direct to him tonight. Is that okay? I would have posted them sooner, but am going to read most of them tonight at the Institute of Contemporary Art and have no other copy' (*Letters* p. 821). In other words, Thomas was reading the proofs without copies of the poems to check them by. He could therefore be making no attempt to have *In Country Sleep* conform exactly to the texts of the poems that had been sent to Dent's for the *Collected Poems* the previous month. Given this circumstance, the variants are surprisingly few.

Thomas made some corrections in Ruthven Todd's copy of *In Country Sleep*: in "Lament" he altered 'fiery' to 'quivering', and 'swaddles my thighs with' to 'hides my thighs in'; in "In the White Giant's Thigh" he altered 'desires' to 'desirers'. We have accepted *In Country Sleep*, so amended, as the best copy-text for our purposes. We have not accepted that the order of the six poems in that volume is preferable, and have restored the basically chronological order of the poems, as indicated by the typescript Contents draft and as followed in the *Collected Poems* (1952) itself.

| | In Country Sleep | Collected (proofs) | Collected (1952) | Present edition |
|---|---|---|---|---|
| **"In Country Sleep"** | | | | |
| (st. 5, l. 2 Sanctum sanctorum) | (not italics) | (italics) | (italics) | (not italics) |
| (st. 5, l. 7) | lord's table | (hyphenated) | (hyphenated) | (not hyphenated) |
| (st. 8, l. 4) | last love | lost love | lost love | last love |
| (pt. II, st. 2, l. 2) | pastoral | pastoral | Pastoral | Pastoral |
| (pt. II, st. 2, l. 5) | the upgiven | The upgiven | The upgiven | The upgiven |

| | *In Country Sleep* | *Collected* (proofs) | *Collected* (1952) | Present edition |
|---|---|---|---|---|
| (pt. II, st. 4, l. 1) | black backed | (hyphenated) | (hyphenated) | (not hyphenated) |
| (pt. II, st. 5, l. 6) | willynilly | willy-nilly | willy nilly | willynilly |

"Over Sir John's hill"

| | | | | |
|---|---|---|---|---|
| (st. 2, l. 8) | dab filled | dab-filled | dab-filled | dab filled |
| (st. 3, l. 1) | hear | hear | read | read |
| (st. 3, l. 3) | hawk eyed | hawk eyed | hawk-eyed | hawk-eyed |
| (st. 3, l. 12) | (not present) | (not present) | shell-hung | shell-hung |
| (st. 5, l. 4) | (end comma) | (dropped) | (dropped) | (restored) |

"Poem on his Birthday"

| | | | | |
|---|---|---|---|---|
| (st. 11, l. 6) | tackle | tackle | tackle, | tackle, |
| (st. 11, ll. 6 and 8) | (no end commas) | (no end commas) | (commas) | (no end commas) |

"Do not go gentle into that good night"

| | | | | |
|---|---|---|---|---|
| (st. 2, l. 2) | had | has | has (early printings) | had |

"Lament"

| | | | | |
|---|---|---|---|---|
| (st. 2, l. 12) | fiery | fiery | quivering | quivering |
| (st. 4, l. 10) | roarer's | roarers' | roarers' | roarer's |
| (st. 5, l. 10) | blesses | blesses | sweetens | sweetens |
| (st. 5, l. 11) | swaddles my thighs with | swaddles my thighs with | hides my thighs in | hides my thighs in |

"In the White Giant's Thigh"

| | | | | |
|---|---|---|---|---|
| (l. 15) | anyone | any one | any one | anyone |
| (after l. 36) | (stanza break) | (no break) | (no break) | (break restored) |
| (l. 50) | bows | bows | kneels | kneels |
| (l. 54) | Beloved | Beloved | Belovéd | Beloved |
| (l. 56) | desires | desires | desires | desirers |
| (l. 59) | forever | for ever | for ever | forever |

In keeping with Thomas's own practice on occasions, we have not felt compelled to use the whole of the first line as a title, but have sometimes used only the first few words. We have also consistently used lower case for titles derived from first lines. Conversely, we have capitalized three titles that are not first-line titles. Other than these minor adjustments, we have changed only two titles from the form in which they appeared in *Collected Poems 1934–1952*. No manuscript of Thomas's uses "Author's Prologue", which was most likely a publisher's decision. "Prologue" was invariably Thomas's title, and we have followed that choice. We have changed "The Conversation of Prayer", the title used in *Deaths and Entrances* and *Collected Poems 1934–1952*, to "The conversation of prayers". This latter title appears in an autograph manuscript of the poem (Texas) and in the copy sent to Vernon Watkins; and also in the two periodical publications of the poem. It is more accurately faithful to the theme of the poem.

The following decisions have also been made in the present edition: 'to-day', 'to-morrow' and 'good-bye' have been normalized to 'today', 'tomorrow', and 'goodbye'; quotation marks at the beginning of stanzas to show that speech is continuing are not used; no stanza break has been allowed to coincide with the bottom of a page, except where the regularity of the stanzaic pattern makes the stanza break obvious.

The prose "Note" which was placed prior to the verse "Prologue" in the *Collected Poems* (1952) came into existence in two stages. There exists in one of the page proof copies at Texas a preliminary version, set up in type at the same time as the first proof of the "Prologue". We conjecture that this text did not issue from the poet's pen:

*Note*
The author's prologue in verse to this collected edition of his poems fulfills the function of an address to his readers (the 'strangers'). It is in two verses of fifty-one lines each, and the second verse rhymes *backwards* with the first.

The poems, arranged and revised by the author, represent all that he has written, and wishes to preserve, up to the present year.

*November 1952.*

We suspect that only a publisher would pre-date a note in anticipation of the publication date. The content of the note echoes Thomas's letter to Bozman of 10 September 1952, and it was presumably set up in type in expectation of the poet's approval. After the usual delay, Thomas returned the note, rewritten, in a letter dated 6 October 1952:

Dear Bozman,
Hope this is satisfactory, and that you can get it in in time. *Do* try, please. And apologies again for my terribleness (*Letters* p. 839).

And a telegram to Bozman the following day read: 'Do really think most vital use new note whatever delay' (*Dent file*). Thomas had made some important changes, but Bozman's formality is still detectable in the note as it was published in *Collected Poems* (1952):

*Note*
The prologue in verse, written for this collected edition of my poems, is intended as an address to my readers, the strangers.

This book contains most of the poems I have written, and all, up to the present year, that I wish to preserve. Some of them I have revised a little, but if I went on revising everything that I now do not like in this book I should be so busy that I would have no time to try to write new poems.

I read somewhere of a shepherd who, when asked why he made, from within fairy rings, ritual observances to the moon to protect his flocks, replied: 'I'd be a damn' fool if I didn't!' These poems, with all their crudities, doubts, and confusions, are written for the love of Man and in praise of God, and I'd be a damn' fool if they weren't.

*November 1952.*

# Notes

## Abbreviations

p. pp.   page, pages
l. ll.   line, lines
st.   stanza
pt.   part

*Notebooks,* ed. Ralph Maud *Poet in the Making* (J. M. Dent 1968) – published in the U.S. by New Directions as *The Notebooks of Dylan Thomas* (1967). Second edition: *The Notebook Poems* (J. M. Dent 1989).

*Letters* ed. Paul Ferris *The Collected Letters of Dylan Thomas* (J. M. Dent 1985).

*Portrait of a Friend* Gwen Watkins *Portrait of a Friend* (Gomer Press 1983).

Tedlock ed. E. W. Tedlock *Dylan Thomas: The Legend and the Poet* (Heinemann 1960).

*Quite Early One Morning* ed. Aneirin Talfan Davies *Quite Early One Morning* (J. M. Dent 1954).

*Early Prose Writings* ed. Walford Davies *Dylan Thomas: Early Prose Writings* (J. M. Dent 1971).

*Letters to Vernon Watkins* ed. Vernon Watkins *Dylan Thomas: Letters to Vernon Watkins* (J. M. Dent and Faber & Faber 1957).

*Prospect of the Sea* Dylan Thomas *A Prospect of the Sea* (J. M. Dent 1955).

Ferris Paul Ferris *Dylan Thomas* (N.Y. Dial Press; London: Hodder & Stoughton 1977).

Treece Henry Treece *Dylan Thomas: 'Dog Among the Fairies'* (Lindsay Drummond 1949).

## Prologue

As the 166 pages of worksheets at Houghton Library, Harvard, show, the origin of this poem was in a verse letter to a friend. Forwarding the worksheets to Oscar Williams on 3 March 1953, Thomas said: 'I've tried to keep the sheets in some sort of order, from the very first germ of the poem – it was going to be a piece of doggerel written to someone in the States on my return from there to Wales, but soon grew involved and eventually serious' (*Letters* p. 875). John Malcolm Brinnin was told by Thomas that the recipient-to-be was himself. The letter-poem was not sent, but Brinnin saw what he believed was a finished poem on two long, legal-sized pages when he visited Thomas in Laugharne in July 1951. (Paul Ferris was puzzled over this and double-checked with Brinnin, who reconfirmed it – see Ferris, *Dylan Thomas* p. 407). If Brinnin is not mistaken, then he must have seen a very early version, for the Harvard worksheets begin with the title "Letter On Returning to Wales from the United States of America, 1952". So the poem was either begun, or taken up completely afresh, in May 1952, after Thomas's second visit. There is reason to think that Ruth Witt-Diamant, his hostess in San Francisco, was to have been the recipient at one stage, for one of the worksheets begins:

> At home sweet Christ at last,
> Wry, Welsh, and far from Scotch,
> My pecker at half mast,
> This unamended potch
> Of poppycock and love
> I send, dear      Ruth

After about twenty-three worksheets, the title "Prologue" begins to appear. Thomas had seen an opportunity to adapt the verse letter to the need to fulfil the promise he had made to E. F. Bozman of Dent's to supply a preface to the *Collected Poems*, then in an advanced stage of preparation for the press. Writing to David Higham on 28 June 1952, Thomas explained:

> I promised him the preface this week, but illness supervened. And now I have to confess that I can't write an ordinary prose-preface at all, having no interest whatsoever in it. What I *am* doing, and doing quickly, is writing a Prologue in verse: not dense, elliptical verse, but (fairly) straightforward and colloquial, addressed to the (maybe) readers of the Collected Poems, & full (I hope) of references to my methods of work, my aims, & the kind of poetry I want to write. I hope it will be interesting; I know I'm interested in writing it. It will be about 160 to 200 short lines of verse, of which I have written about 80 so far (*Letters* pp. 830–831).

In sending the finished "Prologue" to Bozman with a letter of 10 September 1952, Thomas wrote:

> I intended, as you know, to write a more-or-less straightforward & intimate prose preface, and then funked it. And then I began to write a prologue in verse, which has taken the *devil* of a time to finish. Here it is, only a hundred & two lines, and pathetically little, in size & quality, to warrant the two months, & more, I've taken over it. To begin with, I set myself, foolishly perhaps, a most difficult technical task: The Prologue is in two verses – in my manuscript, a verse to a page – of 51 lines each. And the second verse rhymes *backward* with the first. The first & last lines of the poem rhyme; the second and the last but one; & so on & so on. Why I acrosticked myself like this, don't ask me.
>
> I hope the Prologue *does* read as a prologue, & not as just another poem (*Letters* p. 838).

*The Listener* published the poem on 6 November 1952 with the title "Prologue". (The title "Author's Prologue" apparently originated with Dent's; it was never used by the poet, although he allowed it to stand in the *Collected Poems*.)

*you, strangers,* (l.24): The poem, Thomas wrote to Bozman of Dent's on 10 September 1952, 'addresses the readers, the "strangers", with a flourish, and fanfare, and makes clear, or tries to make clear, the position of one writer in a world "at poor peace" ' (*Letters* p. 838). The commas enclosing 'strangers' (omitted in *Collected Poems* of 1952) are here restored on the authority of manuscripts and periodical printing.

*deer* (second half, l.5): Used here in the old, generalized sense of 'beasts, animals' – as in *King Lear* (III, 4, 142), 'mice and rats and such small deer'.

*bryns* (second half, l.6): 'Bryn' is Welsh for 'hill', here pluralized by Thomas in English fashion.

*shall* (12 lines from end): *Collected Poems* (1952) had 'will', but Thomas reads 'shall' in the recording of this poem, following a Dent manuscript.

## 18 POEMS (1934)

### I see the boys of summer

Parts I and II of this poem apparently represent two stages of composition. The 'new poem, just completed, which may be some good to you', which was sent to Geoffrey Grigson in late March 1934 (*Letters* p. 105), was probably the present part I. On returning from a visit to London in early April 1934, when he had apparently discussed the poem with Grigson on the telephone, Thomas expanded it, and then copied it into his notebook as poem "Thirty

Nine" dated 'April '34'. The new version was sent off to Grigson with the comment, 'The poem you said you'd read and tell me about is incomplete in the version you have. I enclose the complete poem' (*Letters* p. 120). Grigson published it in *New Verse* June 1934. Thomas had sent the early version to Pamela Hansford Johnson in late March (*Letters* p. 108); in a letter of 2 May 1934 discussing his choice for *18 Poems*, and saying that "Boys of Summer" would open the volume, Thomas told her that it was now 'altered and double the length' (*Letters* p. 125).

The mood in which at least part II of "I see the boys of summer" was composed was one of depression. Thomas was back in Swansea after his Easter holiday in London with Pamela Hansford Johnson, and wrote a Sunday morning 'soliloquy', looking out from 5 Cwmdonkin Drive:

> I wish I could see these passing men and women in the sun as the motes of virtues, this little fellow as a sunny Fidelity, this corsetted hank as Mother-Love, this abusing lout as the Spirit of Youth, and this eminently beatable child in what was once a party frock as the walking embodiment of Innocence. But I can't. The passers are dreadful. I see all their little horrors (*Letters* p. 111).

And much more. Thomas was himself a very dark 'denier' on Sunday 15 April 1934.

The poem itself, however, expresses this denial with great vitality, recapturing something of the spirit of a letter of 25 December 1933, when he said: 'promise is perhaps the greatest thing in the world' (*Letters* p. 80). The poet considered "I see the boys of summer" one of the two 'best poems in my book' (*Letters* p. 208).

*men of nothing* (st. 4, l.1): Thomas's Swansea friend, A. E. Trick, has said (in conversation) that, walking on the beach, Thomas referred to middle-aged men in Corporation bathing suits as 'boys of summer in their ruin', and began the poem with that scene in mind.

*deniers* (pt. II, st. 2, l.1): Henry Treece in his early study, *Dylan Thomas* (1949), wrote: 'I came upon what I thought to be the archaic term "denier", and asked Thomas why he should think to mention this ancient coin. His reply was that he did not know of such a coin's existence, and that the word was, as far as he knew, his own invention, meaning "One who denies"' (p. 79). There is a copy of Treece's book in the Buffalo Special Collections Library where Thomas has written 'deni-er' in the margin in order to emphasize the point.

*Davy's lamp* (pt. II, st. 2, l.5): A miners' safety lamp was invented by Sir Humphrey Davy. Since the lamp here is associated with the sea, it must belong to Davy Jones, the supposed evil spirit of the sea.

*Man in his maggot* (pt. III, l.2): The Everyman edition of *Blake's Poems and Prophecies* was published in 1927. Thomas was then thirteen, and undoubtedly became influenced by the illustrations from "The Gates of Paradise", including the frontispiece, 'What is Man'.

What is Man

## When once the twilight locks

The early version of this poem was written into a notebook as "Twenty Nine" on 11 November 1933, and sent off to Pamela Hansford Johnson in a letter begun the following day: 'I'm enclosing one poem just finished. It's quite my usual stuff, I'm afraid, and quite probably you won't like it' (*Letters* p. 57). A thorough revision of the poem was made before it was sent off to Geoffrey Grigson in March 1934. This version, published in *New Verse* June 1934, was printed in *18 Poems* with a few minor changes.

*dammed* (l.3): The unborn child's amniotic 'sea' is dammed for the period of pregnancy. In terms of this image, the mother could be considered a dam (or lock). In the notebook version Thomas had written 'damned', which turned up in the Fortune Press resetting of the poem, and thence in the

*Collected Poems* (1952), and has provided one of the difficult textual cruxes. We have opted for the *18 Poems* (1934) 'dammed', while acknowledging that 'damned' may be lurking in the word as a pun. Thomas later, writing to Vernon Watkins on 27 April 1946, described a feeling of depression as a case of being 'locked in these damned days' (*Letters* p. 588).

*cancer* (st. 4, l.2): 'But, honestly, the one "cancer" mentioned *is* necessary' – Thomas to Pamela Hansford Johnson, November 1933 (*Letters* p. 57).

*Christ-cross-row* (st. 4, l.6): ABC. A cross was customarily placed at the head of the alphabet in early spelling-books.

*Sargasso* (st. 5, l.2): The Sargasso Sea in the North Atlantic is made up of masses of floating seaweed with berry-like air-vessels, creating sluggish waters.

*pickthank* (st. 7, l.3): A flatterer – a word used by Shakespeare and Blake. Although Pamela Hansford Johnson has said the word became a joke for the two of them (*Important to Me* p. 140), in the poem it reflects the poet's fervent wish to leave a morbid dream-world and take on a more active life.

## A process in the weather of the heart

Poem "Thirty Five" dated 'February 2. '34' in a notebook supplied the text for publication in *Sunday Referee* 11 February 1934, and in *18 Poems*.

*unangled* (st. 3, l.3): The notebook variant 'unplumbed' makes it clear that 'unangled' means 'unfished'.

## Before I knocked

Poem "Seven" dated 'September 6' (1933) in a notebook was sent, soon after completion, in Thomas's first extant letter to Pamela Hansford Johnson in mid-September 1933, with the comment that she may not like it at all: 'it is distinctly unfashionable' (*Letters* p. 22). He adds: 'The Jesus poem is probably to be printed in T. S. Eliot's Criterion, though, as a rule, the Criterion doesn't print any metaphysic verse at all.' Eliot must have rejected it, for it was not printed until *18 Poems*.

Two of the notebook stanzas were omitted in the *18 Poems* version; other variations are mainly in respect to the capitalization of 'Christ' and the pronouns that might indicate a divine personage. There are further variations in this regard in a British Library typescript of the poem. This seems to suggest that Thomas wavered in his intention to depict the actual Christ figure. In the notebook page opposite "Before I knocked", with an arrow directed to it, are the lines:

> If God is praised in poem one
> Show no surprise when in the next
> I worship wood or sun or none.

Thomas valued this poem more than others he was writing at the time: 'There is more in the poem, "Before I Knocked", more of what I consider to be of importance in my poetry. Please, this isn't boasting. I'm incurably pessimistic and eternally dissatisfied' (*Letters* pp. 39–40).

*Jordan* (st. 1, l.4) ... *Eastern* (st. 3, l.5): In spite of these Biblical references, we cannot be confident that Thomas wanted to give the poem an exclusively Biblical setting. 'Eastern' was 'valley' in an early version, and may be meant to be vague. Jordan could be the name for any river felt to be holy; Thomas knew a farmer near Blaen Cwm (the rural cottage where this poem was written) who believed 'the stream that runs by his cottage side is Jordan water and who can deny him' (*Letters* p. 558).

*Mnetha* (st. 1, l.5): A character in Blake's *Tiriel*. Heva, Mnetha's daughter, is evoked by Blake as sharing kinship with all things. An illustration from "The Gates of Paradise" in the Everyman edition of *Blake's Poems and Prophecies* (1927) p. 308 seems pertinent.

I have said to the Worm: Thou
art my mother & my sister

*the rainy hammer*  (st. 2, l.5): The hammering of rain. In a letter of 25 December 1933, Thomas wrote: 'I think in cells; one day I may think in rains' (*Letters* p. 82). That the image is cosmic and meteorological is made clearer in the British Library typescript, where God is the agent and where 'Father' and 'His dome' are capitalized.

*doublecrossed*  (st. 8, l.4): Apparently Pamela Hansford Johnson objected to this word, for Thomas wrote on 15 October 1933: 'there is always only the one right word: use it, despite its foul or merely ludicrous associations; I used "double-crossed" because it was what I meant' (*Letters* p. 25). He does not further elaborate. Presumably, the 'Him' cheated the speaker's mother's womb by appropriating the 'flesh and blood' for a divine incarnation. If Thomas is addressing normal church-goers ('who bow down at cross and altar'), we should remember his often stated antipathy – for instance, in a letter of November 1933: 'the churches are wrong, because they standardize our gods, because they label our morals, because they laud the death of a vanished Christ, and fear the crying of the new Christ in the wilderness' (*Letters* p. 55).

## The force that through the green fuse

When Thomas began to copy this poem into a notebook as poem "Twenty Three" on 12 October 1933, he still had not settled on its final form. The first stanza, before it was crossed out, was as follows:

> The force that through the green fuse drives the flower
> Drives my green age; that blasts the roots of trees
> Is my destroyer.
> And I am dumb to tell the eaten rose
> How at my sheet goes the same crookèd worm,
> And dumb to holla thunder to the skies
> How at my cloths flies the same central storm.

The imagery of these lines invites us to turn to Blake's "The Sick Rose" for comparison:

> O rose, thou art sick:
> The invisible worm
> That flies in the night
> In the howling storm,

> Has found out thy bed
> Of crimson joy,
> And his dark secret love
> Does thy life destroy.

Blake's influence was acknowledged by the poet: 'I am in the path of Blake' (*Letters* p. 25).

In a long critique of a Pamela Hansford Johnson poem, Thomas revealed his own methodology:

> Though you talk all through of the relationship of yourself to other things, there is no relationship at all in the poem between the things you example. If you are one with the swallow & one with the rose, then the rose is one with the swallow. Link together these things you talk of; show, in your words & images, how *your* flesh covers the tree & the tree's flesh covers you. I see what you have done, of course – 'I am one with the opposites', you say. You are, I know, but you must prove it to me by linking yourself to the opposites and by linking the opposites together (*Letters* p. 79).

*hangman's lime*  (st. 3, l.5): Quicklime in which bodies from the scaffold were disposed of. The image is used again in a notebook poem, "See, says the lime, my wicked milks"; and Thomas comments on it in a letter of December 1933: 'So many modern poets take the *living* flesh as their object, and, by their clever dissecting, turn it into a carcase. I prefer to take the *dead* flesh, and, by any positivity of faith and belief that is in me, build up a living flesh from it' (*Letters* pp. 72–73).

*tell a weather's wind ... round the stars*  (st. 4, ll.4–5): The publication of the poem in *Sunday Referee* 29 October 1933 offers an interesting variant of these lines:

> ... tell the timeless clouds
> That time is all.

This would suggest that when time ticks 'a heaven' in the final revised version of the lines it is a demonstration of the ultimate supremacy of time itself.


## My hero bares his nerves

*18 Poems* was the first publication of this poem, little altered from its notebook version, poem "Thirteen" dated 'September 17 '33 Llangain', except that a last stanza was not used.

*naked Venus* (st. 3, l.2): The image draws on Botticelli's painting, "The Birth of Venus". The heart's veins and arteries are imaged as plaits of hair. Thomas's fondness for the Botticelli painting is suggested by the fact that he pinned two reproductions of it on a wall of his writing-shed at Laugharne. They are still there.

*the cistern moves* (st. 4, l.5): Whatever implications there may be in this last line of the poem – and the phrase 'cistern sex' in notebook poem "Twenty Seven" (February 1933) might indicate one of them – the likelihood cannot be ignored that it is an old-fashioned water-closet image. Around the time of this poem, Thomas wrote to Pamela Hansford Johnson that the refuse of the body is not 'more to be abhorred than the body itself':

> It is polite to be seen at one's dining table, and impolite to be seen in one's lavatory. It might well have been decided, when the tumour of civilisation was first fostered, that celebrations should be held in the w.c., and that the mere mention of 'eating and drinking' would be the height of impropriety. It was decided by Adam and Eve, the first society lawmakers, that certain parts of the body should be hidden and certain be left uncovered (*Letters* p. 39).

It is clearly Thomas's deliberate purpose in "My hero bares his nerves" to uncover what society normally hides.

Since Thomas once said that a poem of his 'is, or should be, a watertight section of the stream that is flowing all ways' (*Letters* p. 282), the dictionary definition of 'cistern' as a 'watertight box' has relevance, and connects the image to the poetry-writing theme in the poem.

## Where once the waters of your face

Poem "Thirty Eight" dated 'March 18. '34' in a notebook was published in *Sunday Referee* 25 March 1934, and, with negligible changes, in *18 Poems*.

The mood of this poem is reflected in a New Year's resolution of January 1934: 'I want to forget all that I have ever written and start again, informed with a new wonder, empty of all my old dreariness, and rid of the sophistication which is disease' (*Letters* pp. 81–82).

*serpents* (st. 4, l.5): Thomas may have been thinking of something like the Loch Ness monster, whose existence, he said in a letter, he does not doubt: 'This new year has brought back to my mind the sense of magic that was lost – irretrievably, I thought – so long ago. I am conscious, if not of the probability of the impossible, at least of its possibility' (letter to Trevor Hughes of early January 1934 – *Letters* p. 91).

## If I were tickled by the rub of love

Poem "Forty One" dated 'April 30, '34' was the last to be copied into the extant notebooks. A copy was immediately sent off, on 2 May 1934, to Pamela Hansford Johnson, with the comment: 'The poem is, I think, the best I've written – I've said that to you about a lot of mine, including all sorts of wormy beasts. It may be obscure, I don't know, but it honestly was not meant to be. It's too – I can't think of the word – for any thing but New Verse to print. I'll get Grigson to do it' (*Letters* p. 126). Thomas revised the poem before sending it to *New Verse*, where it appeared in August 1934.

*Man be my metaphor*  (st. 7, l.7): We take this to be another exhortation to himself to be active in the real world instead of being preoccupied with his degeneration and death. It fits the mood of the New Year, 1934:

> How can I ever lie on my belly on the floor, turning a narrow thought over and over again on the tip of my tongue, crying in my wordy wilderness, mean of spirit, brooding over the death of my finger which lies straight in front of me? How can I, when I have news to scream (*Letters* p. 82).

## Our eunuch dreams

Notebook poem "Thirty Seven" dated March 1934 was revised and sent to Geoffrey Grigson for *New Verse*, where it was published in the April 1934 issue. Thomas tinkered with part I before its appearance in *18 Poems*. He defended the poem half-heartedly to Pamela Hansford Johnson: 'That particular poem isn't as bad as you think' (*Letters* p. 108); and renounced it outright later as 'that silly poem' in a conciliatory gesture to Edith Sitwell, referring to it as 'that Welsh-starch-itch-trash poem' (*Letters* p. 210). Edith Sitwell had picked out "Our eunuch dreams" as 'an appalling affair' in her *Aspects of Modern Poetry* (1934) p. 149. Thomas had apparently written to her then, though the letter is not extant.

*the gunman*  (pt. II, l.1): Pamela Hansford Johnson apparently accused Thomas of being too much a 'thirties' poet in using current diction. He replied in a letter of late March 1934:

> There is no reason at all why I should not write of gunmen, cinemas & pylons if what I have to say necessitates it. Those words & images were essential. Just as some have a complex in regard to lambs & will never mention them even though lambs are necessary for their thought, you, my Christina, refuse to look a pylon in the face. I wasn't conceding anything. I wanted gunmen, and ... I bloody well had them (*Letters* p. 108).

Thomas wanted the 'gunman' because his subject is literally films (or half his subject, the other half being dreams). Thomas had written a serious essay on film as an art form in the *Swansea Grammar School Magazine* (*Early Prose Writings* pp. 87–89). He here sees the film world as unreal, and as debilitating as the dream world.

*Welshing* (pt. III, l.5): Decamping without paying. The word is not usually capitalized. Thomas intends another slap at his Swansea middle-class envionment, confident enough to risk a little self-mockery. In any case, it is an improvement on the line as it was first written:

> The sunny gents who piddle in the porch.

*Have faith* (pt. IV, l.6): With these words, the poem starts its positive note. But the leap within the same line from the rather sarcastic reference to films and dreams as 'This is the world' to the earnest exhortation of 'Have faith' is awkward. Thomas wanted to find some way to avoid the dislocation, and offered Grigson an alternative line (*Letters* p. 106):

> Suffer this world to spin.

The tonal change from cynicism to affirmation would then have begun with the final stanza. But Grigson let the 'Have faith' stand, and Thomas did not change it later.

## Especially when the October wind

This poem began as an early draft, "Especially when the November wind", extant in a British Library typescript. If it is one of Thomas's birthday poems, it became so when revised for publication in *The Listener* 24 October 1934, with the title "Poem in October". There is no notebook draft, but an indication of its early composition (probably in November 1932) is the adolescent heaviness of the typescript's reference to 'the chosen task' of poetry, 'that lies upon/My belly like a cold stone.' The extensive revision produced a final poem of greater rhetorical energy.

*walking like the trees* (st. 2, l.2): One thinks of the 'Sunday-walkers' passing 5 Cwmdonkin Drive or strolling in Cwmdonkin Park (*Letters* p. 110). It might be preferable in this context, however, to hear the Biblical echo: the blind man who is healed by Christ says, 'I see men as trees, walking' (Mark 8:24). The line in the early version was: 'Men in the distance walk like trees.'

*wordy shapes of women* (st. 2, l.3): An early short story, "The Mouse and the Woman", contains a similar image: 'the gestures of women's hands spelling on the sky.' Thomas once said to Alastair Reid (as quoted in Tedlock p. 54): 'When I experience anything, I experience it as a thing and a word at the same time, both equally amazing.'

## When, like a running grave

Thomas considered this poem and "I see the boys of summer" 'the best poems in my book [i.e. *18 Poems*]' (*Letters* p. 208). There is no manuscript or periodical version, since it was written after the extant notebooks were filled, and just before *18 Poems* went to press. A letter of late October 1934 to Pamela Hansford Johnson says: 'I am working very hard on a poem; it is going to be a very long poem; I've completed fifty lines so far; it is by far the best thing I've done; I don't suppose I'll have finished it even when I see you; but you shall read what there is of it then' (*Letters* p. 172). Since this poem is fifty lines long, our assumption is that the poem was allowed to rest at that length.

*tailor age* (st. 2, l.1): A repeated image in Thomas for growing older is the tailor sewing a shroud. Here the tailor stalks like a scissors, ready to cut the human thread like the Greek fate Atropos, or like the 'great tall tailor' of *Struwwelpeter*, a book Thomas read aloud from in his earliest school ("Return Journey" in *Quite Early One Morning* p. 89). It is a book he also lists among his presents in "Memories of Christmas" ('*Struwwelpeter* – oh! the baby-burning flames and the clacking scissorman!'). The rhyme accompanying the following picture from *Struwwelpeter* (Pan Books 1972 p. 20) is, in part:

> The door flew open, in he ran,
> The great, long, red-legged scissor-man.
> Oh! children, see the tailor's come
> And caught out little Suck-a-Thumb.
> Snip! Snap! Snip! the scissors go.

*virgin o* (st. 4, l.4): Thomas in a letter said that this phrase had nothing to do with 'raggletaggle gypsies o', but meant 'a circle, a round complete o' (*Letters* p. 322).

*morsing* (st. 5, l.2): Tapping out a telegraph message in Morse Code.

*Cadaver* (six times in the poem): The word for 'corpse' is here personified: Cadaver has a 'trap', a 'candle', a 'country', a 'hangar', a 'shoot', 'hunger', and other attributes, including being happy. (He also makes an appearance in the poem "I, in my intricate image".) This symbolic figure, so active and prominent in this poem, is associated, according to A.E. Trick (in conversation), with a medieval Italian nobleman, whom Thomas read about in one of his father's books. This historical figure did not want to be still after he was buried, but wanted to keep moving, and prepared a device, which involved a spade under his coffin, to accomplish that end.

## From love's first fever

This poem was begun in the notebooks on 14 October 1933, finished three days later, and sent to Pamela Hansford Johnson soon after. She apparently objected to the ending of the poem, which in the notebook version included the lines:

> Now that drugged youth is waking from its stupor,
> The nervous hand rehearsing on the thigh
> Acts with a woman, one sum remains in cipher.

This arrest of the growth process was unexpected. Thomas replied:

> Your remark about the end of my Feverish poem is entirely justified. I plead guilty to bathos, but offer in excuse the fact that I copied out the poem as soon as I had written it, wanting to get it off to you and too hurried to worry about its conclusion. In the ordinary way I would never have passed it (*Letters* p. 38).

When the poem came to be published in *Criterion* October 1934, the last eleven lines of the notebook version had been dropped.

*breaking of the hair* (st. 2, l.2): The notebook version had 'hatching of the hair', a phrase Pamela Hansford Johnson must have objected to, for Thomas replied in a letter:

> Leave me my 'hatching of the hair'. It's verminous, I know, but isn't it lovely? And what is more refreshing than the smell of vermin? Hardy loved to sit beside a rotten sheep and see the flies make a banquet of it. A dark thought, but good and lively (*Letters* p. 38).

## In the beginning

The development of this poem can be studied in the notebooks, where an early version written at Llangain on 18 September 1933, poem "Forty", has provided the basis for a new version copied into the notebook in April 1934. This was done as part of the 'process of pruning and cutting about' (*Letters* p. 125) in preparation for *18 Poems*, where the revised version was first published.

*crosstree* (st. 2, l.5): A horizontal timber supporting the mast of a ship. The word includes both Adam's tree and Christ's cross; the poem is, in a sense, a rewriting of Genesis.

## Light breaks where no sun shines

Poem "Thirty" dated 'November 20 '33' in a notebook was published in *The Listener* on 14 March 1934. Thomas mentioned to Glyn Jones at the time that the poem was 'a very obscure one' (*Letters* p. 99). Some readers, however, thought it was very clear:

> You'll be interested to know that the B.B.C. have banned my poetry. After my poem in the Listener ("Light Breaks Where No Sun Shines") the editor received a host of letters, all complaining of the disgusting obscenity of two of the verses. One of the bits they made a fuss about was:
>
> > 'Nor fenced, nor staked, the *gushers* of the sky
> > *Spout* to the *rod* divining in a smile
> > The *oil* of tears.'
>
> The little smut-hounds thought I was writing a copulatory anthem. In reality, of course, it was a metaphysical image of rain & grief. I shall never darken Sir John Reith's doors again, for all my denials of obscenity were disregarded (*Letters* p. 108).

Thomas was not really banned, and *The Listener* published "Especially when the October wind" later in the year. Moreover, the publication of the audacious "Light breaks where no sun shines" led to letters of interested inquiry from Geoffrey Grigson, Stephen Spender, and T. S. Eliot; and thus Thomas's London career was launched.

## I fellowed sleep

In a letter of 2 May 1934 Thomas wrote that he had 'rewritten "The Eye of Sleep" almost entirely' (*Letters* p. 125). He is referring to the notebook poem "Twenty Two", which he had sent to Pamela Hansford Johnson on 15 October 1933 (*Letters* p. 28). She must have praised it, for Thomas responded in a letter of 5 November 1933: 'The "dream" poem that you like is *not* the best I have sent you. Only superficially is it the most visionary' (*Letters* p. 39). In revising it, he cut out references to 'the pulse of God' and 'the mysterious order of the Lord', and substituted the plainer, 'I spelt my vision with a hand and hair'.

The revision incorporated the first line and other wording from notebook poem "Thirty One", 'I fellowed sleep who kissed between the brains' (dated 27 November 1933), which expresses the poet's relief at getting over several days of insomnia, a condition he complained of in letters:

> Last night I slept for the first time this month; today I am writing a poem in praise of sleep and the veronal that stained the ravelled sleeve. These twelve November nights have been twelve long centuries to me. Minute by minute through the eight hours of the dark I lay and looked up into the empty corners of this room. First I would seize upon some tiny thought, hug it close to me, turn it over and over in my brain, hoping, by such concentration, to find my senses dropping away into oblivion. But soon my lips would speak sentences aloud, and I listen to them.
>
> 'The man of substance never walks.' Then my lips say, 'He only wheels a truck', and, a thousand years later, I understand what I have spoken. Then I would repeat all the poetry I knew, but if I forgot a word I could never think of another to put in its place, unless it was a mad word and had no meaning. Then I would hear my heart beat, and count its beats, and hear their regularity (*Letters* p. 47).

"I fellowed sleep" has something of the self-cheering quality of "Our eunuch dreams", which ends with the hope that 'we shall be fit fellows for a life'; or of "When once the twilight locks", with its line, 'Awake, my sleeper, to the sun', echoed in the last stanza of "I fellowed sleep": 'There grows the hours' ladder to the sun.' If this poem seems not as clear-cut in its stance as those others, perhaps we should take into consideration the poet's own tentativeness: 'it is now a little better, though still shaky on its rhythms and very woolly as to its intention (if any)' (*Letters* p. 125). He did not apparently attempt to publish it before its inclusion in *18 Poems*, perhaps intending to revise it further.

*nave* (st. 3, l. 1): Compare two lines in the *Criterion* version of "From love's first fever", which were omitted in *18 Poems* and the *Collected Poems*:

> And where one globe had spun a host did circle
> The nave of heaven, each with his note.

A secondary meaning of 'nave' as the 'hub of a wheel' is probably present. The protagonist of the poem is apparently, from the vantage-point of a dreamland, looking down on his 'fathers' globe', the spinning world; but then is reminded in the next line that dreams are also the territory of his fathers. This equality between the two worlds was commented on by Thomas in a letter of 25 December 1933: 'I want to sleep and wake, and look upon my sleeping as only another waking' (*Letters* p. 82). If this thesis is behind 'I fellowed sleep', it would account for the strange symmetry of the two lines (st. 5, ll.4–5):

> How light the sleeping on this soily star,
> How deep the waking in the worlded clouds.

## I dreamed my genesis

Some time in May 1934 Thomas submitted this poem, along with two others, to an editor 'Mr Miles' (probably Hamish Miles of Jonathan Cape, one of the editors of *New Stories*). Thomas commented that they were 'all very similar in subject and approach ... I do hope you'll like one of them, though I admit their constant anatomical symbols can't be to the taste of many, and are, quite often, not even to the taste of myself' (*Letters* p. 117). The other two poems were probably "In the beginning" and "I fellowed sleep", for, like "I dreamed my genesis", these poems were not published before *18 Poems*. Whatever project Mr Miles had in mind, it apparently did not materialize.

Thomas added an interesting comment in his letter: 'The one beginning "I dreamed my genesis" is more or less based on Welsh rhythms, and may seem, rhythmically, a bit strange at first' (*Letters* p. 117). There is a strict syllable count maintained in the lines: 12, 7, 10, 8, consistently. There is an assonantal rhyme-scheme of a very peculiar sort: the last, unaccented syllable of the first line of each stanza rhymes with the last, accented syllable of the second line. Lines 3 & 4 of each stanza rhyme in their accented syllables, e.g. *driving:nerve, metal:night, journey:man*, and so on up to the last stanza, where *vision:sun* breaks the pattern.

This kind of careful, complicated structure to a poem is reminiscent of Welsh prosodic features, although *cynghanedd* in Welsh poetry is always much stricter. Possibly what Thomas was referring to in particular was the enjambment of most of the lines, which is similar in effect to the end of the first line of an *englyn*, where a final word or phrase is tacked on to that line when one would really expect it to take its place at the beginning of the next line.

At the time of writing "I dreamed my genesis" there was a certain amount of acrimony over Victor Neuburg's delay in publishing *18 Poems*. The following passage from a letter to Pamela Hansford Johnson of 9 May 1934 indicates something of Thomas's mood at the time:

> Tell him I write of worms and corruption, because I like worms and corruption. Tell him I believe in the fundamental wickedness and worth-lessness of man, and in the rot in life. Tell him I am all for cancers. And tell him, too, that I loathe poetry. I'd prefer to be an anatomist or the keeper of a morgue any day. Tell him I live exclusively on toenails and tumours. I sleep in a coffin too, and a wormy shroud is my summer suit.
>
> > 'I dreamed the genesis of mildew John
> > Who struggled from his spiders in the grave'
>
> is the opening of my new poem (*Letters* p. 134).

But the delay in the publication of *18 Poems* enabled Thomas to include several poems he was working on between May and October 1934, including "I dreamed my genesis".

*shuffled* (st. 2, l.1): We take it that the subject of the verb 'shuffled' is the 'I' of the first stanza, who is acting in a ghostly fashion.

*Heir to the scalding veins that hold love's drop* (st. 3, l.1): These words appeared in an unpublished notebook poem, "Twenty Seven" of October 1933, which continues:

> My fallen filled, that had the hint of death,
> Heir to the telling senses that alone
> Acquaint the flesh with a remembered itch,
> I round this heritage as rounds the sun
> His winy sky....

## My world is pyramid

Written after the extant notebooks ended, this is presumably the poem sent to Pamela Hansford Johnson on 2 August 1934: 'I took a long time over it, &, at the moment, anyway, I'm a little bit pleased with it. Not much – just a little bit' (*Letters* p. 166). Thomas expected it to be in *New Verse* that month, but it was not published there until December 1934.

*What colour is glory?* (pt. I, st. 5, l.1; compare pt. II, st. 5, l.1): A. E. Trick has described (in conversation) the occasion on which his young daughter asked this question in Thomas's presence. In a notebook draft of "Why east wind chills" dated 1 July 1933 (poem "Thirty Seven"), the poet says:

> I know
> No answer to the children's ghostly cry
> Of glory's colour....

The 'halves' ask in a 'tremble' this and similar impossible questions in "My world is pyramid". In the last stanza of the poem there is offered something of an answer in the 'stammel' (red, as in a kind of cloth) of the veins and in the 'pallor' of the loin.

*Austrian volley* (pt. II, st. 2, l.3): Thomas's review of Stephen Spender's *Vienna* was published in the same issue of *New Verse* as this poem. Thomas considered *Vienna* a bad poem, and in reaction wrote his own poem on the massacre in the workers' quarter of Vienna, when paramilitary formations loyal to the fascistic Chancellor, Dollfuss, crushed Austrian Social Democrats in bloody encounters in February 1934. A remnant of the poem's six stanzas remains, according to A. E. Trick (in conversation), in this reference to 'an Austrian volley'.

*Eloi* (pt. II, st. 2, l.6): 'Lord' (Hebrew) – the cry of Christ upon the Cross.

*Arctic scut* (pt. II, st. 3, l.2): the Arctic hare.

## All all and all

This poem was written after the extant notebooks ended, and was first published in *18 Poems*. It is referred to in a letter to Pamela Hansford Johnson of 20 July 1934: '"Flower", by the way, in my "All all and all" (Bradawl, Nuttall, & Bugger-all) is a two-syllabled word' (*Letters* p. 158). Since a bradawl is a small boring tool, Thomas's remark may be not entirely flippant, but a serious directive as to how to understand other mechanical images in the poem, such as 'milling' (pt. ii, l.4) and 'mauling' (pt. ii, l.6).

*All all and all the dry worlds couple* (pt. iii, l.1): Thomas wrote to Treece on 16 May 1938, 'Sometimes, I think, the influence of Swinburne is more obvious than that of Hopkins in a couple of the quotations from my poetry that you use: "All all and all the dry worlds couple", for instance. This is rhythmically true, at least' (*Letters* p. 297).

## TWENTY-FIVE POEMS (1936)

### I, in my intricate image

When Thomas told Pamela Hansford Johnson in October 1934 that he was working 'very hard' on 'a very long poem', he had finished fifty lines of it (*Letters* p. 172). We have deduced that those fifty lines were included in *18 Poems* as "When, like a running grave". We also deduce that Thomas continued with the intended long poem, and out of that impulse came "I, in my intricate image", which shares certain characteristics with the former poem, including the personage called 'Cadaver'. He presumably finished it when he 'retired home, after a ragged life; for a few weeks' rest' in March 1935 (*Letters* p. 187). It was accepted for *New Verse*. Thomas wrote from Ireland in summer 1935 that it was to be printed there (*Letters* p. 193); and it appeared in the August–September issue.

Speaking of the spring of 1936, Vernon Watkins wrote in his introduction to *Letters to Vernon Watkins* (p. 15):

> Dylan was now preparing his second book of poems, *Twenty-five Poems*, and they were almost finished. He liked these poems, for the most part, much better than the poems of his first book. He read me the first long poem, 'I, in my Intricate Image', a poem in three parts which has seventy-two variations in line-endings on the letter 'l', twenty-four in each part. While he read the poem I did not notice this, which is so obvious to the eye, so subtle was the use of the variations and so powerful the poem's progress. He said afterwards that he did not think it a successful poem, but that he liked it as well as anything he had written up to that time. The statement was modest, but Dylan was always modest about his poems, though he was really very sure of them. It was characteristic of his taste at that time that his favourite lines in the poem were these:

> > *I with the wooden insect in the tree of nettles,*
> > *In the glass bed of grapes with snail and flower,*
> > *Hearing the weather fall.*

Since there is a substantial amount of nature imagery in this poem, we should recall the statement Thomas made on this subject in a letter to A. E. Trick of summer 1935:

little He wotted when he made the trees and the flowers how one of his Welsh chosen would pass them by, not even knowing that they were there. My own eyes, I know, squint inwards; when, and if, I look at the exterior world I see nothing or me (*Letters* p. 192).

*the squirrel stumble*  (pt. II, st. 1, l.4): Thomas wrote to Henry Treece in 1938: 'You are right when you suggest that I think a squirrel stumbling at least of equal importance as Hitler's invasions' (*Letters* p. 310).

*The Cadaverous gravels . . ./The highroad of water*  (pt. II, st. 2, l.2): For a discussion of Cadaver, a figure of mortality (who also appears in the last stanza of this poem), see the note to "When, like a running grave". Here, his substance, dust, surfaces with gravel a roadway in the water.

*Splitting the long eye open*  (pt. II, st. 3, l.2): Through his keen interest in both cinema and surrealism, Thomas would be aware of the Salvador Dali-Luis Buñuel surrealist film, *Un Chien Andalou* (1928), in which a woman's eyeball is slit with a razor.

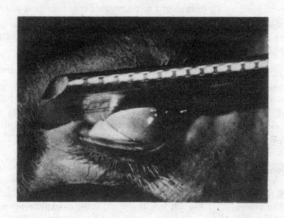

*Lazarus . . . Dead Sea*  (pt. II, st. 4, l.5 and st. 5, l.3): Biblical allusions, emphasizing death. Lazarus's being raised from the tomb (John 11) is here negated.

*triton*  (pt. II, st. 5, l.4): A merman.

*Aran*  (pt. III, st. 1, l.6): A rocky island off the coast of Eire.

*Star-set at Jacob's angle*  (pt. III, st. 2, l.3): Jacob's dream at Bethel (Genesis 28) was of a ladder up to heaven; but here it is 'a stick of folly' more reminiscent, perhaps, of an illustration in the Everyman edition of *Blake's Poems and Prophecies* (1927) p. 301.

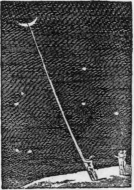

*I want! I want!*

*hophead*  (pt. III, st. 2, l.4): A drug addict, in the American slang of the time.

## This bread I break

Poem "Thirty Three" dated 'Dec: 24 '33' in a notebook was followed closely in the version prepared for *New English Weekly* (published 16 July 1936); only the last two lines were rewritten (probably in January 1936). *Twenty-five Poems* followed the periodical printing, but introduced the misprint 'wind' for 'wine' (st. 2, l.1), which was not finally corrected until after it had appeared in early printings of *Collected Poems*.

A preliminary draft in the notebook had an interesting last line:

> God's bread you break, you drain his cup.

This fixed the poem firmly within the Christian framework; the title given to this draft, "Breakfast Before Execution", suggested the irony of a Christmas poem being written about the Last Supper.

## Incarnate devil

The poem was entitled "Before We Sinned" in the notebook version of 16 May 1933 (poem "Thirty"), which was reduced by half for publication in *Sunday Referee* on 11 August 1935. There it was entitled "Poem for Sunday" – perhaps Victor Neuburg's title, and therefore innocently ironic.

*God* (l.5): Was 'god' in the notebook version and first printing, just as 'Eden' (st. 3, l.3) was 'eden'. The capital letters for these two words serve to emphasize the Biblical setting of the poem, specifically Genesis.

## Today, this insect

Poem "II" dated 18 December 1930 in a notebook was thoroughly revised in 1936 and included in the manuscript *Twenty-three Poems* sent to Dent's on 17 March 1936, and set up in the advance proofs of that volume, preliminary to *Twenty-five Poems*. The final version was sent in the last batch of five additional poems on 22 June 1936. Thomas described it as 'a slightly altered version of a poem you already have' (*Letters* p. 231). The first line had been: 'To-day, this insect, and the plague I breathe'. 'The world I breathe', which became the title of a collection published by New Directions in 1939, was a last-minute change. The only other notable changes occurred in the last two lines, which in the first version were:

> A universe of years notched on my criss-
> Cross tree behind the fabulous curtain.

The final version was published in *Purpose* (October–December 1936) before its appearance in *Twenty-five Poems*.

*Hamlet ... air-drawn windmill ... wooden horse ... John's beast, Job's patience ... Greek in the Irish sea* (last stanza, ll.1–4): These lines are deliberately allusive, illustrating, as it were, the theme of fable versus fact. Macbeth's dagger was 'air-drawn'; the 'windmill' is Don Quixote's; the 'wooden horse' Odysseus's; 'John's beast' is found in Revelation; the conjunction of Greek/Irish sea suggests James Joyce's *Ulysses*.

## The seed-at-zero

Poem "Six" dated 'August 29 '33' in a notebook supplied something of the form and wording of this poem, which, however, far transcends its origin there. There is no manuscript for the revision, and no periodical publication.

A footnote by Thomas in the notebook indicates that the poem had its inception with the story of Johanna Southcott (1750–1814), a domestic servant who identified herself with the 'woman clothed with the sun' of Revelation. Although sixty-four, she promised to give birth to a son, the Shiloh of Genesis 49:10.

## Shall gods be said

This was probably one of the poems sent to *Poetry* (Chicago) in January 1935, but it was not published there, nor anywhere else, before *Twenty-five*

*Poems.* It was a revision, a seemingly hurried one, of a notebook poem of August 1933 (poem "Fifty Two"). It was undoubtedly one of the 'simple' poems approved of by Richard Church of Dent's in his letter to Thomas of 26 November 1935 (*Letters* p. 204).

### Here in this spring

Thomas wrote to Richard Church of Dent's on 9 December 1935 in response to criticism of his difficult poems: 'I have quite a number of poems simple as the three you liked' (*Letters* p. 205). He was thinking of his notebook store. "Here in this spring" was revised from a 9 July 1933 notebook version (poem "Forty Two") without much effort being expended in the revision; the *Twenty-five Poems* version was copied into the notebook, dated 'Jan 1936'. In proposing to send further simple poems on to Church, Thomas cautioned that they were, 'to my mind, not half as good as the ones you cannot stand' (*Letters* p. 205).

### Do you not father me

An early version exists in typescript in the Pamela Hansford Johnson papers at Buffalo. It accompanied a similar typescript, the revised version of "Especially when the October wind"; it was therefore probably a revision (early version unknown) done in September 1934. A final revision was probably done in July 1935, and given to Ruthven Todd for publication in *Scottish Bookman* (October 1935).

*Abraham-man* (st. 3, l. 3): A beggar from Bedlam, allowed out to beg; usually implying a pretence of madness. If the line in the first draft is any guide, this figure should be associated with Christ: 'Master the tower Christ, I am your man'.

*sin-eater* (st. 4, l. 8): One hired to take on himself a dead person's sins by eating and drinking near the corpse. Again, this will have Christian overtones in this context.

### Out of the sighs

This is an amalgamation of two notebook poems, each of two stanzas, dated respectively 7 June 1932 (poem "LVVVI") and 1 July 1932 (unnumbered). These are separated in the notebook, and there is no indication that the second was a continuation of the first. The two were also typed up as separate poems (British Library typescripts). The revising was probably done in Swansea during Christmas 1934. We conjecture that Thomas submitted the final version to *Poetry* (Chicago) at that time, though it was not published there, *Twenty-five Poems* being its first printing.

199

*Were that enough* (st. 3, l.1): In the notebook version, a dash after 'enough' and another dash after 'dog's plate' indicate the list of things referred to in the phrase, 'were that enough'.

## Hold hard, these ancient minutes

Thomas had reason to celebrate spring in Swansea in 1935 – if only because *18 Poems* had received several important favourable reviews. The poem was published before *Twenty-five Poems* in a Majorca magazine, *Caravel* (March 1936), in a supplement edited by a London connection of Thomas's, Oswell Blakeston (*Letters* p. 207).

*the cuckoo's month* (l.1): A folk rhyme includes the lines:

> In April the cuckoo shows his bill;
> In May he sings all day.

*Glamorgan* (l.2): The Glamorgan of this poem reminds one of the symbolic quasi-Welsh landscape of "The Map of Love", a story in which the exhortation, 'Hold hard, the children of love' appears (*A Prospect of the Sea* p. 56).

## Was there a time

Poem "Five" dated 'Feb. 8. '33' in a notebook was edited down from twenty-three lines to nine; the finished revision was copied in and dated December 1935. *Twenty-five Poems* follows the publication in *New English Weekly* on 3 September 1936.

## Now

The biographical account by Trevor Hughes (in a 1960 typescript in the Special Collections Library, Buffalo) has something to say on this poem:

> We had, at one time, been delighted with a burlesque of Gertrude Stein's work which appeared in *The New Statesman*:
>
> > There was a young was a young *Was*,
> > Not *Is*, and not *Will Be*, because . . .
>
> And when, in the tavern, Dylan showed me the manuscript of his poem "Now", and I read:
>
> > Now
> > Say nay,
> > Death to the yes . . .

there remained, obviously, only one thing to say: 'There was a young was a young *Was*' – a criticism which he accepted with such humour as to persuade me that he had written this poem with little serious intent.

It was presumably of this poem that Thomas remarked that 'so far as he knew it had no meaning at all' (reported in the Introduction to *Letters to Vernon Watkins* p. 16). But when Watkins suggested it should be left out of *Twenty-five Poems* because of its 'unwarrantable obscurity', Thomas said him nay.

Associated in style with "How soon the servant sun", it can be dated around May 1935 only because of that association. But already, a year before, Thomas was writing to Pamela Hansford Johnson (*Letters* p. 130) that he was overlabouring his poetry, picking and cleaning his lines so much that 'nothing but their barbaric sounds remained'.

> Or if I did write a line, 'My dead upon the orbit of a rose,' I saw that 'dead' did not mean 'dead', 'orbit' not 'orbit' and 'rose' most certainly not 'rose'. Even 'upon' was a syllable too many, lengthened for the inhibited reason of rhythm.

One might think of "Now" as the poem in which Thomas pays his greatest tribute to words in themselves, paying such fanatical attention to them in the way they weight a line that referential meaning is ultimately lost in the presentational. The stubborn clarity of repeating the same three words at the beginning of each of five stanzas (and thus giving that much theme to the poem) is matched by a stubborn refusal to provide normal syntax for his syllables. Thomas reached the extremity of one direction of his poetry with this poem. Its significance comes from its form and its insistence on form.

## Why east wind chills

Poem "Thirty Seven" dated 'July 1.33' in a notebook was edited down from fifty lines to twenty-six, and the completed revision copied into the notebook 21 January 1936, and published in *New English Weekly* 16 July 1936.

*When cometh Jack Frost?* (st. 2, l.1): In the notebook version, the children also ask: 'What colour is glory?' This is the question once asked by Pamela Trick (aged four) in Thomas's presence (according to A. E. Trick, in conversation), and possibly the initial impetus for the poem. In revising the notebook version, Thomas dropped, 'What colour is glory?' – only to pick it up again later for use in "My world is pyramid".

## A grief ago

A typescript of this poem (at the Humanities Research Library, Texas) is dated January 1935. Thomas apparently submitted the poem to two places; for, when it came out in the Oxford magazine *Programme* on 23 October 1935, Robert Herring of *Life & Letters Today* complained, and a substitute had to be found for him to publish, 'owing to my abominable carelessness' (*Letters* p. 203).

*the rod the aaron/Rose cast* (st. 2, ll. 5–6): Rose of Sharon of the Song of Solomon is combined in this image with Aaron's rod of Exodus. Also utilized is the fact that 'Aaron's rod' is a popular name for several tall plants, especially a mullein.

*the lily's anger* (st. 3, l. 3): The angel Gabriel is pictured as carrying a lily-branch when visiting the Virgin Mary at the Annunciation.

*The country-handed grave boxed into love* (st. 4, l. 7): Edith Sitwell, in reviewing *Twenty-five Poems* in the *Sunday Times* 15 November 1936, referred to this line. Thomas objected in a letter to Henry Treece:

> She makes a few interesting misreadings, or, rather, half-readings. She says the 'country-handed grave' in my poem A Grief Ago is 'that simple nurse of grief, that countryman growing flowers and corn'. My image, principally, did not make the grave a gentle cultivator but a tough possessor, a warring and complicated raper rather than a simple nurse or an innocent gardener. I meant that the grave had a country for each hand, that it raised those hands up and 'boxed' the hero of my poem into love. 'Boxed' has the coffin and the pug-glove in it (*Letters* pp. 300–301).

## How soon the servant sun

This poem was published in *Programme* on 23 October 1935; and our assumption is that it was finished while the poet was staying at the historian A. J. P. Taylor's cottage in Cheshire in May 1935, and forwarded through Taylor's contacts in Oxford.

This is one of the two poems that Vernon Watkins tried to get Thomas to leave out of his *Twenty-five Poems* (see the note to "Now" above). 'He was, however, firm about including them,' writes Watkins in his Introduction to *Letters to Vernon Watkins* (p. 16). 'When I said that reviewers would be likely to pick these out rather than the fine poems in the book he smiled and said, "Give them a bone".'

We do not consider that Thomas's seemingly flippant comment settles the matter, though the poem obviously stands, in itself, as an act of careful eccentricity. Thomas was doing cartwheels with five intricately rhymed and shaped stanzas, and didn't seem to care that he fell, one line short, in the last. This, even without his juggling of parenthetical lines, would be annoying acrobatics. Thomas once called this a 'stunt' poem (*Letters* p. 396).

It is also in Cheshire in May 1935 that Thomas wrote (in a letter to Desmond Hawkins, *Letters* p. 189): 'Those privately coded blocks of feeling, derived from personal, unpoetical, or even anti-poetical complexes must certainly be done away with before I write any more – or, at least, before I write any better.'

## Ears in the turrets hear

The *Twenty-five Poems* printing of this poem is practically identical to the notebook poem "Forty Seven" dated 17 July 1933. When it was published in *John O'London's Weekly* on 5 May 1934, the present second stanza was missing.

In a letter of 9 May 1934 to Pamela Hansford Johnson, Thomas called the poem 'a terribly weak, watery little thing' (*Letters* p. 131); but it was the poem that he read first to Vernon Watkins on opening, at Cwmdonkin Drive, 'a large file, marked in block letters POMES' (*Letters to Vernon Watkins* p. 13); and he sent it later to Thomas Taig as one of the two poems of his most suitable 'for some kind of dramatic presentation' – that is, for recitation (*Letters* p. 399).

Something of Thomas's ambivalence about his isolation is found in his first letter to Vernon Watkins, 20 April 1936: 'living in your own private, four-walled world as exclusively as possible isn't escapism, I'm sure; it isn't the Ivory Tower, and, even if it were, you secluded in your Tower know and learn more of the world outside than the outside-man who is mixed up so personally and inextricably with the mud and unlovely people' (*Letters* p. 222).

## Foster the light

This poem was something of a fosterling. Trevor Hughes tells the story of its inception (in a typescript in the Special Collection Library, Buffalo):

> In January, 1934, Dylan sent me news of his father's first illness, and of some suspected illness of his own. The day passed slowly, and as soon as I reached home I began to type a letter to him. I could not wait for food. There was no time even for the usual formal greeting. I began: 'Not the sympathy of words on news of your father's illness.'
> Then: 'About our own health let us not be perturbed. We shall see no seventh stage, but we shall have our deserts, I doubt not.'

And, later: 'How shall a man die if he has never lived, or see the beauty of the stars through the lenses of his own darkness? For so many God has never lived, the faint glimmer within them the glimmer of their own mean ego. This dies upon them, and they must die in darkness; die in the night and move to eternal fields of darkness. Foster the light, and God be with you.'

With that sentence the long-pent mood deserted me. And I think that Dylan perceived this, for when, six weeks later, he spent a weekend . with me, he handed me a sheet of paper, and muttered shyly, as usual, something about 'a new poem'. I read:

> Foster the light, nor veil. . . .

Thomas had written the finished poem into his notebook (poem "Thirty Six") the day he went up to London to see Hughes on 23 February 1934. One searches for hints that it was derived from Hughes's letter – and 'God' does appear in the last stanza of the notebook draft:

> God gave the clouds their colours and their shapes.

(God will be present in all but name in the final stanza of the poem as we have it.) But the poem urges myriad and cosmic activities, more things, we feel, than were dreamt of in Hughes's philosophy.

Nevertheless, something about this poem made Thomas restive. He had revised it again by September 1935, but called it an unprintable name in submitting it to Desmond Hawkins for *Purpose* (*Letters* p. 203). That magazine did not publish the poem; it appeared in the first issue of *Contemporary Poetry and Prose* (May 1936). There seems to be some truth in Trevor Hughes's remark in the Buffalo typescript: 'This poem is not, nor could it be, amongst his most important poems; and if it had been born of a direct and ecstatic inspiration he would not have felt the same need to amend it.'

*fly-lord* (st. 3, l.1): Beelzebub is literally 'lord of flies'. In the first version the line was

> And father all, nor fail with barren winds.

The altered phrasing still says the same thing: one should not be barren, one should not fail to breed, indeed, like flies.

## The hand that signed the paper

A notebook poem of 17 August 1933 (poem "One") was revised (Thomas lopped off the final stanza of the draft) and sent to Geoffrey Grigson probably in early November 1934. It was published in *New Verse* December 1935.

In the notebook the poem was dedicated to 'A.E.T.', that is, Bert Trick of Swansea. That Trick was an active member of the Labour Party's left wing and stimulated Thomas in that direction makes it appropriate that he should be the dedicatee of Thomas's one acknowledged political poem. Treece wrote that this poem was unique in that regard, and evoked the following response from Thomas in a letter of July 1938 (*Letters* p. 310):

> I was interested in what you said about my lack, except in that little finger-poem, of any social awareness. I suppose I am, broadly, (as opposed to regimented thinkers and poets in uniform) antisocial, but I am extremely sociable. But, surely it is evasive to say that my poetry has no social awareness – no evidence of contact with society – while quite a good number of my images come from the cinema & the gramophone and the newspaper, while I use contemporary slang, cliché, and pun. You meant, I know, that my poetry isn't concerned with politics (supposedly the science of achieving and 'administrating' human happiness) but with poetry (which is unsentimental revelation, and to which happiness is no more important – or any other word – than misery): – (I'll elaborate that, if you'd like me to. Not that it's obscure, but it may, in some way, be helpful to add to it.) But the idea you gave me was that you actually consider me unaware of my surroundings, out-of-contact with the society from which I am necessarily outlaw. You are right when you suggest that I think a squirrel stumbling at least of equal importance as Hitler's invasions, murder in Spain, the Garbo-Stokowski romance, royalty, Horlick's, lynchlaw, pit disasters, Joe Louis, wicked capitalists, saintly communists, democracy, the Ashes, the Church of England, birthcontrol, Yeats' voice, the machines of the world I tick and revolve in, pub-baby-weather-government-football-youthandage-speed-lipstick, all small tyrannies, means tests, the fascist anger, the daily, momentary lightnings, eruptions, farts, dampsquibs, barrelorgans, tinwhistles, howitzers, tiny death-rattles, volcanic whimpers of the world I eat, drink, love, work, hate and delight in – but I *am* aware of these things as well.

## Should lanterns shine

This may be the new poem that Thomas sent to Grigson early in November 1934, 'a bit better than the others, I think' (*Letters* p. 174). The 'others' could have been "The hand that signed the paper" and "I have longed to move away", which were published with "Should lanterns shine" in *New Verse* a year later in December 1935. These conjectures are supported by the fact that, though no titles are mentioned in the correspondence, Thomas added the following comment: 'Do you think it would be better if the enclosed poem were *not* divided into stanzas? I've tried it that way, but it seemed more obscure' (*Letters* p. 174). There is no Thomas poem published by Grigson about which this question could be asked other than "Should lanterns shine".

In any case, its association with the two poems mentioned, both of which were revised from the notebooks, allows us to conjecture that "Should lanterns shine" also came from a notebook, now missing, or perhaps was the torn-out poem "Fifteen" that had followed "Fourteen" dated 1 March 1933, the notebook version of "I have longed to move away".

Vernon Watkins had a hand in preparing the poem for inclusion in *Twenty-five Poems*: 'I persuaded him to cut the last two lines of the poem as it had appeared in *New Verse*.'

These two lines,

> Regard the moon, it hangs above the lawn;
> Regard the lawn, it lies beneath the moon.

seemed to me to echo Eliot, and indirectly Laforgue, and not to belong to the poem, whereas the two previous lines, with their hidden nuances, made a fine autobiographical ending (*Letters to Vernon Watkins* pp. 16–17).

*mummy cloths* (l.8): Gwen Watkins in *Portrait of a Friend* (p. 136) tells of a summer afternoon in 1951 when Vernon Watkins played the part of a grave-robber, Dan Jones a Pharaoh in a mummy case, and Dylan an Egyptologist searching the tombs, in a reenactment of a film, *The Mummy's Claw*, which all three had seen at the Uplands Cinema in Swansea in their youth.

## I have longed to move away

The first version of this poem is a forty-one line, casually rhymed notebook poem "Fourteen" dated 1 March 1933. The eighteen-year-old Swansea youth had not yet flown the coop. It would be five months before his first trip to London: so he was still in the stage of longing to leave, and also afraid of leaving. Something of the sentiment of the poem is summed up in a letter of January 1933 from the poet in Swansea to Trevor Hughes in London, explaining why he has allowed himself to be fired from his newspaper job: 'No, what I feared was the slow but sure stamping out of individuality, the gradual contentment with life as it was, so much per week, so much for this, for that' (*Letters* p. 10).

By 13 January 1936, when the notebook draft was crossed out and a rewritten version copied in, Thomas had become a young celebrity with *18*

*Poems* the year before, and, based in London, was not beset with his previous worry about leaving Swansea. It is clear that he did not spend long in the revision of this poem. It was published in *New Verse* December 1935.

## Find meat on bones

The notebook poem "Forty Six" dated 13 July 1933 was revised inter-linearly in late January 1936. Thomas wrote to Desmond Hawkins, editor of *Purpose*, on 18 January 1936: 'I don't know that I've got anything much good at the moment, but I probably will have by the time I see you' (*Letters* p. 211). He probably brought the revised poem with him to London the following month; it was printed in *Purpose* (April–June 1936). (For all Haw-kins's concern as an editor, this publication had a disastrous misprint in the first line: 'Fine meat on bones'.)

That Thomas took seriously the dramatic dialogue form of this poem is indicated by the fact that he recommended it to Thomas Taig as one of the two poems of his suitable for dramatic recitation on the stage (*Letters* p. 399).

*ram rose* (st. 1, l.8; st. 3, l.8): Desmond Hawkins asked Thomas about the adjective 'ram'. The reply is in a letter of March 1936 (*Letters* p. 218):

> It's funny about ram. Once I looked up an old dictionary and found it meant red, but now I can't find it in any dictionary at all. I wanted ram in the poem to mean red *and* male *and* horny *and* driving *and* all its usual meanings. Blast it, why doesn't it mean red? Do look up and see for me.

Any dictionary defining 'ram' as 'red' has eluded us also.

*Light and dark* (st. 5, l.4): Soon after finishing "Find meat on bones" Thomas started a new notebook with the motto:

> To others caught
> Between black and white.

The attempted resolution: 'no enemies/but one companion' is reminiscent of Blake's 'Contraries are positives', on the title page of the second book of *Milton*.

*Doom on the sun* (st. 5, l.8): In a letter of 9 May 1934, Thomas wrote a description of the novel he was currently writing, tentatively entitled "A Doom On The Sun": 'So far it is rather terrible, a kind of warped fable in which Lust, Greed, Cruelty, Spite etc., appear all the time as old gentle-men' (*Letters* p. 134). Similar anagrammed names are given to characters in Thomas's early story, 'The Holy Six' (*Dylan Thomas: Early Prose Writings*).

## Grief thief of time

The two stanzas of this poem were beginning two separate poems in the notebooks. Poem "Five" dated 26 August 1933, 'Grief, thief of time, crawls off', was revised in Ireland, according to a note appended to the revision: 'Written and copied in later, August 1935. Glen Lough. Donegal.' Thomas apparently took a copy of the notebook poem with him to work on, and wrote the finished revision in the notebook on returning to Swansea, probably in January 1936.

The second stanza of the poem is from notebook poem "Eighteen" dated 26 September 1933, beginning 'Jack my father, let the knaves.' A typescript of this notebook version was sent by Thomas to Glyn Jones in 1934; it had the title "Jack of Christ", and ended:

> All shall remain, and on the cloudy coast
> Walk the blithe host
> Of god and ghost with you, their newborn son.

Any overt Christian reference has been dropped in the revised version.

The two revised poems were amalgamated for publication in *Comment* February 1936.

## And death shall have no dominion

This was one of the poems sent at the last minute to Dent's to fill out *Twenty-five Poems* (*Letters* p. 231). *Letters to Vernon Watkins* p. 16 tells of Thomas's indecision about it:

> The one poem which Dylan hesitated to include in *Twenty-five Poems* was one which afterwards became very well known. When I called at Cwmdonkin Drive one evening he said that he had almost decided to leave out 'And Death Shall Have No Dominion'. Certainly he would leave it out unless he altered it. He read it aloud many times, and I said how necessary it was to the book and how much I admired it, especially its impulsive rhythm. He made a number of small changes that evening...

If Thomas was here reading from the version published previously in *New English Weekly* 18 May 1933, then the changes were not small. He dropped the last stanza, reduced each of the others by one line, and rewrote the last lines of the third stanza. He may, of course, have made these changes before reading the revised poem to Vernon Watkins, for it was copied into the notebook opposite the original version ("Twenty Three" dated April 1933) and dated February 1936, quite a while before it was sent to Dent's on 22 June 1936.

208

*And death shall have no dominion*  (first and last line of each stanza):
Romans 6:9 'Christ being raised from the dead dieth no more; death hath no
more dominion over him.' A. E. Trick has said (in conversation) that this
poem originated when he and Thomas had a competition to see who could
write the best poem on the subject of 'Immortality'. Thomas chose a well-
known Biblical text, though the poem seems more pantheistic than Christian.
Trick's poem ("For Death is Not the End") was published in the *Swansea and
West Wales Guardian* for 15 June 1934:

> For death is not the end!
> Though soul turns sour
> And faith dry-rots,
> Let maggots feed on flesh
> That once was blossom pink
> And memory sink
> Beneath the dust of falling years,
> Yet death is not the end!
> For death is not the end!
>
> Lungs chewed by poison gas
> Attempt to sing.
> Or woman ript with child
> Comfort the smiling flower,
> And good deeds done
> Bring forth dead fruit.
> Hold fast to hope
> For death is not the end!
>
> For death is not the end!
> Moves a soul in some dark cranny
> Like a fluttering bird
> In upward sweep ascends
> To some high altitude,
> Where breathes a living God.
> Then death is not the end!

## Then was my neophyte

Dent's received this poem in the last batch of poems submitted for *Twenty-
five Poems* on 22 June 1936 (*Letters* p. 231). It was published after the volume
was out, in *Purpose* October–December 1936 (*Letters* p. 239).

Thomas wrote to Vernon Watkins on 20 April 1936 about an unnamed poem, probably "Then was my neophyte": 'have more or less finished a poem which I want to send you when I'm better pleased with it.'

> But here again I'm not free; perhaps, as you said once, I should stop writing altogether for some time; now I'm almost afraid of all the once-necessary artifices and obscurities, and can't, for the life or the death of me, get any real liberation, any diffusion or dilution or anything, into the churning bulk of the words; I seem, more than ever, to be tightly packing away everything I have and know into a mad-doctor's bag, and then locking it up: all you can see is the bag, all you can know is that it's full to the clasp, all you have to trust is that the invisible and intangible things packed away are – if they *could* only be seen and touched – worth quite a lot!

He added: 'what I do fear is an ingrowing, the impulse growing like a toenail into the artifice' (*Letters* p. 223).

In spite of these fears, Thomas considered the finished poem the best of the *Twenty-five Poems*. In a letter to Glyn Jones of December 1936, he said: 'Nobody's mentioned it; perhaps it's bad; I only know that, to me, it is clearer and more definite, and that it holds more possibilities of progress, than anything else I've done' (*Letters* p. 243).

*tide-hoisted screen* (st. 3, l.10): Vernon Watkins, who talked to the poet about this poem, summarized it as follows: 'a prophecy of his own melo-dramatic death, shown to him on a film which he as a child, whose character has not been formed, sees unwinding and projected on a screen ... under water' (Gwen Watkins *Portrait of a Friend* p. 33).

## Altarwise by owl-light

We conjecture that the writing of these ten sonnets covered the space of a year, from Christmas 1934 to Christmas 1935. The first two sonnets are nativity poems, and in a letter to Bert Trick of around February 1935 Thomas mentions: 'I have just finished two poems which are, I hope, to appear in the new New Verse, Uncle Geoffrey permitting' (*Letters* p. 184). Geoffrey Grigson apparently was not willing, for no Thomas poems appeared in *New Verse* until the August–September 1935 printing of "I, in my intricate image". It is possible that Thomas withdrew the two sonnets to add to them. Desmond Hawkins had the first seven sonnets early in September 1935. Thomas had to withdraw them from Hawkins to give to Robert Herring for *Life and Letters Today* (*Letters* pp. 203–204), where they were published as "Poems for a Poem" in the December 1935 issue. When Thomas submitted his first batch of manuscripts to Richard Church of Dent's on 8 October 1935 he included only six of the sonnets:

The first poem, divided into six parts of fourteen lines each, (each to be printed on a separate page, for, although the poem as a whole is to be a poem in, and by, itself, the separate parts can be regarded as individual poems) is so far incomplete; there will be at least another four parts (*Letters* p. 202).

In the twenty-three poems sent to Church on 17 March 1936 Thomas included eight sonnets. The eighth was published separately in *Contemporary Poetry and Prose* May 1936. In the last batch of poems to Dent's on 22 June 1936 he sent 'the last two sections, IX & X, of my long poem' (*Letters* p. 231). These two were published in *Contemporary Poetry and Prose* July 1936.

There is reason to think that these ten sonnets marked the end of Thomas's early period. Responding to Glyn Jones's review of *Twenty-five Poems* in *Adelphi* (December 1936), Thomas wrote in a letter:

> You're the only reviewer, I think, who *has* commented on my attempts to get away from those rhythmic and thematic dead ends, that physical blank wall, those wombs, and full-stop worms, by all sorts of methods – so many unsuccessful. But I'm not sorry that, in that Work in Progress thing, I did carry 'certain features to their logical conclusion'. It had, I think, to be done; the result had to be, in many of the lines and verses anyway, mad parody; and I'm glad that *I* parodied those features so soon after making them, and that I didn't leave it to anyone else (*Letters* p. 243).

Thomas here recognizes that his early style had become so fixed as to be parodiable. We cannot, however, believe that the poet deliberately set out to parody himself in "Altarwise by owl-light". If Thomas, in this letter, sees something like parody in the sonnets, it can only be that, almost immediately on publishing them, he saw them as representative of a style which he had relegated to the past. Or, as he put it in a reply to questions at the University of Utah on 18 April 1952, 'Those sonnets are only the writings of a boily boy in love with shapes and shadows on his pillow' (Tedlock p. 61).

That Thomas disparaged these sonnets is disturbing. Even as one tries to take them at their own evaluation on a level of high seriousness, one cannot help being aware that the poet considered them, in some respects, an unsuccessful attempt at an ultimate statement of his methods and beliefs up to 1936. Even in defending them against Richard Church's criticism, Thomas acknowledged certain 'faults':

> I think I do know what some of the main faults of my writing are: immature violence, rhythmic monotony, frequent muddleheadedness, and a very much overweighted imagery that leads too often to incoherence. But every line *is* meant to be understood; the reader *is* meant

to understand every poem by thinking and feeling about it, not by sucking it in through his pores, or whatever he is meant to do with surrealist writing. Neither is the new group on which I'm working influenced, in any way, by an experiment with which I am totally unfamiliar. You have, and no doubt rightly, found many things to object to in these new poems; all I wish to do is to assure you that those faults are due neither to a delirious following of intellectual fashion nor to the imitation of what, to my ignorance, appears a purposely 'unreasonable' experiment inimical to poetry (*Letters* p. 205).

*Abaddon* (sonnet I, l.3; also sonnet II, l.7): The angel of the bottomless pit in Revelation 9:11. We can take it that the devil in the flesh (*a bad 'n in* the hang-nail) cracks off from man at the moment of Christ's redemption on the cross. This act is equivalent to that in the next three lines of the poem, which Thomas himself explicated in a letter to Henry Treece of 1 June 1938, refuting a statement of Edith Sitwell's:

> Edith Sitwell's analysis, in a letter to the Times, of the lines 'The atlas-eater with a jaw for news/Bit out the mandrake with tomorrow's scream', seems to me very vague and Sunday-journalish. She says the lines refer to 'the violent speed and the sensation-loving, horror-loving craze of modern life'. She doesn't take the literal meaning: that a world-devouring ghost creature bit out the horror of tomorrow from a gentleman's loins. A 'jaw for news' is an obvious variation of a 'nose for news', & means that the mouth of the creature can taste already the horror that has not yet come or can sense it coming, can thrust its tongue into news that has not yet been made, can savour the enormity of the progeny before the seed stirs, can realise the crumbling of dead flesh before the opening of the womb that delivers that flesh to tomorrow. What is this creature? It's the dog among the fairies, the rip and cur among the myths, the snapper at demons, the scarer of ghosts, the wizard's heel-chaser. This poem is a particular incident in a particular adventure, not a general, elliptical deprecation of this 'horrible, crazy, speedy life' (*Letters* p. 301).

The context indicates that the 'particular adventure' is a castration with momentous future import – i.e. the Crucifixion. Thomas once used the phrase, 'the cross of a castrated Saviour' (*Letters* p. 54).

*Capricorn and Cancer* (sonnet I, l.14): Signs of the zodiac; or, in astronomy, the two corresponding circles on the celestial sphere where the sun appears to turn after reaching its greatest declination – probably, therefore, related in the poet's mind to 'the antipodes' of sonnet III (last line).

*pelican* (sonnet II, l.3): The folk belief that the pelican pierced its own breast to feed its young with its blood has been taken as an emblem of Christ's sacrifice.

*Jacob* (sonnet II, l.10): A reference to Jacob's ladder of Genesis 28. In the poem, the horizontal bones of Abaddon provide the rungs of the ladder, and thus climb, or 'Jacob' (intransitive verb), to the stars.

*Hairs of your head* (sonnet II, l.11): Thomas wrote in a letter: 'The greatest description I know of our own "earthiness" is to be found in John Donne's *Devotions*, where he describes man as earth of the earth, his body earth, his hair a wild shrub growing out of the land' (*Letters* p. 39).

*First there was the lamb ... The black ram* (sonnet III, ll.1 and 11): These lines are to be found in notebook poem "Twenty Eight" dated 13 May 1933, a poem whose subject is youth growing into age. A dramatic representation of this theme is the story of Rip Van Winkle (l.9), who, in Washington Irving's story, wakes up an old man after twenty years of sleep.

*nagging the wounded whisper* (sonnet IV, l.4): In a letter to A.E. Trick from Donegal, where this sonnet may have been composed, Thomas wrote: 'I'm lonely as Christ sometimes and can't even speak to my Father on an ethereal wave-length' (*Letters* p. 190). There is no evidence for the notion that, in the questions of this sonnet, the poet was, as has been suggested, consciously acting out the role of doubting Thomas.

*Love's a reflection* (sonnet IV, ll.11–12): In Edith Sitwell's copy of *Twenty-five Poems*, now at Texas, Thomas wrote a marginal gloss on these lines:

> Love is a reflection of the features (the features of
> those you will know and love *after* the womb) which are
> photographed before birth on the wall of the womb
>     the womb being surrounded by food; a field being its
> own field, and the womb being its own food.

*Gabriel* (sonnet V, l.1): The Annunciation story as told by 'the fake gentleman', the devil, has the angel Gabriel as a card-sharping cowboy.

*Byzantine Adam* (sonnet V, l.6): An Adam connected with Constantinople would perhaps rise like a minaret or a dome.

*For loss of blood I fell* (sonnet V, l.7): A notebook poem "Seventeen" dated 25 September 1933 begins with the lines: 'For loss of blood I fell where stony hills/Had milk and honey flowing from their cracks.'

*Ishmael ... Jonah's Moby snatched me by the hair* (sonnet V, ll.7 and 10): Ishmael of Genesis 16 is connected, via Melville, with the 'Moby Dick' which swallowed Jonah. In *Moby Dick* (ch. 78) Queequeg restrains Tashtego by the hair from disappearing into the sperm whale's head.

213

*the white bear quoted Virgil* (sonnet V, l.13): In *Penguin Island* by Anatole France, St. Mael sees a white bear reciting Virgil's Fourth Eclogue, which foretells a virgin birth.

*our lady's sea-straw* (sonnet V, l.14): 'Our lady's bed-straw' is a plant.

*house of bread* (sonnet VII, l.12): Bethlehem literally translated means 'house of bread'.

## THE MAP OF LOVE (1939)

### Because the pleasure-bird whistles

> The poem begins with a queer question about a bird and a horse: because one thing is made sweeter (qualify this word) through suffering what it doesn't understand, does that mean everything is sweeter through incomprehensible, or blind, suffering? (Later, the poem has a figure in it standing suffering on the tip of the new year and refusing, blindly, to look back at, if you like, the *lessons* of the past year to help him; and the case, which is really a case for a prayer, begins to make itself clear.) (*Letters* p. 396)

As this comment to Desmond Hawkins indicates, "Because the pleasure-bird whistles" is concerned with thoughts at the year's end. It is literally a New Year poem, entitled "January 1939" in *Twentieth Century Verse* February 1939 and *Delta* Easter 1939, and probably the poem promised to Vernon Watkins in the postscript to a letter of 8 January 1939 (*Letters* p. 351).

When Thomas finally sent the poem to Watkins on 4 February 1939, he worried that it may be too short: 'do I end before the point? does it need more room to work to a meaning, any expansion?' (*Letters* p. 354). Thomas had been undoubtedly gearing up to look back at the year in some detail. 'I intended it as a longer and more ambitious thing, but stopped it suddenly thinking it was complete' (*Letters* pp. 354–355). The poem, then, is a 'grace' to begin a meal, but complete in itself as a statement of how the simple idea of looking back can be symbolized in terms of food for thought. The poem is quite self-conscious about its own processes. The above letter to Desmond Hawkins continues:

> Then I, the putter of the question, turn momentarily aside from the question and, in a sort of burst of technical confidence, say that the bird and beast are merely convenient symbols that just *have* to suffer what my mood dictates, just *have* to be the objects my mood (wit or temper?

but here 'mood' alone) has decided to make a meal upon and also the symbolic implements with which I cut the meal and objects up.

As an announcement rather than a full retrospective, the poem was appropriate as a prologue to *The Map of Love*.

*blind horse* (l.2): Gwen Watkins, writing from Vernon Watkins's notes, says in *Portrait of a Friend* (p. 68): 'The image of the singing horse came from a dream of Dylan's, in which a horse stood in a cage made of wires which gradually became red-hot, on which a man standing by said, "He sings better now."'

*bum city ... frozen wife ... salt person and blasted place* (ll.13–20): Lot's wife looked back on Sodom and was turned into a pillar of salt (Genesis 19:26). Thomas was thinking of London; he had just written to Watkins on 20 December 1938 (*Letters* p. 343):

> I've just come back from three dark days in London, city of the restless dead. It really is an insane city, & filled me with terror. Every pavement drills through your soles to your scalp, and out pops a lamp-post covered with hair. I'm not going to London again for years; its intelligentsia is so hurried in the head that nothing stays there; its glamour smells of goat; there's no difference between good & bad.

## I make this in a warring absence

Thomas wrote to Desmond Hawkins, editor of *Purpose*, in September 1937, after being married for two months: 'I am lost in love and poverty, and my work is shocking. I can let you have one longish and very good poem, unprinted, for an immediate guinea. It is this week's masterpiece, it took two months to write, and I want to drink it' (*Letters* p. 260). He added, later in the letter: 'If you want that poem, it's yours for a pound. I've come down one shilling, and it's forty lines.' Thomas offered what is presumably the same poem to Julian Symons, editor of *Twentieth Century Verse*, on 22 October 1937: 'I can send you a longish poem in about a week' (*Letters* p. 260). On 25 October 1937 he wrote to Vernon Watkins: 'My poem is continuing. You shall have it next week' (*Letters* p. 261). On 28 October, to Symons again: 'I'll let you have the poem very shortly' (*Letters* p. 262). On 30 October, to Desmond Hawkins again: 'The poem I have to revise. I thought it was perfectly correct – as to detail – before I read it again early one morning ... I'm now working hard on the poem, and it should be complete in some days' (*Letters* p. 262). Vernon Watkins, who saw the poem 'at many stages on its way to completion' (*Letters to Vernon Watkins* p. 30), received the finished sixty-eight lines, "Poem to Caitlin", with a letter of 13 November 1937: 'Here, after so long, is my own new poem' (*Letters* p. 263). Thomas indicated that he wanted to send the typed poem off to *Criterion*. However, it was published in *Twentieth Century Verse* January–February 1938, with the title "Poem (For Caitlin)".

Thomas included the poem in a reading at Goldsmiths' College, London University, on 27 January 1938. Hermann Peschmann of the College wrote afterwards asking for help with the poem. Thomas replied on 1 February 1938: 'I can give you a very rough idea of the "plot". But, of course, it's bound to be a most superficial, and, perhaps, misleading, idea, because the "plot" is told in images, and the images *are* what they say, not what they stand for' (*Letters* p. 269). Thomas offers a stanza by stanza summary (see notes below), with a general introduction as follows:

> The poem is, in the first place, supposed to be a document, or narrative, of all the emotional events between the coming and going, the creation and dissipation, of jealousy, jealousy born from pride and killed by pride, between the absence and the return of the crucial character (or heroine) of the narrative, between the war of her absence and the armistice of her presence (*Letters* p. 269).

When Desmond Hawkins was preparing to review *The Map of Love* he wrote to Thomas, who endeavoured to answer his 'questions and natural bewilderments' in a letter of 14 August 1939. The general comments on "I make this in a warring absence" are as follows (*Letters* p. 397):

> The next things you wanted to discuss were stanzas three and four of the poem (page 4) beginning 'I make this In A W.A.' (Work of Art, Workshop of Agony, Witbite of Agenwar). The stanzas are a catalogue of the contraries, the warring loyalties, the psychological discrepancies, all expressed in physical and/or extra-narrative terms, that go towards making up the 'character' of the woman, or 'beloved' would be wider & better, in whose absence, and in the fear of whose future unfaithful absences, I jealously made the poem. I didn't just say in one line that she was cold as ice and in the next line that she was hot as hell; in each line I made as many contraries as possible fight* together, in an attempt to bring out a *positive* quality; I wanted a peace, admittedly only the armistice of a moment, to come out of the images on *her* warpath. Excuse me, but this note I wrote for a my-eye essay by H. Treece may as well come in now: 'I make one image, though "make" is not the word; I let, perhaps, an image be made emotionally in me & then apply to it what intellectual and critical forces I possess; let it breed another; let that image contradict the first, make, of the third image bred out of

the other two together, a fourth contradictory image, and let them all, within my imposed formal limits, conflict'. A bit smug, and old stuff too, but it applies here. And the conflict is, of course, only to make peace. I want the lasting life of the poem to come out of the destroyers in each image. Old stuff again. Here, in this poem, the emotional question is: Can I see clearly, by cataloguing and instancing all I know of her, good and bad, black and white, kind & cruel (in coloured images condensed to make, not a natural colour, but a militant peace and harmony of all colours), the emotional war caused by her absence, and thus decide for myself whether I fight, lie down and hope, forgive or kill? The question is naturally answered by the questions in the images and the images in the questions – if the vice-versa makes any different sense.

* negate each other, if they could; keep their individualities & lose them in each other.

### *her pride in mast and fountain ... to her blind mother drawn* (st. 1, l.4 – st. 2, l.14):

The 'I', the hero, begins his narrative at the departure of the heroine, at the time he feels that her pride in him and in their proud, sexual world has been discarded. All that keen pride seems, to him, to have vanished, drawn back, perhaps, to the blind womb from which it came (letter to Peschmann, *Letters* p. 269).

### *She makes for me ... Is maiden* (st. 3, ll.1 and 6)

Yes, the syntax of stanza 3 is difficult, perhaps 'wrong'. SHE makes for me a nettle's innocence and a soft pigeon's guilt; she makes, in the fucked, hard rocks a frail virgin shell; she makes a frank (i.e. imprisoned, and candid and open) and closed (contradiction again here, meaning virgin-shut to diving man*) pearl; she makes shapes of sea-girls glint in the staved (diver-poised) & siren (certainly non-virgin) caverns; *SHE IS* a maiden in the shameful oak–: (here the shameful oak *is* obscure, a mixture of references, half known, half forgotten, nostalgic romantic undigested and emotionally packed, to a naughty oracle, a serpent's tree, an unconventional maypole for conventional satyrate figures). The syntax *can* be allowed by a stretch or rack-stretches; the difficulty is the word Glint. Cut out 'Glint' and it's obvious; I'm not, as you know too well, afraid of a little startling difficulty.

* This is adding to the image, of course, digging out what is accidentally there on purpose (letter to Hawkins, *Letters* p. 397).

*Proud as a sucked stone and huge as sandgrains* (st. 3, l.8): In a BBC broadcast on Thomas on 5 March 1958, Vernon Watkins said of this stanza:

> I suppose that verse took him perhaps three weeks, and the last line three or four days, of fairly continuous work, because he wanted an image of stability at the end of the stanza after 'Is maiden in the shameful oak'. The last line that I remember he put was 'proud as a mule's womb and huge as insects', and gradually 'insects' was altered to 'sandgrains', and about two days later the other part was altered to 'Proud as a sucked stone' (*BBC script*).

*her contraries* (st. 4, l.1):

> He sees her as a woman made of contraries, innocent in guilt & guilty in innocence, ravaged in virginity, virgin in ravishment, and a woman who, out of a weak coldness, reduces to nothing the great sexual strengths, heats, & prides of the world (letter to Peschmann).

*priest's grave foot ... molten* (st. 4, ll.2 and 3): The word 'molten' was apparently suggested by Watkins, and 'priest's grave foot' a phrase Watkins criticized – as implied in Thomas's letter to Watkins of 13 November 1937: 'I've used "molten", as you suggested, but kept "priest's grave foot", which is not, I'm sure, really ugly' (*Letters* p. 263).

*I make a weapon of an ass's skeleton* (st. 5, l.1):

> Crying his visions aloud, he makes war upon her absence, attacks and kills her absent heart, then falls, himself, into ruin at the moment of that murder of love (letter to Peschmann).

Samson slew a thousand men with the jawbone of an ass (Judges 15:15).

*the room of errors* (st. 6, l.1): A letter to Desmond Hawkins of 30 October 1937 describes how Thomas thought the poem was finished, when he saw that the then third verse, 'which dealt with the faults and mistakes of death, had a brilliant and moving description of a suicide's grave as "a chamber of errors"' (*Letters* p. 262), i.e. too close to 'a chamber of horrors'. He changed it to the present phrase.

*scraped of every legend* (st. 6, l.5):

> He falls into the grave; in his shroud he lies, empty of visions & legends; he feels undead love at his heart (letter to Peschmann).

*His mother's womb had a tongue that lapped up mud* (st. 7, l.1): This

line occurs in a 'four-line epitaph' that Thomas enclosed 'just written' in a
letter to Vernon Watkins of 25 October 1937 (in the British Library):

> He fed on the fattened terror of death, and died.
> (And his mother's womb had a tongue that lapped up mud).
> The terrible grave was lesson for the suicide:
> He slit his throat in the coffin and shed dry blood.

The above are the four deleted lines mentioned in *Letters* p. 261. The fourth
line was soon afterwards adapted for "After the funeral".

*fork him back* (st. 7, l.5)

> The surrounding dead in the grave describe to him one manner of death
> and resurrection: the womb, the origin of love, forks its child down to
> the dark grave, dips it in dust, then forks it back into light again (letter
> to Peschmann).

*a man is tangled* (st. 7, l.8): Thomas repudiates any notion of Frederick
Prokosch as a source for this phrase: 'It was weeks after writing that line
that I remembered Prokosch's "man-entangled sea": but I don't think any
apologies are necessary, anyway' (*Letters* p. 263). The phrase occurs in Prokosch's poem 'The Baltic Shore' in his *The Assassins*.

*These once-blind eyes . . . mild as pardon* (st. 8, l.1):

> And once in the light, the resurrected hero sees the world with penetrat-
> ing, altered eyes; the world that was wild is now mild to him, revenge
> has changed into pardon (letter to Peschmann).

*With loud, torn tooth and tail and cobweb drum* (st. 8, l.4): Almost
exactly the same line exists in an uncollected poem "Your Breath Was Shed" –
'With biter's tooth and tail/And cobweb drum' (*Poetry* (*London*) April 1944).

*my love . . . Walks with no wound* (st. 9, ll.2–3):

> He sees his love walk in the world, bearing none of the murderous
> wounds he gave her (letter to Peschmann).

*A calm wind blows . . . turned to ice* (st. 9, ll.4–5): In sending the poem
to Vernon Watkins on 13 November 1937, Thomas wrote:

> Lines 4 & 5 of the last verse might, perhaps, sound too fluent: I mean,
> they might sound as though they came too easily in a manner I have
> done my best to discard, but they say exactly what I mean them to. Are
> they clear? Once upon a time, before my death & resurrection, before

the 'terrible' world had shown itself to me (however lyingly, as lines 6 & 7 of the last verse might indicate) as not so terrible after all, a wind had blown that had frightened everything & created the first ice & the first frost by frightening the falling snow so much that the blood of each flake froze. This is probably clear, but, even to me, the lines skip (almost) along so that they are taken in too quickly, & then mainly by the eye (*Letters* p. 263).

The lines were still troubling him in the letter of 20 November 1937: 'I agree with you entirely as to the (apparently) hurried ending of my sixty-line-year's work, and will alter the middle lines of the last stanza' (*Letters* p. 264). They were apparently left unaltered.

*Prides of tomorrow ... forgiving presence* (st. 9, ll.8–9):

Forgiven by her, he ends his narrative in forgiveness: – but he sees and knows that all that has happened will happen again, tomorrow and tomorrow (letter to Peschmann).

## When all my five and country senses

In discussing the poems proposed for *The Map of Love*, Thomas wrote to Richard Church of Dent's on 8 March 1939: 'The sonnet I am not sure about, it seems mechanical' (*Letters* p. 363). "When all my five and country senses" is the only poem in the volume to which this comment could apply. He had called it 'a conventional sonnet' in sending it to Vernon Watkins on 21 March 1938 (*Letters* p. 279). We conjecture that it was a revised early poem (perhaps from a missing notebook), since it was submitted with three other revised poems to *Poetry* (Chicago), and published there, August 1938. Thomas was still wanting to revise it in May 1939 when proofs of *The Map of Love* arrived. He wrote to Watkins: 'One poem I want to rewrite, *with* your assistance; but I must do it quickly. Can you come down Saturday – for, if possible, the weekend? Please try, I need your help a lot. It really is important to me' (*Letters* p. 376). Watkins's visit produced some changes from the *Poetry* version, chiefly a new line 4, which in the periodical printing had been: 'In the ten planted towers of their stalk.'

*the lynx tongue cry* (l.8): Was 'the eyed tongue talk' in *Poetry* (Chicago). In a letter to Watkins of 1 April 1938, Thomas said: ' "eyed" tongue shall, momentarily, become "lashed" ' (*Letters* p. 287); later, probably in the rewriting session of May 1939, 'lashed' was used earlier in the line, and 'lynx' supplied instead of 'eyed'.

## We lying by seasand

This poem was initially written as notebook poem "Twenty Nine" on 16 May 1933. In a letter later that year, Thomas describes a local landmark, Worm's Head, as follows:

> I often go down in the mornings to the furthest point of Gower – the village of Rhossilli – and stay there until evening. The bay is the wildest, bleakest, and barrennest I know – four or five miles of yellow coldness going away into the distance of the sea. And the Worm, a seaworm of rock pointing into the channel, is the very promontory of depression ... There is one table of rock on the Worm's back that is covered with long yellow grass ... (*Letters* p. 62).

If there were not this location for the poem, we would have to imagine one with a similar feeling of doom about it.

The version published in *Poetry* (Chicago) January 1937 (an 'English Number' edited by W. H. Auden and Michael Roberts) was the short notebook poem, rewritten, with nine added lines (ll. 9–17).

## It is the sinners' dust-tongued bell

This is the first poem Thomas composed after the publication of *Twenty-five Poems* (September 1936). Writing on 10 November 1936 to Julian Symons, Thomas said: 'I haven't got a poem at the moment; I expect that I'll have one finished in a week or ten days; by the end of the month certainly' (*Letters* p. 240). Symons published "It is the sinners' dust-tongued bell" in the January 1937 issue of *Twentieth Century Verse*.

*dark directly under the dumb flame* (st. 3, l. 1): Vernon Watkins in a BBC broadcast, 5 March 1958, told of the inception of this line:

> He came to my house one day and he said, 'I've been reading a thriller, a very bad thriller, but I came on the most wonderful line in the middle of a lot of trash, which was "the shadow is dark directly under the candle"'. And he said, 'Out of that line I'm going to make a new poem which is going to be my best, about churches' (*BBC typescript*).

*a white child ... Scales the blue wall of spirits* (st. 4, ll. 1–3): Thomas spoke of this image in response to a query from Desmond Hawkins (*Letters* p. 398):

> This is a very decorative poem, a poem, if you'll pardon me, on stained glass. There are many ornamental designs, but all, I hope, utilitarian. And I really can't get down to explaining it; you just have to, or just

221

don't have to, let the poem come to you bit by bit through the rather obvious poetry of it. It's not a really satisfactory poem, but I like it. The blue wall of spirits is the sky full of ghosts: the curving crowded world above the new child. It sounds as though it meant the side of a chemist's bowl of methylated spirits, & I *saw* that too and a child climbing up it.

*hyleg image* (st. 5, l.4): The position of the planets influencing the fate of the 'sinners' – according to astrology.

*plagued groom and bride* (st. 5, l.5): The adjective 'plagued' was 'clapped' in the periodical printing of this poem, which, along with the 'claps' of l.1 of the poem, suggests the theme of venereal disease. *Caitlin: Life with Dylan Thomas* (p. 35) reveals that this was a concern for them at this time: 'I know that Dylan did have the disease because he told me about it, and soon after I met him I had to go into hospital myself when I caught gonorrhoea.' Caitlin adds that she 'didn't catch that from Dylan'; but he perhaps did not know that she didn't. A letter, written to Caitlin in hospital, is full of real concern (dated late 1936 in *Letters* p. 241). The couple were not yet married; the 'rascal' and 'urchin grief' of this last stanza cannot refer to a pregnancy, but quite possibly to the disease which had been the result of their sexual activity.

## O make me a mask

Probably some time in November 1937, after receiving the manuscript of a 'London Letter' from D. S. Savage in which Thomas was called 'outstanding among the younger poets', *Poetry* (Chicago) wrote requesting poems. This was the first such attention Thomas had received from across the Atlantic. He wanted to respond to it promptly, and turned to the notebook poems. The early version of "O make me a mask" (poem "Eighteen", undated, but of March 1933) was crossed through, and the revision copied in and dated 'Nov 1937 Blashford'. He had not gone beyond the first nine lines of the notebook poem, rewording extensively and not worrying if some of the lines were left unrhymed in the outcome. He did not push beyond the simple request of the early poem: a mask to protect his feelings from being seen by others while allowing him to see theirs. This was undoubtedly one of the 'short simple' poems sent to Vernon Watkins on 21 March 1938 (*Letters* p. 279) to be typed for submission to *Life and Letters Today* (printed there September 1938) after acceptance by *Poetry* for the May issue (but not published until the August issue).

*rebellion in* (l.3): Apparently Watkins did not like the phrase, and Thomas said in a letter that he would 'conquer' it (*Letters* p. 287), but it remained in the poem.

222

## The spire cranes

Poem "IX" dated 27 January 1931 in a notebook was revised, and sent to Watkins on 13 November 1937:

> I've done another little poem: nothing at all important, or even (probably,) much good: just a curious thought said quickly. I think it will be good for me to write some short poems, not bothering about them too much, between my long exhausters (*Letters* p. 264).

Published in *Wales* March 1938, and in *Poetry* (Chicago) August 1938.

*spire* (l.1): Keidrych Rhys has said (in conversation) that Thomas was thinking of the old ruined tower of Llanybri church. This location is, however, a mile inland from the sea.

*carved birds* (l.3): 'My poems *are* formed,' Thomas wrote in refutation of a remark by Stephen Spender (*Letters* p. 298): 'they are not turned on like a tap at all ... the last thing they do is to flow; they are much rather hewn.'

*that priest, water* (l.6): Thomas presumably knew the lines from Keats's 'Bright star' sonnet: 'waters at their priestlike task/Of pure ablution round earth's human shores.'

## After the funeral

Poem "Six" dated 'Feb 10. '33' in a notebook was revised, and a fifteen-line draft sent to Watkins on 21 March 1938. In a letter of 1 April 1938 Thomas said: 'The poem in memory of Anne Jones I am completely rewriting; and again the "weather" shall drop out: I'm making it longer and, I hope, better than any of my recent simple poems' (*Letters* p. 287). The finished poem came soon after (Watkins says in his notes that the poem was finished 'in a rush'), presumably in April 1938, with the following comment:

> Now here is the Anne Jones poem, & now I think it is more of a poem; will you type it for me? I knew it was feeble as it stood before, & the end of it – that is the part that becomes the new brackets – was too facile &, almost, grandiosely sentimental. (By the way, when you type it, will you spell Anne as Ann: I just remember that's the right way: she was an ancient peasant aunt.) I think there are some good lines, but don't know abt the thing as a whole (*Letters* p. 288).

The poem was published in *Life and Letters Today* Summer 1938.

The Caseg Broadsheet printing of this poem in June 1942 omitted the first nine lines. Theodore Roethke remembers that Thomas thought "After the funeral" 'creaked a bit at the beginning: that he had not worked hard enough on it' (in Tedlock p. 51).

*Ann Jones*  (title): In introducing this poem in a BBC reading, Thomas said it was 'the only one I have written that is, directly, about the life and death of one particular human being I knew' (*Quite Early One Morning* p. 137).

'*In loving memory of Annie Jones, Mount Pleasant, Llangain, died 7 Feb. 1933, 70 years old. Also her husband James Jones, died 3 Sept. 1942, 78 years old.*' (Translation of the Welsh.)

We know the circumstances of his aunt's death by cancer from a letter Thomas was writing to Trevor Hughes on 6 February 1933 when a telegram arrived. The young poet has conflicting reactions, or rather a puzzling non-reaction:

But the foul thing is I feel utterly unmoved, apart, as I said, from the pleasant death-reek at my negroid nostrils. I haven't, really, the faintest interest in her or her womb. She is dying. She is dead. She is alive. It is all the same thing. I shall miss her bi-annual postal orders. That's all. And yet I like – liked – her. She loves – loved – me. Am I, he said, with the diarist's unctuous, egotistic preoccupation with his own blasted psychological reactions to his own trivial affairs, callous & nasty? Should I weep? Should I pity the old thing? For a moment, I feel I should. There must be something lacking in me. I don't feel worried, or hardly ever, about other people. It's self, self, all the time. I'm rarely interested in other people's emotions, except those of my pasteboard characters. I prefer (this is one of the thousand contradictory devils speaking) style to life, my own reactions to emotions rather than the emotions themselves. Is this, he pondered, a lack of soul? (*Letters* p. 13).

The notebook version of "After the funeral" is dated 10 February 1933, perhaps the day of the funeral. In the early poem the young Thomas maintains a rather jaded view of life and death: 'Another gossip's toy has lost its use.'

*sheds dry leaves* (l.8): A similar image describing suicide appears in an 'epitaph' of October 1937; see notes to "I make this in a warring absence".

*a room with a stuffed fox and a stale fern* (l.11): Said to be an accurate description of the front parlour of Fernhill farm (see also the story "The Peaches" in *Portrait of the Artist as a Young Dog*). The mood is antithetical to that of the later poem "Fern Hill".

*Storm me forever over her grave until* (l.38): In the letter to Vernon Watkins of April 1938, Thomas says: 'The 38th line may seem weak, but I think I wanted it like that' (*Letters* p. 288).

*twitch and cry Love* (l.39): Watkins's notes indicate that Thomas was thinking of a passage in *Nightwood* (by Djuna Barnes), one of his favourite books: 'if one gave birth to a heart on a plate, it would say "Love," and twitch like the lopped leg of a frog' (Gwen Watkins, *Portrait of a Friend* p. 35).

## Once it was the colour of saying

A Christmas poem for 1938, looking back to Swansea, if not written there, Thomas called it 'this Cwmdonkin poem' when he sent it to Watkins on 29 December 1938. Responding to Watkins's comments, he wrote on 8 January 1939:

> I shan't alter anything in it except, perhaps but probably, the 'close & cuckoo' lovers ... I see your argument about the error of shape, but the form was consistently emotional and I can't change it without a change of heart (*Letters* p. 351).

'Close' was changed to 'cold' for the publication in *Wales* March 1939.

*mitching* (l.7): A dialect colloquialism for 'truant', appearing also in the notebook version of "The hunchback in the park" and the BBC broadcast "Return Journey" (*Quite Early One Morning* p. 84).

## Not from this anger

Poem "Twenty Five" dated 'April 20 '33' in a notebook was edited down from forty-two lines to fourteen; the revised poem was copied into the notebook, dated 'January 1938 Blashford', and sent to Watkins as one of 'two short simple ones' on 21 March 1938 (*Letters* p. 279).

*strapped by hunger* (l.4): The notebook revision had 'without weather'. Thomas, responding to comments by Vernon Watkins, wrote him on 1 April 1938: 'Before your letter came, I had cut out the ubiquitous "weather" from the anticlimactic poem, and am revising it all' (*Letters* p. 287). The phrase 'without weather' is crossed out in the notebook, and 'strapped by hunger' substituted. However, this was not done before Thomas sent the poem off to *Poetry* (Chicago), for the earlier phrase appears there in the issue of August 1938.

## How shall my animal

This is the poem on which Thomas said he had 'spent a great deal of time' when he enclosed it in a letter to Vernon Watkins of 21 March 1938 (*Letters* pp. 278–279). In the same letter he referred, in another context, to the line 'I build a flying tower, and I pull it down', which is to be found in the early notebook poem "42" of 9 December 1930, a poem which begins:

> How shall the animal
> Whose way I trace
> Into the dark recesses,
> Be durable
> Under such weight as bows me down.

The final "How shall my animal" is far removed from this early poem; Thomas 'had worked on it for months' (*Letters* p. 287). It is probably the revision of this poem that Thomas is referring to in a letter to Desmond Hawkins of 16 March 1938: 'The poem that was meant for your stupendous number ... died, twisted in its mysteries and I am trying now to bury it in another poem' (*Letters* p. 276).

The poem was sent on 30 August 1938 for publication in the New Directions annual for 1938. It was also published in *Criterion* October 1938.

*lionhead's* (st. 2, l.3): A word supplied by Vernon Watkins as an alternative for a word not known. 'I'm as sure now as you are of the "lionhead"' – letter to Watkins of 1 April 1938 (*Letters* p. 287). It is a neologism, possibly alluding to Revelation 9:17 – 'The heads of the horses were like lions' heads.'

*my beast* (st. 4, l.9):

> I hold a beast, an angel, and a madman in me, and my enquiry is as to their working, and my problem is their subjugation and victory, downthrow & upheaval, and my effort is their self-expression. The new poem I enclose, 'How Shall My Animal', is a detailed enquiry; and the poem too is the result of the enquiry, and is the furthest I can, at present, reach or hope for. The poem is, as all poems are, its own question and answer, its own contradiction, its own agreement. I ask only that my poetry should be taken literally. The aim of a poem is the mark that the poem itself makes; it's the bullet and the bullseye; the knife, the growth, and the patient. A poem moves only towards its own end, which is the last line (letter to Henry Treece 16 May 1938, *Letters* p. 297).

*whinnying* (st. 4, l.10): Was 'blowing' in the version sent to Vernon Watkins on 21 March 1938. Thomas asked: 'About "blowing" light in the last verse. Can you think of anything better?' (*Letters* p. 280). In his next letter to Watkins, he thanks him for a suggestion: ' "whinnying" is certainly far better than my word and may – I am coming to think it is – be the best' (*Letters* p. 287).

## The tombstone told

A notebook poem ("Thirty Six" dated July 1933) was expanded from one stanza to three, and the revision copied in, dated 'Sept 1938. Laugharne'. Thomas had already sent the poem to Watkins, as one of '2 short ones of mine, just done', and calling it 'the ballad-like poem' (*Letters* p. 326), and later 'the Hardy-like one' (*Letters* p. 327). It apparently came from a story that Thomas personally heard, of a Welsh farmer's bride dying in her wedding dress.

*Through the devilish years and innocent deaths* (st. 2, l.4): In the notebook this was 'Through the small years and great deaths'. Thomas wrote to Vernon Watkins in response to suggestions (*Letters* p. 328):

> I agree with your objection to 'small'; 'innocent' is splendid, but 'fugitive' & 'turbulent' are, for me in that context, too vague, too 'literary' (I'm sorry to use that word again) too ambiguous. I've used 'devilish', which is almost colloquial.

*hurried* (st. 3, l.1): Was 'winding' in the notebook draft, and stayed 'winding' in the poem as published in *Poetry* (Chicago) November 1939 and *Seven* Winter 1938 and *Voice of Scotland* December–February 1938–39. The word had been 'hurried' in a draft, but Thomas told Watkins: ' "Hurried" film I just couldn't see; I wanted it slow and complicated, the winding cinematic works of the womb' (*Letters* p. 328). Thomas reverted to 'hurried' for *The Map of Love* printing.

*my womb was bellowing*  (st. 3, l.7): Apparently Watkins objected to this word, for Thomas replied: 'No, I still think the womb "bellowing" is allright, exactly what I wanted; perhaps it looks too much like a stunt rhyme with heroine, but that was unavoidable' (*Letters* p. 328).

*blazing red harsh head ... dear floods*  (st. 3, ll.9–10): In the notebook these phrases were 'strange and red harsh head' and 'great floods'. In sending the poem to Watkins, Thomas wrote: 'I'm not *quite* sure of several words, mostly of "great" floods of his hair. I think it's right, though; I didn't want a surprisingly strong word there. Do tell me about it, soon' (*Letters* p. 326). In his next letter he wrote (*Letters* pp. 327–328):

> I considered all your suggestions most carefully. A 'strange & red' harsh head was, of course, very weak & clumsy, but I couldn't see that the alliteration of 'raving red' was effective. I tried everything, & stuck to the commonplace 'blazing', which makes the line violent enough then, if not exactly good enough, for the last. In the last line you'll see I've been daring, & have tried to make the point of the poem softer & subtler by the use of the dangerous 'dear'. The word 'dear' fits in, I think, with 'though her eyes smiled', which comes earlier. I wanted the girl's *terrible* reaction to orgiastic death to be suddenly altered into a kind of despairing love. As I see it now, it strikes me as very moving, but it may be too much of a shock, a bathetic shock perhaps, & I'd like very much to know what you think.

## On no work of words

Poem "Eight" of February 1933 was revised in the notebook, and the completed revision is dated there 'Laugharne. Sept. 1938'. It was published in *Wales* March 1939.

*three lean months*  (l.1): Specifically, the summer months of 1938, when Thomas and family had taken up residence in a fisherman's cottage in Gosport Street in Laugharne. The notebook draft had begun with three lines that stylistically forecast the later Laugharne poetry:

> For three lean months now, no work done
> In summer Laugharne among the cockle boats
> And by the castle with the boatlike birds.

*Puffing the pounds of manna up* ... (st. 2, l.2): It is likely that Thomas would have known George Herbert's images for prayer in his poem "Prayer" 'reversed thunder', 'exalted manna'.

*ogre* (st. 4, l.1): Watkins must have objected to the word when Thomas sent him the poem in September 1938. In his next letter, 14 October 1938, Thomas states emphatically: 'The word is OGRE, not orge or orgy & ... I'll listen to no criticism of it' (*Letters* p. 329).

*woods of my blood ... nut of the seas* (st. 4, l.2): In answer to queries from Desmond Hawkins, Thomas wrote on 14 August 1939 (*Letters* p. 396):

> 'Nut', yes, has many meanings, but here, in the same line as 'woods', I can't really see that it can have any but a woody meaning. The actual line is a very extravagant one, an overgrand declamatory cry after, in my opinion, the reasoned and quite quiet argument of the preceding lines. The *sense* of the last two lines is: Well, to hell and to death with me, may my old blood go back to the bloody sea it came from if I accept this world only to bugger it up or return it. The oaktree came out of the acorn; the woods of my blood came out of the nut of the sea, the tide-concealing, blood-red kernel. A silly, far-fetched, if not, apparently, far-fetching shout – maybe – but, I think, balanced in the poem.

## A saint about to fall

In a letter to John Davenport of 24 August 1938, Thomas referred to his expected child as 'our saint or monster' (*Letters* p. 318). Sending the poem to Vernon Watkins on 14 October 1938, he said: 'Remember this is a poem written to a child about to be born – you know I'm going to be a father in January – and telling it what a world it will see, what horrors and hells' (*Letters* p. 328). It was published in *Poetry (London)* February 1939 with the title "Poem in the Ninth Month", a title which had been suggested by Watkins (*Letters* p. 344).

*his father's house in the sands* (st. 1, l.7): The Thomases were living in Sea View, Laugharne, during September 1938.

*On the angelic etna of the last whirring featherlands* (st. 1, l.11): To Desmond Hawkins on 14 August 1939 Thomas wrote:

> I wanted to get the look of this stanza right: a saint about to fall, *to be born*, heaven shifting visionarily under him as he stands poised: (changingly, the landscape moving to no laws but heaven's, that is: hills moving, streets flowing etc) the stained flats, the lowlying lands, that is, *and* the apartment houses all discoloured by the grief of his going, ruined for ever by his departure (for heaven must fall with every

falling saint): on the last wave of a flowing street before the cities flow to the edge of heaven where he stands about to fall, praising his making and unmaking & the dissolution of his father's house etc – (this, as the poem goes on to talk about, is his father-on-the-earth's veins, his mother's womb, *and* the peaceful place before birth): Standing on an angelic (belonging to heaven's angels & heavenly itself) volcanic hill (everything is in disruption, eruption) on the last feathers of his father-lands (and whirring is a noise of wings). All the heavenly business I use because it makes a famous and noble landscape from which to plunge this figure on to the bloody, war-barbed etc earth. It's a poem written on the birth of my son. He was a saint for a poem's sake (hear the beast howl) (*Letters* p. 398).

*Glory cracked*  (st. 2, l.1): Thomas wrote to Vernon Watkins: 'Does "Glory cracked like a flea" shock you? I think you'll see it *must* come there, or some equally grotesque contrast' (*Letters* p. 328).

*carbolic ... Strike*  (st. 2, l.11; st. 3, l.1): 'I agree that "carbolic" and "strike" could be bettered, but, at the moment, I'll just leave them; I may be able to go back clearly to the poem some time soon, but I'll publish it now as it is' (*Letters* p. 333).

*war of burning brains and hair*  (st. 2, l.17): Thomas thought that this line 'might appear just a long jumble of my old anatomical clichés, but if, in the past, I've used "burning brains and hair" etc too loosely, this time I used them – as the only words – in dead earnest' (*Letters* p. 328). He provisionally called the poem "In September" – 'and called that at all only because it was a terrible war month' (*Letters* p. 328). September 1938 saw the war scare and the Munich Pact; Thomas refers to Prime Minister Chamberlain in a letter of 1 September 1938 (*Letters* p. 325). The war that was actually going on – and Thomas refers to it in a letter of 23 September 1938 (*Letters* p. 327) – was the Spanish Civil War; the 'thundering bullring' of the last line of the poem may be an oblique reference to Spain.

*herods*  (st. 3, l.5): Herod ordered all the newborn children of Bethlehem killed (Matthew 2:16).

*Cry joy*  (st. 3, ll.14–17): Thomas wrote to Watkins about these lines (*Letters* p. 328):

> The last four lines of the poem, especially the last but two, may seem ragged, but I've altered the rhythm purposely; 'you so gentle' must be very soft & gentle, & the last line must roar. It's an optimistic, taking-everything, poem. The two most important words are 'Cry Joy'. Tell me about this, please, very soon. I'm surer of the *words* of this poem than of the words in any recent one.

### If my head hurt a hair's foot

Thomas wrote to Vernon Watkins on 3 March 1939 (*Letters* p. 359) that the proofs of *The Map of Love* had arrived, but he wanted to include this poem 'just finished': 'Please, can I have a quick criticism. It's deeply felt, but perhaps clumsily said.' There were a few changes (see below) before the poem was sent to *Poetry (London)* for immediate publication in the issue of April 1939.

In introducing a reading of the poem on the BBC, Thomas said the following, as found in *Quite Early One Morning* p. 133:

> The next poem tells of a mother and her child who is about to be born. It is not a narrative, nor an argument, but a series of conflicting images which move through pity and violence to an unreconciled acceptance of suffering: the mother's *and* the child's. This poem has been called obscure. I refuse to believe that it is obscurer than pity, violence, or suffering. But being a poem, not a lifetime, it is more compressed.

*glove on a lamp ... the ghost with a hammer* (st. 2, ll.2 and 4): The South Wales coal miner and world champion fly-weight boxer Jimmy Wilde was known as 'the ghost with a hammer in his hand'.

*And the endless beginning of prodigies suffers open* (st. 6, l.5): Thomas in a letter to Watkins 3 March 1939 asked of this line: 'is the last line too bad, too comic, or does it *just* work? Have you any alternatives for the *adjectives* of that last line?' (*Letters* p. 359). The last line as given by Watkins in *Letters to Vernon Watkins* p. 59 was: 'And the endless, tremendous beginning suffers open'. In a letter of 20 March 1939 Thomas agreed with what Watkins had said about the poem:

> The 2nd person speaks better than the first, & the last line is false. I haven't been able to alter the first part, & will have to leave it unsuccessful. The last line is now: 'And the endless beginning of prodigies suffers open'. I worked on from your suggestion (*Letters* p. 366).

### Twenty-four years

Entitled "Birthday Poem" when published in *Life and Letters Today* December 1938, this poem was written on a postcard for Vernon Watkins and sent on 24 October 1938, 'for my birthday just arriving' (*Letters* p. 334).

*(Bury the dead for fear that they walk to the grave in labour.)* (l.2): Vernon Watkins must have made a suggestion about this line; Thomas responded on 20 December 1938:

sorry about that bracketed line in the birthday poem, but, until I can think of something else or feel, it will have to stay. I thought your alternative line clumsier & more bass-drum (rather muffled, too) than mine. I do realise your objections to my line; I feel myself the too selfconscious flourish, recognize the Shakespeare echo (though echo's not the word). If ever I do alter it, I'll *remember* your line (*Letters* p. 344).

*like a tailor* (l.3): 'In the first version I had "like a stuffed tailor". I think stuffed is wrong, don't you?' (letter to Vernon Watkins, *Letters* p. 334).

*for as long as forever is* (l.9): The Humanities Research Center (Texas) has a manuscript of an unpublished poem beginning with this line.

> For as long as forever is
> And the fast sky quakes in the web, as the fox in the wave,
> With heels of birds and the plumed eyes,
> Shakes in its stride the partridge fence and the sea-duck rows,
> And a flame in a wheel jumps the nave,
> As a dozen winds drop the dark by the one moonrise,
> And a stag through a trap grave,
> Forever the hunted world at a snail's gallop goes.
>
> Over the packed nests now, the snare and the she-bear's floes,
> Through the cat's mountain and the cave
> By the market and a feather street near the townspires,
> Narrowly time's slow riders shove.

Thomas referred to this undated poem in sending "Twenty-four years" to Watkins:

> I know you'll hate the use of the 'Forever' line, but there it is. I scrapped the poem beginning with that line long ago, and at last – I think – I've found the inevitable place for it: it was a time finding that place. I'm pleased, terribly, with this – so far. Do tell me, & type please ... Try to read the end of the poem as though you didn't know the lines. I do feel they're right. In the old 'Forever' poem they were completely out of place – & the rest of the poem wouldn't stand without them. So bang went the whole poem, obviously, & here at last is what it should be (*Letters* p. 334).

## DEATHS AND ENTRANCES (1946)

[From here on, where necessary, we have reduced first-line titles to lower case, in keeping with the vast majority of such titles in Thomas's poetry. Conversely, three titles that are not first-line titles, formerly lower case, are here capitalized.]

### The conversation of prayers

We have restored the plural title "The conversation of prayers", which Thomas used in sending the poem to Vernon Watkins with a letter of 28 March 1945, and in the two periodical printings, *Life and Letters Today* July 1945, and *New Republic* 16 July 1945. *Deaths and Entrances* had "The Conversation of Prayer", which runs counter to the intention of the poem, where two prayers are converting, one into the other.

*his true grave* (st. 4, l.3): The poem as sent to Vernon Watkins had 'his made grave', which is more successful in connecting the phrase to the theme of bedtime. The emotive 'true' is Thomas's later and considered choice.

### A Refusal to Mourn the Death, by Fire, of a Child in London

This poem was sent in its completed form to Vernon Watkins on 28 March 1945 (*Letters* p. 548), and published in *New Republic* 14 May 1945, and in *Horizon* October 1945.

*A Refusal* (title): A provisional title for the second part of "Ceremony After a Fire Raid", written in the year previous to this poem, was "Among Those Burned To Death Was A Child Aged A Few Hours" (manuscript in Ohio State University), which in turn was modelled on the 1941 poem, "Among Those Killed In The Dawn Raid Was A Man Aged 100" (the title found in a Buffalo manuscript). The form of these titles draws upon the immediacy and yet formality of certain kinds of newspaper headlines.

*the first death* (st. 4, l.6): Thomas possibly had in mind several references in Revelation to a 'second death' (e.g. Revelation 21:6–8).

### Poem in October

The poem Thomas announced to Watkins in a letter of 26 August 1944 as 'a Laugharne poem: the first place poem I've written' (*Letters* p. 518) was sent in the next letter, 30 August 1944 (*Letters* p. 519), 'a month & a bit premature. I do hope you like it, & wd like very much to read it aloud to you ... It's got, I think, a lovely slow lyrical movement'. In his notes, Watkins said that the poem 'had been contemplated for three years' (*Letters to Vernon Watkins* p. 115). This would take us back to the time of a preliminary list Thomas made for *Deaths and Entrances*, when a "Birthday Poem" was to be the last in the book. But if the poem was conceived and begun literally as a birthday poem, and in Laugharne, then its inception goes back to October 1939, when Thomas and family were resident at Sea View.

Published in *Horizon* February 1945 and *Poetry* (Chicago) February 1945.

*winged trees* (st. 2, l.2): Was 'bare trees' in the copy sent to Watkins (*Letters to Vernon Watkins* p. 116). Thomas noticed, 'on copying out, that I have made October trees bare. I'll alter later' (*Letters* p. 519).

*leaved with October blood* (st. 7, l.7): Was 'brown with October blood' in the version sent to Watkins. The change was made in response to Watkins's criticism (Gwen Watkins, *Portrait of a Friend* p. 120).

## This side of the truth

Sent to Vernon Watkins on 28 March 1945, this poem was published in *New Republic* on 2 July 1945 and in *Life and Letters Today* July 1945.

In her book *Caitlin: Life with Dylan Thomas* p. 93, Caitlin Thomas recalls something of the background to this poem:

> One of the poems he wrote at New Quay, 'This Side of the Truth', was written for Llewelyn [their first child, born January 1939]. It is not a very clear poem and I was a bit surprised that he wrote it, but pleased that he did. I think Dylan was disappointed that Llewelyn wasn't more of a natural boy. He was always brooding and introspective, sensitive and vulnerable. Dylan wanted a straightforward boy who kicked a ball.... I can't remember what led Dylan to write that poem, although I imagine that there must have been a certain amount of guilt, because Llewelyn had not had decent treatment.

## To Others than You

'Here is a new short poem, nothing very much' is how Thomas described this poem in sending it to Watkins in June 1939 (*Letters* p. 383). Since there is no record of Thomas sending the poem to anyone else, the title might be taken as excluding Watkins from the accusations in the poem. It could, however, be tongue-in-cheek.

Publication in *Seven* Autumn 1939.

*sucked* (l.8): 'The word I used too much – "sucked" – is here bound, I think, to be' (letter to Watkins, *Letters* p. 383).

*desireless familiar* (l.15): Thomas said this was 'a phrase in my "Orchards" and what caused me to write the poem' (letter to Watkins, *Letters* p. 383). The phrase can be found in *A Prospect of the Sea* p. 90: 'They sat in the grass by the stone table like lovers at a picnic, too loved to speak, desireless familiars.'

*While you displaced a truth in the air* (l.17): 'The best thing is, as you'll perhaps agree, the simple last line of the middle bit' (letter to Watkins, *Letters* p. 383).

*friends were enemies on stilts* (l.20): An early notebook poem "Twenty Two" dated 2 April 1933 contained the lines:

> A friend is but an enemy on stilts
> Striding so high above the common earth
> ....
> You cannot see his eyes or know his faults.

## Love in the Asylum

Writing to the editor of *Poetry (London)*, Tambimuttu, on 19 February 1941, Thomas said: 'I haven't finished my own thing for the next number. Will it do for the number after next?' (*Letters* p. 927). He apparently sent "Love in the Asylum" at the end of April 1941: 'I haven't heard a word from you yet about the poem I sent you at the end of last month' (letter of 21 May 1941 – *Letters* p. 928). The poem was printed in the May–June 1941 issue of *Poetry (London)*.

*mazed* (st. 2, l.2): Was 'mad' in the Buffalo draft of the poem, and in the periodical printing. Early in his relationship with Caitlin, Thomas was quite willing to use the word 'mad', as in a letter of late 1936, where he speaks of 'a sort of sweet madness about you and me' and tells of 'an Irish book' he has just read:

> innocent Rory falls in love with innocent Oriana, and, though they're
> both whimsy and talk about the secret of the language of the hills and
> though Rory worships the moon and Oriana glides about in her garden
> listening to the legendary birds, they're not as mad as we are, nor as
> innocent (*Letters* p. 242).

*First vision that set fire to the stars* (st. 6, l.3): The notebook poem "Fifty One" of August 1933 included the line: 'First vision that set fire to the stars'. But the context there is quite different from this poem, which is more in keeping with the early story, "The Mouse and the Woman": 'The woman had shown him that it was wonderful to live ... He opened his eyes, and looked up at the stars. There were a million stars spelling the same word' (*A Prospect of the Sea*, p. 76).

## Unluckily for a death

The first version is printed in full as "Poem (To Caitlin)" in *Letters to Vernon Watkins* pp. 64–65; the same version was published in *Life and Letters Today* October 1939, with the same title. In sending the poem to Watkins in May 1939, Thomas made comments on some specific words in the poem, but added: 'Don't bother too much about other details in it; apart from what I've mentioned, it's the spirit of this poem that matters' (*Letters* p. 377). We cannot concern ourselves too much with this first version, because it was greatly changed. The poem worried Thomas (*Letters* pp. 382–383), and he revised it thoroughly at the proof stage, 'retaining only the title line and one or two others', sending it with the corrected proofs to Dent's on 18 September 1945 (*Letters* p. 569). The result is, incidentally, one of only two unrhymed poems in the *Collected Poems*.

*tigron* (st. 3, l.1): A neologism, tiger plus lion, 'striped' and 'maned' – a creature equivalent to the phoenix, used in the poem as a symbol of one kind of death.

## The hunchback in the park

An early notebook poem "LVVV" dated 9 May 1932 was revised in the notebook in July 1941, converting a thirty-one-line free verse poem into a regularly rhymed poem of seven six-line stanzas. This was the last use Thomas made of the notebooks before he sold them. Copies of the revised poem were sent to both Charles Fisher and Vernon Watkins on 15 July 1941. 'Just a poem, finished today,' he said to Fisher (*Letters* p. 493). The poem was published in *Life and Letters Today* October 1941.

*truant* (st. 3, l.4): Was the dialect 'mitching' in the notebook version.

*the park keeper* (st. 4, l.5): Like the hunchback himself, an actual figure – a council employee called Mr Smallcombe, generally referred to as 'Old Smalley' (Ferris p. 57).

*woman figure without fault* (st. 6, l.2): The BBC broadcast,"Reminiscences of Childhood", included a recitation of this poem, and a comment about Cwmdonkin Park, Swansea, its setting: 'the bushy Red-Indian-hiding park, where the hunchback sat alone, images of perfection in his head' (*Quite Early One Morning* p. 6). The original notebook version carried a cancelled line that said of the 'figure without fault' that 'It is a poem and it is a woman figure.'

## Into her lying down head

In March 1940 Thomas announced in a letter to Watkins that he was beginning 'an ambitious new poem' (*Letters* p. 445). On 5 June 1940 he sent the first version of "Into her lying down head" (*Letters to Vernon Watkins* pp. 93–95 prints it in full):

> Here's a poem. I showed you the beginning, or *a* beginning, months – is it? – ago in Laugharne. Tell me straight away. I consider, at the just-finished illusionary glowing moment, it's good. I've never worked harder on anything, maybe too hard: I made such a difficult shape, too. Points: (I) I want a title for it. Can you suggest? Modern Love? Wd that be affected? I've often wanted to use other people's titles, & once began my Ode On The Intimations Of Immortality. It is a poem about modern love. For some reason, I wrote a note under the poem in my copybook:
>
> All over the world love is being betrayed as always, and a million years have not calmed the uncalculated ferocity of each betrayal or the terrible loneliness afterwards. Man is denying his partner man or woman and whores with the whole night, begetting a monstrous brood; one day the brood will not die when the day comes but will hang on to the breast and the parts and squeeze his partner out of bed. Or, as a title, One Married Pair. It's a poem of wide implications, if not of deep meanings, and I want a matter-of-fact, particular title (*Letters* p. 455).

*Juan . . . young King Lear,/Queen Catherine* (pt. I, ll. 11–12): King Lear, in Shakespeare's play, gives hints of a Don Juan youth. Catherine the Great of Russia was well known for her sexual activities. Her appearance in the poem may also be due to the fact that Caitlin is a form of Catherine.

*domed and soil-based* (pt. III, l. 5): Was 'helled and heavened' in the first version. Thomas wrote to Watkins: ' "Helled and heavened shell". Is this too clumsy? I like it, but it may be' (*Letters* p. 455).

*With the incestuous secret brother* (pt. III, l. 20): There was one notable change made for the publication of the poem in *Life and Letters Today* in November 1940. Thomas had asked Watkins: 'The longest line in the last verse: is this too – prosy? I wanted a very direct statement, but perhaps this straggles' (*Letters* p. 455). The line read (*Letters to Vernon Watkins* p. 95):

> The filth and secret of death is sweeter with the
> sun than these inconstancies.

This was changed in the periodical printing to

> Damned damned go down or caress to death the
> sun-sized bridal bed's cruellest brood.

In sending the poem to Robert Herring (probably around July 1940), Thomas wrote: 'The poem may look very sprawly, but it's really properly formed' (letter in the Rosenbach Library, Philadelphia). But the last lines of the third part were not yet properly formed, and Thomas worked on the version published in *Life and Letters Today* in November 1940 to have them conform to the stanzaic pattern of the previous two parts. Thus, the version in *Deaths and Entrances* had a completely rewritten last ten lines.

## Paper and sticks

First published in *Seven*, Autumn 1939, this poem was collected into *Deaths and Entrances*, but dropped from the *Collected Poems 1934–1952* at the last minute. 'Proofreading the Collected Poems,' Thomas wrote to Dent's on 10 September 1952, 'I have the horrors of "Paper and Sticks" on page 116. It's *awful*. I suppose it's *quite* impossible to cut it out? I shd so like it, somehow, to be omitted' (*Letters* p. 839). The publishers were able to oblige, but only by bringing "Do not go gentle into that good night" from its place towards the end of the volume into p. 116. In the present edition we have restored "Paper and sticks" and "Do not go gentle into that good night" to their previously assigned places. Reasons for this decision are given in the General Preface to the Notes.

## Deaths and Entrances

The poem had its inception with Thomas's experience of a London air attack in the summer of 1940. He described to Vernon Watkins the nightmares it produced: 'I get nightmares like invasions' (*Letters* p. 463). In his next letter he announced that he had finished his 'poem about invasion, but it isn't shapely enough to send you yet' (*Letters* p. 464). In November 1940 Thomas brought the poem to Watkins's house and 'spent the evening completing it' (*Portrait of a Friend* p. 88). It was published in *Horizon* January 1941.

*Deaths and Entrances* (title): From Donne's last sermon, *Death's Duell*: 'Deliverance from that death, the death of the wombe, is an entrance, a delivery over to another death.' Gwen Watkins records in *Portrait of a Friend* p. 88 that Thomas intended in May 1940 to call his next book by the same title, 'because that is all I ever write about or want to write about'.

*mount your darkened keys* (st. 3, l.9): In the letter to Watkins describing his nightmares about 'invasions' (*Letters* p. 463), Thomas wrote, 'I went to see a smashed aerodrome. Only one person had been killed. He was playing the piano in an entirely empty, entirely dark canteen.'

*Samson of your zodiac* (st. 3, l.12): 'The last line', according to Gwen Watkins in *Portrait of a Friend* p. 88, 'was based on a suggestion of Vernon's, and Dylan remained uncertain about it; because, he said, '"zodiac" is a Watkins word, not a Thomas word.' Samson, here as destroyer, is certainly a Thomas word.

## A Winter's Tale

Sending the poem to Watkins on 28 March 1945, Thomas wrote:

The long one doesn't, I think, come off, but I like it all in spite of that. It isn't really one piece, though, God, I tried to make it one and have been working on it for months (*Letters* p. 548).

He sent it to Oscar Williams in New York on the same day: 'The longish one, I'm glad to say, has taken a great deal of time and trouble' (*Letters* p. 550). Williams sent it on to *Poetry* (Chicago), where it was printed in July 1945.

## On a Wedding Anniversary

The first version of this poem was published in *Poetry* (*London*) 15 January 1941. The poem was revised, presumably just before Thomas returned proofs of *Deaths and Entrances* to Dent's on 18 September 1945: 'The poem on page 32 is substantially altered. In form, it is now three stanzas of four lines each' (*Letters* p. 569). However, it remained the least satisfactory of the volume's poems to Thomas; in a letter to Dent's of 28 September 1945 he indicated that it 'could be cut out' if need be (*Letters* p. 572).

*three years* (l.3): Dylan and Caitlin were married on 11 July 1937; the poem clearly is celebrating their third wedding anniversary, 11 July 1940.

## There was a saviour

In a letter to Watkins of 30 January 1940, Thomas announced: 'Now I'm working on a new poem, a poem which is giving me more pleasure than I've got out of any work for months, or even years' (*Letters* p. 437). The poem was sent to Watkins soon after, perhaps with the letter of 3 February 1940 (*Letters* p. 439); for in the letter after that, dated 6 March 1940, Thomas is responding to Watkins's comments on his 'austere poem in Milton measure' (*Letters* p. 443). The stanza used by Thomas is that of Milton's "On the

Morning of Christ's Nativity", which Kathleen Raine once said was Thomas's favourite poem.

*Letters to Vernon Watkins* did not print the draft version on which Thomas commented in detail, nor does it exist in the Watkins papers in the British Library. The comments themselves, however, often reveal what the wording was before it was changed.

Publication in *Horizon* May 1940.

*hindering man* (st. 2, l.4): In response to Watkins's suggestion, Thomas replied, 'I'll think of "stupid kindred", which is right, of course, in meaning and which prevents any ambiguity, but kindred seems a little pompous a word: it hasn't the literal simplicity of hindering man' (*Letters* p. 442). In a postscript, after reading the poem 'very carefully', Thomas indicated an adjustment: 'To avoid ambiguity, and also the use of the word "kindred" I've turned "his" in line 6 of verse 2 into "that"' (*Letters* p. 443).

*cloud-formed shell* (st. 3, l.7): 'This harder word, "formed", balances the line, avoids the too-pretty internal rhyme of "laid" and "made", and stops the too-easy flow, or thin conceited stream' (*Letters* p. 443).

*blacked* (st. 4, l.1): 'I like the word "blacked", by the way, in spite of its, in the context, jarring dissonance with "locked". I had, quite apart (that is absurd, I mean secondarily to) from the poem, the blackout in mind, another little hindrance on the scene, and the word seemed, to me, to come rightly. But I'll think about it' (*Letters* p. 442).

*Brave deaths of only ones but never found* (st. 5, l.3): According to *Letters to Vernon Watkins* p. 81, this line was originally 'Deaths of the only ones, our never found.' Watkins must have commented on it, for Thomas replied: 'about line 3 of the last verse, you're right as can be and somehow I must make "death" the second word. I'll let you know what I can work out … Your criticism's always terribly suggestive, and in that particular "death line" you showed quite clearly to me the one big misbalance in the poem' (*Letters* p. 442). Later in the letter Thomas indicated he had altered the line to the present reading, 'which I believe to be right' (*Letters* p. 443).

*dust/Ride through the doors* (st. 5, ll.6–7): 'No, I can't see "seep" with dust, and unless a better word can be made will remain true to "fly"' (*Letters* p. 442). Later: 'For "fly" in the last line but 2 of the last verse I have now "ride". I'm sure of that: it's mysteriously militant, which is what I wanted' (*Letters* p. 443).

## On the Marriage of a Virgin

Poem "Sixteen" dated 'March 22 '33' in a notebook was edited down from forty-two lines to fourteen, and the revision copied in the notebook, and dated January 1941. The first half of the poem was sent to Watkins on the back of a letter of 21 June 1941, with the comment: 'Here is a tiny poem I've just done. Not very well formed; just a poem between bits of my unfortunately forced novel' (*Letters* p. 490). The whole revised poem came in the next letter, 4 July 1941: 'I'm enclosing the short, now finished, poem' (*Letters* p. 491). Without further revision, it was published in *Life and Letters Today* October 1941.

The early version was begun at a time when Thomas knew that his sister Nancy was to be married; he was possibly planning it as a prothalamion for her wedding in May 1933.

*Galilee* (l.7): The inland sea where, in Thomas's image, Christ left his 'footprints' when he walked on the water.

## In my craft or sullen art

We do not hear about this poem until 18 September 1945, when Thomas is correcting proofs of *Deaths and Entrances*, and he tells A. J. Hoppé of Dent's: 'I have crossed out the poem on page 36 *entirely*, and am substituting another, and shorter, poem – *"In My Craft or Sullen Art"* – which I enclose' (*Letters* p. 569). (It is hard to think what extant single-page poem longer than this one could have previously been on p. 36.) The poem was published in *Life and Letters Today* October 1945.

*sullen* (l.1): From the Latin *solus* 'alone', 'sullen' means not only morose but also solitary, emphasizing that the poet's task is essentially companionless, without the rewards and comforts of society.

## Ceremony After a Fire Raid

Probably written just prior to publication in *Our Time* May 1944, during the months when Thomas moved his family to Bosham, Sussex, because of the heavy bombing on London.

*Give* (st. 3, l.3): A manuscript had 'Give/Over your death'. This is a powerful image of asking the child to offer itself as a sacrifice.

*cinder of the little skull* (pt. II, l.8): According to manuscripts (Ohio State; University of Texas), part II of the poem was to have been given the title, "Among Those Burned To Death Was A Child Aged A Few Hours."

*Into the organpipes* (pt. III): In sending a copy of the published poem to Vernon Watkins in a letter of 27 July 1944, Thomas wrote: 'It really is a Ceremony, and the third part of the poem is the music at the end. Would it be called a voluntary, or is that only music at the beginning?' (*Letters* p. 518).

## Once below a time

This poem, published in *Life and Letters Today* in March 1940, was originally intended for *Deaths and Entrances*, but was not finally included, perhaps because Thomas thought he should do more work on the poem. He had meant to do so, ever since Watkins's criticisms of January 1940 (*Letters* p. 437).

"Once below a time" was sent to James Laughlin for *New Poems* (Norfolk, Connecticut: New Directions 1943), and thence got into the *Selected Writings of Dylan Thomas* (1946), as part of the editor's list, not Thomas's. The pressure of these American publications of the poem may have led to its inclusion in the *Collected Poems*, where the decision was Thomas's; he even specified where it should take its place in the volume among the poems of *Deaths and Entrances*.

*kangaroo* (st. 2, l.9): 'Yes, the Lawrence calling-up-of-memory in the kangaroo lines was intentional, but if in any way it seems feeble, perhaps a little tame, in such a poem (strenuously resisting conventional associations) then, of course, I must change it' (letter to Watkins 30 January 1940, *Letters* p. 436). Thomas and Watkins had a shared interest in Lawrence's poem, "Kangaroo". Not many readers would be compelled to think of that association, but would simply take the 'hopping' kangaroo, like the dancing bear, as an image of the young swanky Thomas, described so well in the BBC broadcast, "Return Journey", as 'a bit of a shower-off; plus-fours and no breakfast, you know' (*Quite Early One Morning* p. 75). Written in Swansea during Christmas 1939, "Once below a time" is itself something of a poetic return journey.

*Up through the lubber crust of Wales* (st. 2, l.12): Vernon Watkins had criticized this line; Thomas responded:

> I agreed with your criticism of the 'lubber crust of Wales' but have, so far, done nothing about altering it. Gaels is good, but that sounds to me facetious. Actually, although I thought the pun out quite coldly, I wanted to make the lubber line a serious one, and I'm glad that you like it apart from its joke. I'll tell you, later, what I do about it: I shall probably use Gaels, anyway (*Letters* p. 437).

He added: 'changing only the word "Wales" I might print the poem in L & Letters just as it is, alterable bits and all, and then work on it later.'

*Shabby and Shorten* (st. 2, l.15): A suitably Dickensian name for an imaginary Swansea haberdasher's, symbolic of all in the provincial life that required the young Thomas either to inhibit himself or to cut his cloth in stylish defiance. The names should be taken to summarize a great deal that the poem contains, since Thomas habitually referred to the poem as having the title "Shabby and Shorten".

*Columbus on fire ... Cold Nansen's beak* (pt. II, st. 2, ll.3 and 6): Two famous explorers are utilized in an image of the young Thomas's downfall from a hot high-flyer to a dejected 'boy' exposed by stern examination.

*Never never oh never to regret the bugle I wore* (pt. II, st. 3, l.7): In a letter to Vernon Watkins of 30 January 1940, Thomas states: 'I didn't much like "I do not regret the bugle I wore" but its omission makes the end too vague. I'll either retain the line or alter it – alter it, that is, in a worked-on version later' (*Letters* p. 437). He did not wait, and in a letter of 3 February 1940 states:

> For 'I do not regret' in my much discussed poem I have put 'Never never oh never to regret the bugle I wore' (all one line), so that the repetition, the pacific repetition, of 'I would lie down, lie down, lie down and live' is loudly and swingingly balanced. When you see the poem again, I think you'll like the alteration (*Letters* p. 439).

If the last five lines of the poem are taken as a unit, the balancing desired by the poet has certainly been achieved, though nothing in the poem really prepares us for the contrasting quietness of the final image. No doubt Thomas's desire to 'live as quiet as a bone' was heartfelt; during these first months of the war, fearing call-up, he would have preferred to be invisible: 'I'm not doing anything about the war; resigned to personal neutrality, I wait' (*Letters* p. 434).

## When I woke

This poem seems to have escaped being sent to Vernon Watkins; so that it cannot be dated with any precision. It may be the 'nice new poem' that Thomas, in a letter of July 1939 to John Davenport, promised to send when finished (*Letters* p. 386). Inside the back cover of his own copy of *Wales* (the issue dated March 1938, which really came out in mid June 1938) Thomas tried a few lines, including the following:

> When I woke, the dawn spoke.

Thomas had quoted this line to Vernon Watkins on 1 April 1938, saying it was 'one of those very youth-fully made phrases ... that often comes to mind and which one day I shall use' (*Letters* p. 287). He was thinking back to a notebook poem "Fifty One" of August 1933 into which he had interpolated the line: 'You woke and the dawn spoke.'

In any case, the poem was finished in time to be submitted for the Autumn 1939 issue of *Seven*. It is not, therefore, eligible to be considered a war poem. It could, however, have something to do with rumours of war; in a letter to Vernon Watkins, on 25 August 1939, Thomas wrote: 'This war, trembling even on the edge of Laugharne, fills me with such horror and terror and lassitude' (*Letters* p. 401). Four days later, he wrote to his father: 'It is terrible to have built, out of nothing, a complete happiness – from no money, no possessions, no material hopes – and a way of living, and then to see the immediate possibility of its being exploded and ruined' (*Letters* p. 402). In its publication in *Seven* the poem ended with a rather more definite picture of doom. There, the voice he hears 'in the erected air' is

> Shaking humanity's houses:
> Wake to see one morning breaking:
> Bulls and wolves in iron palaces:
> Winds in their nests in the ruins of man.

## Among those Killed in the Dawn Raid was a Man Aged a Hundred

A statement by Charles De Lautour accompanying a manuscript of this poem in the Humanities Research Library, Texas, describes his working on location with Dylan Thomas for Strand Films in Bradford 'about 1940–41' and seeing a newspaper account of an air-raid death in Hull:

> I remember we were both very taken up with this story of the old man, and talked wildly about it, the script forgotten. After a while Dylan turned over the script and on the back of the page wrote down words, changed them, crossed out and re-wrote. In a very short time he took a clean sheet and, using the incredible short stub of pencil he always wrote with whenever at least I saw him writing or he was working with me, wrote out complete the enclosed poem and gave it to me.

De Lautour's copy of the poem was as published in *Life and Letters Today* in August 1941.

*Assembling* (l. 11): This word was not in the version he first sent to Vernon Watkins on 15 July 1941 (*Letters* p. 491), asking him for his opinion: 'I am a bit dubious about "Through ruin" in the third line of the sextet. Originally I had "All day".' It was apparently Watkins who suggested the word 'Assembling', for Thomas thanks him for it in the next letter, about 23 July 1941: 'Thank you for "Assembling." Of course' (*Letters* p. 492). Since Watkins's letters are not extant, we cannot know what arguments made that particular word so compelling.

## Lie still, sleep becalmed

The version of this poem published in *Life and Letters Today* in June 1945, which appeared unchanged in *Deaths and Entrances*, was a revision of a draft sent to T. W. Earp in April 1944 from Bosham, Sussex, where Thomas had moved his family when the air attacks on London were resumed in what was called the 'Little Blitz' (*Letters* pp. 513–515). The manuscript draft in Ohio State University Library has not been printed; it deserves to be examined for its more explicit war-time imagery. (Another manuscript of the poem, in the Humanities Research Library, Texas, is identical to this.)

Lie Still, You Must Sleep

Lie still, you must sleep, sufferer with the wound
In the throat, burning and turning. All night afloat
On the silent sea we have heard the sound
That came from your wound. Your wound is a throat.
Under the mile off moon we trembled listening
To music pouring like blood from the loud wound
And when the bandages broke in a burst of singing
It was to us the music of all the drowned.

Open a pathway through the sails, open
Wide the gates of the wandering boat
For my journey to the end of my wound,
The voices cried when the bandages were broken.
Lie still, you must sleep, hide the night from your throat,
Or we shall obey, and ride with you through the drowned.

*throat* (st. 3, l.5): Thomas's father had had a case of malignant though curable cancer of the throat during 1933–34; the poem may have had its inception then, being given a more general significance ten years later by the war casualties. His father's complaint may have been ongoing. On 27 October 1935 Thomas wrote to his married sister: 'Dad has a very painful throat' (*Letters* p. 202).

245

## Vision and Prayer

"A saint about to fall" was a poem to Llewelyn before his birth (*Letters* p. 332); "Vision and Prayer" quite possibly is a celebration of the birth itself, on 30 January 1939. It would not be the only long poem that Thomas kept unfinished through the war years and was able to finish only with the promise of peace. There had been another birth, a daughter Aeronwy, in London, on 3 March 1943; but Thomas's life was very hectic then, and he could probably no more start a poem for her than he could finish one for Llewelyn. We should also note that the poem refers to a son.

The poem was called 'finished' by August 1944 (*Letters* p. 518), but it received more work, and was sent to Vernon Watkins on 28 October 1944 (*Letters* p. 527). On receiving Watkins's reaction on 15 November 1944, Thomas wrote:

> I am so glad you liked the 'Vision & Prayer' poem; and that the diamond shape of the first part seems no longer to you to be cramped & artificed. I agree that the second part is, formally, less inevitable, but I cannot alter it, except, perhaps, in detail … Yes, the Hound of Heaven is baying there in the last verse, but, at the moment, and again from memory, I don't remember seeing any Hopkins after the poem was finished (Letters pp. 531–532).

He is here acknowledging some influence from Francis Thompson, but not from Hopkins, nor from George Herbert, for that matter, who has been thought of as a source for the idea of patterning the poem according to its theme.

In the periodical printings, *Horizon* January 1945 and *Sewanee Review* Summer 1945, Thomas obtained a fairly satisfactory shaping of the stanzas of the poem, preferring the latter, and sending it to Dent's as the model for *Deaths and Entrances* (*Letters* p. 572). In a letter of 6 November 1945 Thomas, returning final proofs of the book, thanks Dent's 'for printing the poem as it is' (*Letters* p. 572). When *Deaths and Entrances* was reprinted and reset in February 1947, however, all the lines of both parts were wrongly rectified by the printer to the left margin.

*in the next room* (st. 1, l.4): *Portrait of a Friend* p. 119 quotes Vernon Watkins's note about this poem: 'Dylan told me, when he was just beginning to write it, that he had read a most wonderful statement of Rilke about God being born in the next room. (This must, I think, have been the poem Du Nachbar Gott from the Stundenbuch.)'

*One. The sun roars at the prayer's end* (last line): Watkins apparently criticized the stresses of this last line of the poem, for Thomas replied: 'I will read the very last line again, and see what, if anything, can be done about the stresses. I haven't a copy of the poem with me but, as I remember, I liked the last line *for* the awkward stressing, for the braking, for the slowing up of the last two same-vowelled words' (*Letters* p. 532).

## Ballad of the Long-legged Bait

'A young man goes out to fish for sexual experience, but he catches a family, the church, and the village green': this is how Thomas summarized "Ballad of the Long-legged Bait" for William York Tindall (*The Literary Symbol* [1955] p. 155). Another time, in public, Thomas phrased it differently: his 'one sentence explanation of the central meaning of his *Ballad* was so lewd and searing as to stop conversation altogether' (John Malcolm Brinnin, *Dylan Thomas in America* p. 16).

Thomas had undoubtedly read Norman Cameron's translation of Rimbaud's "*Bateau ivre*" ("The Drunken Boat") in *New Verse* (June–July 1936), and his friend Vernon Watkins had preceded him in the use of the ballad genre; but the worksheets at Buffalo indicate that Thomas went about this poem, unaided by sources, in his customary arduous way. As Watkins says in the notes to *Letters to Vernon Watkins*: 'I had watched it grow from fifteen lines to its full length during the stay in Bishopston where he worked at it continuously' (p. 103). That would be the months of January to April 1941; the March issue of *Horizon* announced its publication, but it did not appear until the July issue. Thomas wrote to John Davenport on 8 January 1941: 'Today the pipes burst, and Caitlin, in a man's hat, has been running all day with a mop from w.c. to flooded parlour, while I've been sitting down trying to write a poem about a man who fished with a woman for bait and caught a horrible collection' (*Letters* pp. 471–472). And in a letter of 28 April 1941: 'I've just finished my ballad. Too late, unfortunately, for the May Horizon. It's about 220 lines long, a tremendous effort for me, and is really a ballad. I think you'll like it. At the moment, I think it's the best I've done' (*Letters* pp. 482–483).

Vernon Watkins in his notes wrote: 'The poem is full of visual imagery. It was so much a visual poem that he made a coloured picture for it which he pinned on the wall of his room, a picture of a woman lying at the bottom of the sea. She was a new Loreley revealing the pitfalls of destruction awaiting those who attempted to put off the flesh' (*Portrait of a Friend* p. 91).

*Jericho* (st. 14, l.2): The extraordinary lung-power of the Israelites caused the walls of the city of Jericho to collapse (Joshua 6:20).

*bulls of Biscay* (st. 17, l.4): Biscay is not notable for its bull-rearing but for being a Bay; its bulls will therefore be found at sea.

*Susanna ... Sheba* (st. 27, ll.3–4): As one of the bearded elders spying on the bathing Susanna (Old Testament Apocrypha) or as Solomon giving the visiting Queen of Sheba 'all she desired' (I Kings 10:13), the protagonist of the "Ballad" has been enflamed with desire; but no longer.

*walked on the earth in the evening* (st. 40, l.3): 'Lord God walking in the garden in the cool of the day' (Genesis 3:8). 'The church' i.e. religion, is one of the things that Thomas said 'the young man' caught (see quotation above, and also next-to-last stanza of the poem).

## Holy Spring

In sending this poem to Vernon Watkins on 15 November 1944, Thomas said: 'Here is a poem of mine which I started a long time ago but finished very recently, after a lot of work' (*Letters* p. 532). "Out of a war of wits," notebook poem "Ten" of 22 February 1933, seems to have been the origin of the poem, and the revision would have begun before the notebooks were sold in 1941. We can take it that the poem was worked on through stages during the war. A manuscript offered for sale in a House of Books catalogue is stated to differ substantially from the version finally published in *Horizon* in January 1945. The following signed autograph fair copy of an early version of the poem, from the collection of James Gilvarry, was offered for sale in a bookseller's catalogue in 1988 (William Reese Company, catalogue 61, item 1084):

*O Out of A Bed Of Love*

O out of a bed of love
When that immortal hospital made one more move to soothe
The cureless, counted body
And ruin and his causes
Winging over the gunpowdered sea assumed an army
And walked into our wounds and houses,
I climb to greet the war in which I have no heart but only
That one dark I owe my light,
Call for confessor and wiser mirror but there are none
To purge after the planed rough night
And I am struck as dumb as cannonfire by the sun.

Praise that the springtime is all
All all in a flower fire of peace and songs after the evil
Leaves of the clanging fall
O prodigal sun the father his quiver full of green trees

> Praise to the blood of days
> That uncalm still it is sure alone to stand and sing
> Dumb by the chanted blaze
> By the mother and showering voice of the mortal spring
> Hail and upheaval of the judge-blown drowned of the sun,
> If only for a last time.

## Fern Hill

This was the last poem written before *Deaths and Entrances* was published; it was added to the volume at the proof stage, according to a letter to Dent's of 18 September 1945:

> I am enclosing a further poem, 'Fern Hill', not so far included in the book, which I very much *want* included as it is an *essential* part of the feeling and meaning of the book as a whole (*Letters* p. 572).

Dent's managed to include it, as the final poem of the volume. It was published in *Horizon* October 1945, prior to *Deaths and Entrances*, which came out in February 1946.

*Fern Hill* (title): The farm referred to here and in the story "The Peaches" and elsewhere in Thomas's works is an actual farm, Fernhill, occupied at one time by his aunt and uncle, but not at the time of the poem's composition. Thomas told Edith Sitwell in a letter of 31 March 1946 that "Fern Hill" was finished the previous September, 'in Carmarthenshire, near the farm where it happened' (*Letters* p. 583). This would be the cottage at Blaen Cwm, Llangain, still in the hands of the Thomas family, and to where Thomas's parents retired from Swansea. Thomas visited them there for long periods during the summer of 1945. On 30 July 1945 when he was there, he wrote to Oscar Williams (*Letters* p. 558):

> A farmyard outside the window, sows and cows and the farmer's daughters, what a day of dugs. I've been reading all Lawrence's poems, some aloud to no-one in this bombazine room, and liking them more and more. Do you remember:-
>
> > O the green glimmer of apples in the orchard,
> > Lamps in a wash of rain!
> > O the wet walk of my brown hen through the stackyard!
> > O tears on the window pane!

Thomas once said of "Fern Hill": 'it's a poem for evenings and tears' (*Letters* p. 565).

## IN COUNTRY SLEEP (1952)

## In Country Sleep

Thomas wrote from Rapallo to his agent David Higham on 24 April 1947: 'I'm working on a long poem' (*Letters* p. 626). It was the first sign of new poetry since *Deaths and Entrances* of a year before. He wrote again on 24 May 1947, settled in Florence: 'The long poem is coming on slowly' (*Letters* p. 632). He had written up to a hundred lines by 20 June 1947 (*Letters* p. 644). By 11 July 1947 he is willing to declare it almost finished:

> My poem, of 100 lines, is finished, but needs a few days' work on it, especially on one verse. Then I'll send you a copy. The manuscript is thousands and thousands of foolscap pages scattered all over the place but mostly in the boiler fire. What I'll have to send you will be a fair copy. I think it's a good poem. But it has taken so long, nearly three months, to write, that it may be stilted. I hope not (*Letters* p. 651).

As published, "In Country Sleep" has two parts, but a third was envisaged: 'The first two parts of my poem are finished. I'm working on the third' (*Letters* p. 652 – letter of 14 July 1947). Becoming rather less ambitious, Thomas wrote to Margaret Taylor on 3 August 1947: 'I have altered several words in my poem' (*Letters* p. 657). The next we hear is that *Atlantic* has asked him for a poem, and he has sent "In Country Sleep" (*Letters* p. 659), which was published there in December 1947. It was published the same month in *Horizon*, with '16 misprints, including Jew for dew' (*Letters* p. 669).

Paul Ferris, in his biography *Dylan Thomas*, summarizes some of the explanations of the poem that seem to have emanated, however remotely, from the poet himself:

> The critic William York Tindall told Thomas he thought it was about 'how it feels to be a father'. Thomas is said to have wept at this remark – 'but whether from vexation, beer or sentimental agreement I could not tell'. The poet is reassuring someone and warning her at the same time. She is threatened by an unidentified figure, the Thief, generally assumed to be Time or Death. Thomas told a woman who admired the poem that it was not addressed to a child at all, but to his wife, and that the Thief was jealousy. A third explanation was given in New York to a reporter. Thomas said, 'Alcohol is the thief today. But tomorrow he could be fame or success or exaggerated introspection or self-analysis. The thief is anything that robs you of your faith, of your reason for being.'
>
> The idea that faith is being threatened runs through the poem. The year before he died he told an American student that it was started 'in cold blood', and that he 'never thought it would work' (pp. 211–212).

*three Marys*  (pt. I, st. 5, l.1): Three Marys were present at the crucifixion (Matthew 27:56).

*Sanctum sanctorum*  (pt. I, st. 5, l.2): Latin for 'holy of holies', usually referring to the part of the Jewish Temple most inaccessible.

*Thief*  (pt. I, st. 6, and elsewhere): 'For yourselves know perfectly that the day of the Lord so cometh as a thief in the night' – I Thessalonians 5:2.

*heeled wind*  (pt. II, st. 3, l.6): On 1 July 1933 Thomas wrote in his notebook a "Children's Song" for Pamela Trick, his friend's young daughter, which includes the lines:

> I think of the night when the owl is still
> And the moon is hid and the stars are dim,
> And that is the night that death will call,
> And the night that I most fear him.
> Let the owl hoot and the sheep complain;
> Let the brotherly wind speak low;
> Death shall not enter in west wind and rain,
> Let the wind blow.

*riding high*  (pt. II, st. 7, l.2): Thomas actually reads 'riding thigh' on the Caedmon recording, which gives support to the idea that the poet's wife as well as his daughter are figured in the protagonist of the poem. However, the child may prefigure the woman.

A manuscript at Texas contains what appear to be a few lines of a continuation of the poem, or notes towards it:

### III

> Who will teach you that the child
> Who sucks on innocence
> Is spinning fast and loose on a fiery wheel?

The manuscript then continues with two prose paraphrases of the final passage of "In Country Sleep" as published:

> If you believe (and fear) that every night, night without end, the Thief comes to try to steal your faith that every night he comes to steal your faith that your faith is there – then you will wake with your faith steadfast and deathless.
> If you are innocent of the Thief, you are in danger. If you are innocent of the loss of faith, you cannot be faithful. If you do not know the Thief as well as you know God, then you do not know God well. Christian

251

looked through a hole in the floor of heaven and saw hell. You must look through faith, and see disbelief.

## Over Sir John's hill

This poem was begun during the first few weeks of residence in the Boat House at Laugharne, provided for the Thomases through the generosity of Margaret Taylor, to whom Thomas wrote on 11 May 1949, referring to Laugharne as 'this place I love and where I want to live and where I can work and where I have started work (my own) already' (*Letters* p. 706). On

5 August 1949 he reports that he is 'beginning to work hard again' (*Letters* p. 716). The poem was sent to *Botteghe Oscure* the following day, 6 August 1949: 'I finished, only this week, the poem I enclose' (*Letters* p. 716). It was published there before the end of the year. It was published in *Hudson Review* in Autumn 1950 and *Times Literary Supplement* on 24 August 1951.

*Sir John's hill* (title): The name of a low headland just along the shore from the Boat House at Laugharne.

*dilly dilly ... Come and be killed* (st. 2, ll. 10–11): In the nursery song "Mrs Bond" occur the lines

> John Ostler, go fetch me a duckling or two;
> Cry Dilly, dilly, dilly, dilly, come and be killed.

*Aesop* (st. 3, l. 11): The supposed author of *Aesop's Fables*, a collection of very ancient stories.

*in the tear of the Towy* (st. 5, l. 1): *Portrait of a Friend* (p. 138) tells that, in a reading in Vernon Watkins's presence, Thomas pronounced 'tear' as 'tare', as in 'to tear'.

> Caitlin abruptly put in 'Tear!' (pronouncing it as 'tier'.) Dylan became – with some reason – furious. They screamed their own versions of the word back and forth, until Dylan, his face congested, bawled, 'But, for Christ's sake, the bloody word is *there* – I wrote it!'

The Towy is one of the two rivers running into the estuary at Laugharne.

*Wear-willow* : (st. 5, l. 10): Was 'wear-the-willow' in a draft of the poem (Buffalo Library), meaning 'pertaining to a desolate lover'. 'Wear', incidentally, rhymes with 'tear' in Thomas's pronunciation, as heard by Vernon Watkins (*Portrait of a Friend* p. 139).

## Poem on his Birthday

Since 'thirty-five bells sing' in this birthday poem, we should take it that the poem was begun for Thomas's thirty-fifth birthday, i.e. October 1949. One manuscript worksheet at Harvard is headed "Poem in October (1950)" indicating a continuing attention to the poem. But it was not finished until 1951. In a letter of 18 July 1951 to Princess Caetani, editor of *Botteghe Oscure*, Thomas wrote:

> I hoped to finish the longish (about 100 lines) birthday poem I was – and still am – writing. I wanted to send it to you ... I like it better than anything I have done for a very long time (*Letters* p. 802).

On 31 August 1951 he tells the Princess a sad story:

> I took the new poem – it is the first of three poems linked together by
> the occasion of a birthday – up to London with me on my last, just-
> over visit, meaning to typewrite it there and send it straight to you.
> Nothing, however, went right with my plans – it was my hope to
> arrange a job for myself for the winter, when we must move from here
> to London – and I decided to go, with no hopes, home. But I hadn't the
> money to go home, couldn't arrive home with no money, and was
> forced to sell my poem to a London magazine for ten pounds (*Letters*
> p. 807, see also p. 809).

This is how the poem came to be published in *World Review* October 1951.
It was a version shorter by three stanzas than that published in *Atlantic*
March 1952, sent there via Oscar Williams in October or November 1951
(*Letters* p. 817).

Thomas gave to Bill Read, when he was working on his book *The Days of
Dylan Thomas* (1964), a synopsis of "Poem on his Birthday" as follows
(p. 149):

> Before he began the poem at all, he had the plan all worked out: it was
> to be about a poet who realizes he has arrived at 'half his bible span.'
> He means both to celebrate and spurn his birthday in a house high
> among trees, overlooking the sea. Birds and fishes move under and
> around him on their dying ways, and he, a craftsman in words, toils
> 'towards his own wounds which are waiting in ambush for him.' The
> poet 'sings in the direction of his pain.' Birds fly after the hawks that
> will kill them. Fishes swim toward the otters that will eat them. He sees
> herons walking in their shrouds, which is the water they fish in; and
> he, who is progressing, afraid, to his own fiery end in the cloud of an
> atomic explosion knows that, out at sea, animals who attack and eat
> other sea animals are tasting the flesh of their own death. Now exactly
> half of his three score and ten years has gone. He looks back at his
> times – his loves, his hates, all he has seen – and sees the logical progress
> of death in everything he has been and done. His death lurks for him,
> and for all, in the next lunatic war. And, still singing, still praising the
> radiant earth, still loving, though remotely, the animal creation also
> gladly pursuing their inevitable and grievous ends, he goes toward his.
> Why should he praise God and the beauty of the world, as he moves to
> horrible death? He does not like the deep zero dark, and the nearer he
> gets to it, the louder he sings, the higher the salmon leaps, the shriller
> the birds carol.

*house on stilts* (st. 1, l.4): The Boat House, Laugharne. In a draft, Thomas specifies the location as the shed at the top of the cliff, where he worked on his poetry-writing in the company of a number of photographs of certain poets:

> In this estuary room
> With Walt Whitman over my head....

*Through wynds and shells of drowned* : (st. 3, l. 5): In one of the worksheets at Houghton Library, Harvard University, is a drawing of this scene as the poet envisaged it.

## Do not go gentle into that good night

Thomas wrote to Vernon Watkins on 28 March 1945:

> My Father is awfully ill these days, with heart disease and uncharted pains, and the world that was once the colour of tar to him is now a darker place (*Letters* p. 548).

The poem could have had its inception as far back as 1945. It is not a poem that was written quickly, one suspects. Thomas did not make a fuss about it in letters, submitting it to *Botteghe Oscure* on 28 March 1951 with the comment: 'I have just finished the short poem I enclose' (*Letters* p. 800), adding in a postscript: 'The only person I can't show the little enclosed poem to is, of course, my father, who doesn't know he's dying.' It was published in that periodical in November 1951.

In the last stages of production of the *Collected Poems*, "Do not go gentle into that good night" was moved from its position as the last-but-two poem in the volume to take the place of "Paper and sticks", which Thomas asked to have removed (*Letters* p. 839). This edition restores it to its previous place.

Thomas is reported as speaking of this poem, introducing a reading of it at the University of Utah 18 April 1952 (Tedlock, p. 66). He

> began to talk in a soft voice about his father, who, he said, had been a
> militant atheist, whose atheism had nothing to do with whether there
> was a god or not, but was a violent and personal dislike for God. He
> would glare out of the window and growl: 'It's raining, blast Him!' or
> 'The sun is shining – Lord, what foolishness!' He went blind and was
> very ill before he died. He was in his eighties, and he grew soft and
> gentle at the last. Thomas hadn't wanted him to change. . . .

The villanelle form for this poem is something Thomas would have picked
up from William Empson, if nowhere else. Thomas's parody of Empson,
"Request to Leda (Homage to William Empson)" published in *Horizon* July
1942 (and not in the *Collected Poems*) is itself, as far as it goes, in the villanelle
form:

> Not your winged lust but his must now change suit
> The harp-waked Casanova rakes no change
> The worm is (pinpoint) rational in the fruit.
>
> Not girl for bird (gourd being man) breaks root.
> Taking no plume for index in love's change
> Not your winged lust but his must now change suit.
>
> Desire is phosphorous: the chemic bruit
> Lust bears like volts, who'll amplify, and strange
> The worm is (pin-point) rational in the fruit.

*on the sad height* (st. 6, l.1): Vernon Watkins wondered aloud whether
there was a reminiscence of Kierkegaard learning that his father had once
stood upon a hill and cursed God. Thomas 'only smiled and remained silent'
(*Portrait of a Friend* p. 139).

## Lament

This punning poem comes out of the same mood as the plans for a BBC
comedy show that Thomas was hoping to participate in with Ted Kavanagh
in 1951 (*Letters* pp. 789–790). On 20 March 1951 Thomas wrote to Princess
Caetani about this poem 'nearly finished',

> which will be about 50 or 60 lines long and is coarse and violent: I will
> send it along as *soon* as it is done . . . and the poem will come: the
> crotchety poem not quite clean, but worked at, between the willies,
> very hard (*Letters* p. 791).

He sent it on 17 May 1951 (*Letters* p. 797), and it was published in *Botteghe Oscure* before the end of 1951. The Princess omitted the fourth stanza; Thomas made no objection in sending back proofs (*Letters* p. 803), but restored it for *Partisan Review* (January–February 1952) and *In Country Sleep*.

*coal black* : (st. 1, l.12, and in each subsequent stanza): In one draft of this poem in the Humanities Research Library, Texas, the title was "The Miner's Lament", and included are such phrases as 'the skinbare pit' and 'the moon shaft slag'. The origin of the poem in this specific mode accounts for some of the colliery allusions in the poem ('black spit', 'ram rod', 'wick' etc.).

## In the White Giant's Thigh

This poem was 'half completed' in October 1949 (*Letters* p. 718). In a letter to Helen and Bill McAlpine of 12 November 1949 Thomas said: 'I have finished my poem, a hundred lines, but it may need a second part' (*Letters* p. 727). But the poem was reduced rather than lengthened. On 28 November 1949 it was 'now 80 lines long' (*Letters* p. 735); it was its present sixty lines when sent to *Botteghe Oscure* in the late summer of 1950, with a Note about "In Country Heaven", 'where this poem will, one day, I hope, find its place' (*Letters* pp. 768–769). Thomas explained some of the circumstances of the revision in a letter to Oscar Williams of 28 May 1951:

> I'm sending you only one poem – and that only the first section of a poem, though nobody need know that. I mentioned the title and idea

of this poem over a year ago, in pretty New York, but scrapped all of it
I had written on my return. I have only recently finished this version
(*Letters* p. 798).

He adds: 'It's a conventionally romantic poem & perhaps you won't like it at
all.' It was published in *Atlantic* September 1951.

*white giant*  (title, and line 3): probably the 'Mighty Giant of Cerne Abbas',
a figure cut into hillside chalk soil in Dorset, about twenty-five miles from
Blashford, Hampshire, where the Thomases often stayed with Caitlin's
mother.

*gambo*  (l.37): 'GAMBO means a farm-cart' (letter to Oscar Williams, *Letters*
p. 798). It is a dialect word of frequent use in West Wales.

*desirers*  (l.56): Readers of *In Country Sleep* (1952) and the *Collected Poems*
(1952) had 'desires' at this spot in the poem, and probably felt comfortable
with that word. The change to 'desirers' is undoubtedly correct. A worksheet
had: 'hay haired phantoms'.

# *Notes to*
# In Country Heaven *and* Elegy

## In Country Heaven

It was Thomas's intention to include a poem called 'In Country Heaven' in some future collection. In a notebook dated October 1951 (at Texas) there is a draft list of titles for such a volume. The six poems of *In Country Sleep* are listed; then "Shabby and Shorten", which, as "Once Below a Time", was included in the 1952 *Collected Poems*. The list continues:

> In Country Heaven
> Where Have the Old Words Got Me
> Poem to Caitlin
> Poem to Colm
> Continuation of White Giant.

We know nothing of four of these poems beyond the poet's intention to write them. Of "In Country Heaven" we have an early draft of forty-three lines, and a rewritten section of sixteen lines, the latter of such accomplishment as to make us happy to present it in the present volume as a valued part of the corpus of Thomas's poems.

"In Country Heaven", haunted by the vision of the destruction of the world, could have had its inception any time after the dropping of the atom bombs in 1945. But there is no hint of a start on any poetry, let alone a major undertaking like "In Country Heaven", during 1946. It was a year of very heavy pressure of BBC work. Relief came with the news that Edith Sitwell had arranged for Thomas to have an award of £150 to travel to Italy. Thomas learned of this around 1 March 1947, and had six weeks of relative ease and pleasant anticipation before leaving. We conjecture that it was in this lull, while living at Holywell Ford, Oxford, that Thomas was able to work on a poem after over a year's stop, a poem for which he set himself even more extreme formal requirements than the last poem he had completed, "Fern

259

Hill". The stanzas were to run in two's, according to syllable count and rhyme-scheme, as follows:

9 a
4 b
11 c
7 d
8 e

11 b
7 d
9 e
8 a
4 c

repeated for the next two stanzas, and so on. Worksheets exist (at Texas) where the poet puts against the lines the numbers and letters for syllables and rhymes as above. The poem got through four of these dual stanzas, plus four further lines, before it was abandoned. One of the Texas manuscripts, a holograph fair copy of what was completed up to that time, is transcribed here:

### In Country Sleep

Always, when he, in Country Heaven,
(Whom my heart hears),
Crosses the breast of the praising East, and kneels,
Humble in all his planets,
And weeps on the abasing hill,

Then in the delight and groves of beasts and birds
And the canonized valley
Where the dewfall stars sing grazing still
And the angels whirr like pheasants
Through aisles of leaves,

Light and his tears glide down together
(O hand in hand)
From the country eyes, salt and sun, star and woe
Down the cheek bones and whinnying
Downs into the low browsing dark.

Doused in hamlets of heaven swing the loft lamps,
In the black buried spinneys
Bushes and owls blow out like a spark,

260

And the seraphic fields of shepherds
Fade with their rose-

White, God's bright, flocks, the belled lambs leaping,
(His gentle kind);
The shooting-star hawk locked blind in a lame cloud
Over the blackamoor shires
Hears the belfries and the cobbles

Of the twelve apostles' towns ring in his night;
And the long fox like fire
Prowls flaming among the cockerels
In the plunged farms of Heaven's keeping,
But they sleep sound.

For the fifth element is pity,
(Pity for death);
No fowl or field mouse that night of his kneeling
Lies in the fox's fires
Or twice dies in the screech-owl's eyes;

All the canterbury tales in the wild hedge-
Row of the small, brown friars,
The lithe reeve and the rustling wife
Blithe in the tall telling of his pitch
Time go sleeping

Under the switchback glide of his tears,
(And the salt light).

Young Aesop fabling by the coracled Towy....

The "Sleep" in the title of this Texas manuscript was crossed through by Thomas, and "Heaven" written above it. This change presumably took place after he had used the "In Country Sleep" title for the poem he had spent all his three months in Italy composing. To Margaret Taylor, who had been his hostess at Holywell Ford, Oxford, Thomas wrote from Florence on 11 July 1947: 'I'll send you my poem ["In Country Sleep"] this week. It isn't the one whose beginning I showed you' (*Letters* p. 651). We are assuming that, before leaving Oxford for Italy, Thomas had shown Margaret Taylor the unfinished manuscript transcribed above. Clearly, this manuscript had provided something of the tone of the new "In Country Sleep", and some words, such as 'spinneys', used twice in the later poem.

261

Even more clear are the phrases from this ur-manuscript utilized in "Over Sir John's hill" (for instance, the 'hawk' and the 'Young Aesop') and in "In the White Giant's Thigh" ('doused', 'small, brown friars', 'fox's fires'). It is as though these poems of 1949 grew tangentially from the "In Country Heaven" draft. In sending the finished "In the White Giant's Thigh" for publication in *Bòtteghe Oscure* VI (November 1950), Thomas added a prose "Note", which refers to the inception of his poem about the end of the world, to the old manuscript of "In Country Heaven", and to his renewed intention to develop it as a frame within which the long lyrical poems he had just done could have a place:

> The preceding sixty lines compose the first part of a poem, 'In the White Giant's Thigh', which is intended to be a part of a long poem, 'In Country Heaven', which is in preparation. I mean, by 'in preparation', that some of the long poem is written down on paper, some of it is a rough draft in the head, and the rest of it is radiantly unworded in ambitious conjecture.
>
> The plan of this long poem-to-be is grand and simple, though the grandeur will seem, to many, to be grandiose, and the simplicity crude and sentimental.
>
> The godhead, the author, the first cause, architect, lamp-lighter, the beginning word, the anthropomorphic bawler-out and black-baller, the quintessence, scapegoat, martyr, maker – He, on top of a hill in Heaven, weeps whenever, outside that state of being called His country, one of His worlds drops dead, vanishes screaming, shrivels, explodes, murders itself. And, when He weeps, Light and His tears glide down together, hand in hand. So, at the beginning of the poem-to-be, He weeps, and Country Heaven is suddenly dark. Bushes and owls blow out like candles. And the countrymen of heaven crouch all together under the hedges, and, among themselves, in the tear-salt darkness, surmise which world, which star, which of their late, turning homes in the skies has gone for ever. And this time, spreads the heavenly hedge-row rumour, it is the Earth. The Earth has killed itself. It is black, petrified, wizened, poisoned, burst; insanity has blown it rotten; and no creatures at all, joyful, despairing, cruel, kind, dumb, afire, loving, dull, shortly and brutishly hunt their days down like enemies on that corrupted face. And, one by one, these heavenly hedgerow men who once were of the Earth, tell one another, through the long night, Light and His tears falling, what they remember, what they sense in the submerged wilderness and on the exposed hairs-breadth of the mind, of that self-killed place. They remember places, fears, loves, exultation, misery, animal joy, ignorance and mysteries, all you and I know and do not know. The poem-to-be is made of these tellings.

And the poem becomes, at last, an affirmation of the beautiful and terrible worth of the earth.

It grows into a praise of what is and what could be on this lump in the skies.

It is a poem about happiness.

I do not, of course, know how this first part of the poem called 'In the White Giant's Thigh,' will, eventually, take its place in that lofty, pretentious, down-to-earth-and-into-the-secrets, optimistic, ludicrous, moony scheme. I do not yet know myself its relevance to the whole, hypothetical structure. But I do know it belongs to it.

In sending this "Note" to Princess Caetani, editor of *Botteghe Oscure*, in the summer of 1950, Thomas declared: 'All I want to do is to be able to write that long, intended poem' (*Letters* p. 769). On 25 September 1950 Thomas introduced a BBC reading of "In Country Sleep", "Over Sir John's hill", and "In the White Giant's Thigh" with remarks very similar to the published "Note", and added a further comment on the relationship between the frame story and its parts:

> The remembered tellings, which are the components of the poem, are not all told as though they are remembered; the poem will not be a series of poems in the past tense. The memory, in all tenses, can look towards the future, can caution and admonish. The rememberer may live himself back into active participation in the remembered scene, adventure, or spiritual condition.

We conjecture that a reworking of the old "In Country Heaven" manuscript was begun about this time. The few worksheets at Texas indicate revision of the first part of the poem, leading up to the fair copy of a finished sixteen lines found in the notebook dated October 1951. We have taken this notebook version as our copy-text, and have published it without emendation.

The worksheets indicate that, if Thomas had continued with the poem, it would have followed the direction of the prose "Note". It would have set the scene in 'country heaven' where the 'heavenly hedgerow' countrymen tell their stories about the Earth, sitting in a darkness that has been produced in heaven by the Earth's self-destruction. As they stand, the finished sixteen lines of "In Country Heaven" are a beautifully crafted poem, which, in the present volume, joins the rest of Thomas's collected poems. Even incomplete, this first part has accomplished what the poet intended for the whole; it has become an affirmation of the worth of the Earth, 'beautiful and terrible'.

## Elegy

Vernon Watkins included a version of Thomas's last, unfinished poem,

"Elegy", as an appendix to the *Collected Poems* in printings after 1956. In the Humanities Research Center, University of Texas, is a notebook, eighteen pages of which contain drafts of lines belonging to this poem; there are also thirty-three numbered sheets, twenty of which have verso workings. Sheet number 31 has on the verso a draft of a letter to E. F. Bozman dated 15 September 1953, indicating that Thomas was working on the poem up to a month before his final visit to America. There are also two worksheets at the Pierpont Morgan Library, and one in the National Library of Wales.

The most finished version, as Watkins identified, is the Texas sheet numbered 2, where the poem is given the title, "Elegy", and, though rhymed in quatrains, is written in six verses of three lines each, plus an extra incomplete line. We have kept strictly to this version, taking one liberty: we have retained the last two lines, though Thomas was apparently dissatisfied with them, and struck them out. They are valuable lines; and there is reason to think that they would have been utilized in some similar form, if the poet had had a chance to return to the poem. We have concluded that there is no justification for extending the poem as Vernon Watkins did, as all the extant worksheets lead up to the version printed here. Thomas outlined his intentions in a prose note, on sheet 30:

(1) Although he was too proud to die, he *did* die, blind, in the most agonizing way but he did not flinch from death & was brave in his pride.

(2) In his innocence, & thinking he was God-hating, he never knew that what he was was: an old kind man in his burning pride.

(3) Now he will not leave my side, though he is dead.

(4) His mother sd that as a baby he never cried; nor did he, as an old man; he just cried to his secret wound & his blindness, never aloud.

Undoubtedly, Thomas intended at one stage to use these thoughts in sequence, but as the writing progressed, the original scheme was conflated, and all the worked-over phrases were either discarded or incorporated into the Texas p. 2, adopted as our copy-text. Indeed, if the poem had continued, it would have been in a new direction. The last two lines of Texas p. 2 take up a theme not previously hinted at in the prose summary or any of the worksheets. They are a benediction from the poet to his recently dead father:

> Go calm to your crucifixed hill, I told
> The air that drew away from him.

This exhortation contrasts conspicuously with that of the previous poem that Thomas had written on his father's death, "Do not go gentle into that good night". This final "Elegy" is proposing that a calmness is possible in the face of death.

# Index of Titles and First Lines

Titles of poems are in italics.
Where the first line of a poem is exactly the same as the title, it is not repeated.